1980

W9-ACF-967

3 0301 00009652 5

Contexts
for
Ethical Discussion

Contexts
for
Ethical Discussion

Edited by
Alfred Dewey Jensen
Northern Arizona University

LIBRARY
College of St. Francis
JOLIET, ILL.

Charles E. Merrill Publishing Company
A Bell & Howell Company
Columbus, Ohio

Published by
Charles E. Merrill Publishing Company
A Bell & Howell Company
Columbus, Ohio 43216

This book was set in Baskerville and Optima.
The Production Editor was Sharon Thomason.
The cover was designed by Will Chenoweth.
The cover photograph was by Larry Hamill.

Copyright © 1977 by Bell & Howell Company. All rights reserved. No part of this book may be reproduced in any form, electronic or mechanical, including photocopy, recording, or any information storage and retrieval system, without permission in writing from the publisher.

ISBN: 0–675–08491–1

Library of Congress Catalog Card Number: 76–24609

1 2 3 4 5 6 7 8 9 10—83 82 81 80 79 78 77

Printed in the United States of America

170
J529

7-15-79 Dr. Elgar Reach B. J.

92020

To my great-grandmothers and grandmothers, who first taught me to read;
My parents, readers both, who encouraged a love of reading;
Peggy, who can read for herself, but with whom I love to read; and
O.K. Bouwsma, who taught me to read a second time,

With Love and Thanks.

Acknowledgments

I should like to express my appreciation to:

Oxford University Press
Harvard University Press
Encyclopaedia Britannica, Inc.
Mc-Graw Hill Book Company
Princeton University Press
Macmillan Publishing Company
Fawcett Publications, Inc.
Doubleday & Company, Inc.
International Creative Management
Little, Brown and Co.
St. Martin's Press, Inc.

for permission to reprint materials included in this book; Mr. Fred Kinne (of Charles E. Merrill Publishing Company) whose help came just in time; Ms. Audrey Wood (of International Creative Management) and Professor Frederick A. Pottle (of The Yale Editorial Committee) who allowed me to persuade them; and, lastly, Professors Richard A. Wood and Charles A. Peek (of Northern Arizona University) whose friendship and encouragement have given me strength, and whose insight has added to the book.

Contents

Preface

Benjamin Franklin was once asked, "What kind of man deserves the most pity?" He answered, "A lonesome man on a rainy day who does not know how to read." In these days of too easy familiarity, television, and continual consultation of the crowd (which insures that each of us thinks just what everyone else thinks and that we all think in the simple phrases of the pollsters), it may be that we have lost the precious capacity for solitude. To be alone has become for us synonymous with loneliness. Certainly the art of reading has suffered. For, as with any art, reading is also a task—a task to which the person must bring that which only he or she can bring *as an individual.* Be that as it may, if someone not altogether bereft of imagination, one who still hears the pure crystal tones of individual existence (which is a tintinnabulation lost in the gong-like clamor of numbers and "groups"), one not completely "massified" by what passes for ideas in our time—if such a person should find oneself alone in the company of this book, I believe there would be company enough.

And what company!

The moral beauty of Plato, the uncompromising depth of Augustine, the hard paradox of Kierkegaard—all are here to confront the individual.

The reader will find characters as diverse as Socrates and Sherlock Holmes, Diogenes and Dr. Johnson. While on the other end of the scale of reflection and conduct are mobs, Jacob Horner, and Smerdyakov.

One will find here, by turns, the descriptive power of Dickens, the sheer force of Dostoevsky, the simplicity of Tolstoy.

I am almost moved to exclaim, "All this and more await you!" In the midst of my enthusiasm, however, I must add a word of caution. Although this book is designed as a text, its purpose is not to present a body of instruction, but to provide bases for the discussion of moral questions. Perhaps there are answers to such questions, perhaps not. If there are answers, you must provide them.

Alfred Dewey Jensen
Bennet, Nebraska

Notes

To the Instructor

This book may find use in several ways. All of them, however, rest upon commitment to the use of discussion. Given this commitment, one naturally searches for tools to serve it. We hope that this book might be such a tool. It may be used as the sole text in an introductory ethics course. This may be the most satisfactory use for the teacher able to "lecture on the move" in order to supply the theoretical structures implied be the issues raised. On the other hand, it may be used to supplement the more standard texts that present ethical theories and/or moral problems. The book has a short introductory essay, and each chapter is followed by questions designed to arouse and focus discussion. These "literary episodes" confront us with something of the stuff of human life. Choices we make or allow to be made for us and, thus, the characters that we cultivate or neglect, are made manifest. That, we believe, is something worth talking about.

To the Student

Your instructor would not be using this book without an interest in *discussing* issues with you. He or she wishes to assist you—perhaps it is impossible to teach directly—in learning the art of discussion. What does that require of you? Socrates said that to discuss "these matters" requires knowledge, goodwill, and outspokeness. The knowledge of what is really is at issue and how to deal with it will become clear to you only gradually, because philosophy is different from anything you have studied. In the meantime, you will need to have the goodwill to persevere in your work. You are responsible for being outspoken when you are confused or disagree. Speak up!

The questions following each selection are there to aid in beginning your discussions. You will add many questions of your own. What you gain from this study will be determined by your effort. There is not one laborsaving device in the book, for any apparent shortcut would ultimately shortchange you. At the least, you are in for the "fifty-drachma course."

Introduction

Our primary concern in bringing together the selections in this book is the cultivation of moral reflection. By "moral reflection," we mean seriously thinking about ourselves as at least *potentially* responsible agents. (There can be no question of morality without the recognition of responsibility.) Kierkegaard, a great thinker and writer of the nineteenth century, has one of his literary creations say of those he sees around him, "The thoughts of their hearts are too paltry to be sinful." It may well be that "sin" is not an ethical category at all. However, if Socrates is right in saying that "the unexamined life is not worth living," then we *must* think about our lives before there is even the possibility of morality. Otherwise we do not "act"—and thus cannot be responsible for our acts in a moral sense—we simply "behave." "Behavior" is the subject matter of the so-called social sciences and, when properly understood and presented, is purely and at best descriptive. The point of moral reflection is to give us insight into how we *ought* to think and act, not to record what we already are doing or what our attitudes and opinions are. That is, moral reflection is prescriptive rather than descriptive. It does not report our lives; we direct our lives by means of it.

But how do we cultivate moral reflection? How do we examine our lives?[1] It would be misleading to give the impression that these questions can be answered in the space of a brief essay, or, indeed, that an answer can be *guaranteed* even if we are willing to devote months to finding it. Such is not the case. What we *can* offer are some remarks on the difficulty of answering these questions and the uses to which this book might be put in our philosophizing.

First of all, it must be seen that these are not questions requiring more information. They are not information questions at all, but questions of character and commitment. If this is not clear from the very beginning, all our effort will be misdirected. Thus, it must be assumed that nothing less is to be attempted than the acquisition of beginning philosoph-

---

[1] We are not suggesting that these two are *exactly* the same by any means. Rather, it seems that without the latter, the former cannot be accomplished at all.

ical skills. For philosophy is something that we as individuals *do*. The philosopher Ludwig Wittgenstein described philosophy as an "activity." It is by means of this activity that we commit ourselves, as reflective beings, to one sort of life rather than another. (*Nota bene:* This is not a matter of "life-styles" in conflict. In fact, the difference between a change of life-style and an essential change in a life might be a subject for philosophical reflection.) We will not be helped in developing these skills simply by being confronted with various ethical theories or a list of current (or "contemporary") moral problems. While problems tempt us to "take a stand" and only devote thought to defending our position, it is often difficult to see the importance in the theoretical approach. In neither case do we really come to understand ethics; nor do we cultivate moral reflection.

Ethics—the branch of philosophy dealing with morality—might be said to arise from a certain dissatisfaction with our lives. This dissatisfaction is not a matter of our different places in society, nor still less of our physical or mental characteristics (though the distribution of wealth, for example, or how we use our bodies and minds *might become* matters of moral concern). Rather, we would characterize the dissatisfaction in terms of a desire for some sort of ultimate grounding and direction in our lives. It is as if we *should* be able to present to ourselves certain answers, or kinds of answers, and yet cannot do so. Perhaps the more ardently we search for these answers, the more dissatisfied we become. This dissatisfaction is usually expressed in the form of certain very general questions:

What is justice?
What is good?
What is good in itself?
What is the highest good?
What is right?
What is truth?

Notice, now, that though we began by taking our lives seriously, the questions are not about our lives. They are about justice and right and good and truth. (A few years ago, a student expressed this tendency most forcefully by saying: "I don't care what you [or even I, for that matter] *think* is right; I want to know what *is* right.") It seems that in order to take our lives seriously we must first answer these abstract questions.

But how do we answer these questions? *How* and *where* do we look for our answers? If we accept the theory (often stated in arguments) that the answers are matters of opinion, we seem to be giving up before we begin. And notice what we are giving up: knowing ourselves! We began by seeking self-knowledge, but as soon as the road to this was understood in terms of answering the abstract questions, we were at a loss.

Being confronted with the difficulty of answering these abstract, though apparently straightforward, questions is perhaps the surest indication that we are in the realm of philosophy. For it is well known, in some quarters notorious, that philosophical questions do not get settled. Like the poor they are always with us. There may be a temporary settlement here and there, but essentially it is the questions, not the answers, that are permanent. Ethics is simply one area of philosophy; there are several others as well. Indeed, many philosophers would claim that ethical questions are answerable, if at all, only after other, more fundamental, questions have been asked and answered. Thus, we seem to be led further afield into questions dealing with the nature of ultimate reality and how reality is known. The areas of philosophy dealing with these questions are metaphysics and epistemology. Here too, we might say, the concern is grounded in what we *as individuals* are faced with and what we have or need to develop in order to meet reality. But for most of us, ethics is the first and perhaps only area of philosophy in which we are ultimately interested. The desire for self-knowledge, the dissatisfaction with our lives, and the difficulty of answering the abstract philosophical questions may be given direction and focus by considering *meaning*. For this consideration will help us to think about *how* to philosophize. And in philosophizing, we hope these concerns may be addressed.

What are we asking *for* when we ask a philosophical question (e.g., What is justice?)? Philosophers as different in style, content, and time as Socrates, Heidegger, Aristotle, and Wittgenstein have agreed that when we ask a philosophical question we are asking for the meaning of a word (or concept). The point is never, however, simply to add to our store of knowledge. Rather, we believe that by coming to understand the meaning, our *lives* will be given direction. The understanding, as it were, will provide the very substance of our lives. This is the point of seeking the meaning of a word.

But what is the *meaning?* Perhaps the answer which first occurs to us is that it is a definition. Again, we have all argued, "Let's define our terms," or "It depends on your definition of _____." But did this help our understanding? Usually these disputes end with the grudging admission that you have your definition and I have mine (which, if you were not so unenlightened, you would accept). The argument is not interrupted to consult a dictionary. Rather, each of us assumes the Websterian mantle with all its prerogatives. The chief benefit to be derived from this stance is that we think we can safely ignore our opponent. We did not win the argument, but then we did not lose it either, and that, at least, is something.

But it is not much. We began by asking *important* questions, questions whose answers would give direction and substance to our lives, and we ended with the shallow satisfaction of not losing an argument. Here we are only one step removed from the level of saying, "It's all a matter of opinion." Formerly, we were saying that it is only a matter of opinion what justice *is.* Now we have reached the not very advanced point of saying that it is a matter of individual definition what "justice" *means.* But this much advantage has been gained: We have tacitly recognized that our questions concern the meanings of the words we wish to use and *do* use. So let us consider: *Are* definitions meanings?

Perhaps the answer is both yes and no. Yes, a definition might help us to understand the meaning in the case of a sentence such as, "Hippocrates was the first to practice nosography."[2] If we do not understand the sentence because we have never seen the word "nosography" before, and the context surrounding the sentence does not help, we might consult a dictionary. There we would find a definition of nosography—"the systematic description of disease." But the words about which we have become concerned—"justice," "good," "bad," "evil," "right," "wrong," and so on—are not new to us. We have been using them for some time now. We have even argued by means of them. Yet when confronted with a question, "What is justice?" for example, we apparently are at a loss. It is as if all along we have not known what we were talking about.[3]

We are confronted, then, with the difficulty of being required to present the meaning of a well-known word. How do we do that? Suppose we consult a dictionary. We would find "justice" defined as:

> 1. the quality of being righteous. 2. impartiality; fairness. 3. the quality of being right or correct. 4. sound reason; rightfulness; validity. 5. reward or penalty as deserved; just deserts. 6. the use of authority and power to uphold what is right, just, lawful. 7. the administration of law; procedure of a law court. 8. a judge: abbreviated jus., just., j. 9. a justice of the peace.[4]

Would any of this help? Now we are inclined to say, "It depends on what was being asked." So far, the question is still up in the air. Our question was supposed to be important, not merely an exercise in the use of the dictionary. What has gone wrong? What does it take to make the question, and our answer, important? What is required to give our search direction and, at the same time, relate it to our lives?

---

[2]That is false, by the way, but we are concerned here with meaning rather than either truth or falsity. We must understand the former before we can evaluate the latter.

[3]In many cases this may well be so, but for reasons other than our inability to offer a definition.

[4]*Webster's New World Dictionary of the American Language,* College Edition (Englewood Cliffs, N.J.: The World Publishing Company, 1956), p. 795.

Perhaps the following has helped to mislead us. When we were unable to understand the sentence, "Hippocrates was the first to practice nosography," we referred to the dictionary. It is as if we asked the series of questions:

1. What is nosography? that is,
2. What does "nosography" mean? that is,
3. What is the definition of "nosography"?

This served us well in the case of an unfamiliar word, but in the case at hand it does not seem to help. For if we ask the series of questions:

1. What is justice? that is,
2. What does "justice" mean? that is,
3. What is the definition of "justice"?

the definitions that follow do not seem to add to our understanding and insight. We got the definitions from the dictionary; perhaps we could have done just as well by ourselves. The whole business seems flat, stale, and unprofitable. Perhaps we grow weary, too. What has happened to our important question?

The qualification, "It depends on what is being asked," suggests that there is a concrete answer to our question. But we are not asking something *in general;* we *already* know that. In order to be important the question needs some *human* point. It needs a context in which something is really at issue. Suppose we consider (chapter 13 of this book) Sherlock Holmes' release of Dr. Sterndale when it is evident that the latter has killed ("murdered"?) Mortimer Tregennis. Holmes, in trying to determine what he should do, asks, "Now, Dr. Sterndale, how do you justify such conduct, and what were the motives for your actions?" Clearly he is after something more than a definition. In a sense, two definitions are in conflict. For in part, Holmes is torn between the use of authority in administering law (Webster's definitions 6 and 7), and what Dr. Sterndale really deserves (Webster's definition 5). That is, given Dr. Sterndale's remarkable background (the details of which form part of the context for the question),

Holmes is confronted with something more than another case of murder. A different series of questions is to be considered:

1. What is justice?
2. What does "justice" mean *in this case?*
3. How do I (Sherlock Holmes) do what is just?

Now it is not supposed that the meaning of "justice" is simply a definition, but rather something that can be seen only in the full context of a human life. In this instance, to the question "Are definitions meanings?" we would answer "no."

If we are to undertake moral reflection, then, our first philosophical task is to learn how to present the meaning of a word. Since philosophical questions are about the meanings of familiar words, the presentation of their meanings will require full-blown contexts. We should be sure that we learn to really look at the contexts in order to understand the meanings of the words that puzzle us. Otherwise we will only be consulting our moods, prejudices, inclinations, and feelings, all of which are irrelevant to the philosophical issue of the meaning of a word.

This, however, should not be understood to mean that (1) the philosophical questions are only about words, or that (2) just any context will lead us to a correct understanding. This collection will serve as a starting point for moral reflection, but, finally, the most important skill we can develop is that of supplying and looking at contexts for ourselves.

Further, the *moral* issue is about something more than the meaning of a word. Suppose we find someone who apparently is not concerned about right and wrong, good and evil. (Or suppose we discover this is the case with ourselves!) Surely here we would say the issue is not one of the meaning of words; it is one of the meaning (or lack of meaning) of a life. Perhaps this would best be described as a question of character. For what clearer indication of character could there be than the depth and seriousness with which questions of good and evil, right and wrong are confronted or shirked?

1

Trying to Drive Arrogance to Thought

Euthyphro

Persons of the Dialogue: Socrates; Euthyphro. Scene: The Porch of the King Archon

[2] Euthyphro. Why have you left the Lyceum, Socrates? and what are you doing in the Porch of the King Archon? Surely you cannot be concerned in a suit before the King, like myself?

Socrates. Not in a suit, Euthyphro; impeachment is the word which the Athenians use.

Euth. What! I suppose that some one has been prosecuting you, for I cannot believe that you are the prosecutor of another.

Soc. Certainly not.

Euth. Then some one else has been prosecuting you?

Soc. Yes.

Euth. And who is he?

Soc. A young man who is little known, Euthyphro; and I hardly know him: his name is Meletus, and he is of the deme of Pitthis. Perhaps you may remember his appearance; he has a beak, and long straight hair, and a beard which is ill grown.

Euth. No, I do not remember him, Socrates. But what is the charge which he brings against you?

Soc. What is the charge? Well, a very serious charge, which shows a good deal of character in the young man, and for which he is certainly not to be despised. He says he knows how the youth are corrupted and who are their corruptors. I fancy that he must be a wise man, and seeing that I am the reverse of a wise man, he has found me out, and is going to accuse me of corrupting his young friends. And of this our mother the state is to be the judge. Of all our political men he is the only one who seems to me to begin in the right way, with the cultivation of virtue in youth; like a good husbandman, he makes the young shoots his first care, and *[3]* clears away us who are the destroyers of them. This is only the first step; he will afterwards attend to the elder branches; and if he goes on as he has begun, he will be a very great public benefactor.

Euth. I hope that he may; but I rather fear, Socrates, that the opposite will turn

Reprinted from *The Dialogues of Plato* translated by Benjamin Jowett, third edition, (London: Oxford University Press, 1892).

6   Trying to Drive Arrogance to Thought

out to be the truth. My opinion is that in attacking you he is simply aiming a blow at the foundation of the state. But in what way does he say that you corrupt the young?

Soc. He brings a wonderful accusation against me, which at first hearing excites surprise: he says that I am a poet or maker of gods, and that I invent new gods and deny the existence of old ones; this is the ground of his indictment.

Euth. I understand, Socrates; he means to attack you about the familiar sign which occasionally, as you say, comes to you. He thinks that you are a neologian, and he is going to have you up before the court for this. He knows that such a charge is readily received by the world, as I myself know too well; for when I speak in the assembly about divine things, and foretell the future to them, they laugh at me and think me a madman. Yet every word that I say is true. But they are jealous of us all; and we must be brave and go at them.

Soc. Their laughter, friend Euthyphro, is not a matter of much consequence. For a man may be thought wise; but the Athenians, I suspect, do not much trouble themselves about him until he begins to impart his wisdom to others; and then for some reason or other, perhaps, as you say, from jealousy, they are angry.

Euth. I am never likely to try their temper in this way.

Soc. I dare say not, for you are reserved in your behaviour, and seldom impart your wisdom. But I have a benevolent habit of pouring out myself to everybody, and would even pay for a listener, and I am afraid that the Athenians may think me too talkative. Now if, as I was saying, they would only laugh at me, as you say that they laugh at you, the time might pass gaily enough in the court; but perhaps they may be in earnest, and then what the end will be you soothsayers only can predict.

Euth. I dare say that the affair will end in nothing, Socrates, and that you will win your cause; and I think that I shall win my own.

Soc. And what is your suit, Euthyphro? are you the pursuer or the defendant?

Euth. I am the pursuer.

Soc. Of whom?

[4] Euth. You will think me mad when I tell you.

Soc. Why, has the fugitive wings?

Euth. Nay, he is not very volatile at his time of life.

Soc. Who is he?

Euth. My father.

Soc. Your father! my good man?

Euth. Yes.

Soc. And of what is he accused?

Euth. Of murder, Socrates.

Soc. By the powers, Euthyphro! how little does the common herd know of the nature of right and truth. A man must be an extraordinary man, and have made great strides in wisdom, before he could have seen his way to bring such an action.

Euth. Indeed, Socrates, he must.

Soc. I suppose that the man whom your father murdered was one of your relatives —clearly he was; for if he had been a stranger you would never have thought of prosecuting him.

Euth. I am amused, Socrates, at your making a distinction between one who is a relation and one who is not a relation; for surely the pollution is the same in either case, if you knowingly associate with the murderer when you ought to clear yourself and him by proceeding against him. The real question is whether the murdered man has been justly slain. If justly, then your duty is to let the matter alone; but if unjustly, then even if the murderer lives under the same roof with you and eats at the same table, proceed against him. Now the man who is dead was a poor dependent of mine who worked for us as a field labourer on our farm in Naxos, and one day in a fit of drunken passion he got into a quarrel with one of our domestic servants and slew him. My father bound him hand and foot and threw him into a ditch, and then sent to Athens to ask of a diviner what he should do with him. Meanwhile he never attended to him and took no care about him, for he regarded him as a murderer; and thought that no great harm would be done even if he did die. Now this was just what happened. For such was the effect of cold and hunger and chains upon him, that before the messenger returned from the diviner, he was dead. And my father and family are angry with me for taking the part of the murderer and prosecuting my father. They say that he did not kill him, and that if he did, the dead man was but a murderer, and I ought not to take any notice, for that a son is impious who prosecutes a father. Which shows, Socrates, how little they know what the gods think about piety and impiety.

Soc. Good heavens, Euthyphro! and is your knowledge of religion and of things pious and impious so very exact, that, supposing the circumstances to be as you state them, you are not afraid lest you too may be doing an impious thing in bringing an action against your father?

Euth. The best of Euthyphro, and that which distinguishes him, Socrates, *[5]* from other men, is his exact knowledge of all such matters. What should I be good for without it?

Soc. Rare friend! I think that I cannot do better than be your disciple. Then before the trial with Meletus comes on I shall challenge him, and say that I have always had a great interest in religious questions, and now, as he charges me with rash imaginations and innovations in religion, I have become your disciple. You, Meletus, as I shall say to him, acknowledge Euthyphro to be a great theologian, and sound in his opinions; and if you approve of him you ought to approve of me, and not have me into court, but if you disapprove, you should begin by indicting him who is my teacher, and who will be the ruin, not of the young, but of the old; that is to say, of myself whom he instructs, and of his old father whom he admonishes and chastises. And if Meletus refuses to listen to me, but will go on, and will not shift the indictment from me to you, I cannot do better than repeat this challenge in the court.

Euth. Yes, indeed, Socrates; and if he attempts to indict me I am mistaken if I do not find a flaw in him; the court shall have a great deal more to say to him than to me.

Soc. And I, my dear friend, knowing this, am desirous of becoming your disciple. For I observe that no one appears to notice you —not even this Meletus; but his sharp eyes have found me out at once, and he has indicted me for impiety. And therefore I adjure you to tell me the nature of piety and impiety, which you said that you knew so well, and of murder, and of other offences against the gods. What are they? Is not piety in every action always the same? and impiety, again—is it not always the opposite of piety, and also the same with itself, having, as impiety, one notion which includes whatever is impious?

Euth. To be sure, Socrates.

Soc. And what is piety, and what is impiety?

Euth. Piety is doing as I am doing; that is to say, prosecuting any one who is guilty of murder, sacrilege, or of any similar crime— whether he be your father or mother, or whoever he may be—that makes no difference; and not to prosecute them is impiety. And please to consider, Socrates, what a notable proof I will give you of the truth of my words, a proof which I have already given to others:—of the principle, I mean, that the impious, whoever he may be, ought not to go unpunished. For do not men regard Zeus as the best and most righteous of the gods? *[6]*—and yet they admit that he bound his father (Cronos) because he wickedly devoured his sons, and that he too had punished his own father (Uranus) for a similar reason, in a nameless manner. And yet when I proceed against my father, they are angry with me. So inconsistent are they in their way of talking when the gods are concerned, and when I am concerned.

Soc. May not this be the reason, Euthyphro, why I am charged with impiety—that I cannot away with these stories about the gods? and therefore I suppose that people think me wrong. But, as you who are well informed about them approve of them, I cannot do better than assent to your superior wisdom. What else can I say, confessing as I do, that I know nothing about them? Tell me, for the love of Zeus, whether you really believe that they are true.

Euth. Yes, Socrates; and things more wonderful still, of which the world is in ignorance.

Soc. And do you really believe that the gods fought with one another, and had dire quarrels, battles, and the like, as the poets say, and as you may see represented in the works of great artists? The temples are full of them; and notably the robe of Athene, which is carried up to the Acropolis at the great Panathenaea, is embroidered with them. Are all these tales of the gods true, Euthyphro?

Euth. Yes, Socrates; and, as I was saying, I can tell you, if you would like to hear them, many other things about the gods which would quite amaze you.

Soc. I dare say; and you shall tell me them at some other time when I have leisure. But just at present I would rather hear from you a more precise answer, which you have not as yet given, my friend, to the question, What is "piety"? When asked, you only replied, Doing as you do, charging your father with murder.

Euth. And what I said was true, Socrates.

Soc. No doubt, Euthyphro; but you would admit that there are many other pious acts?

Euth. There are.

Soc. Remember that I did not ask you to give me two or three examples of piety, but to explain the general idea which makes all pious things to be pious. Do you not recollect that there was one idea which made the impious impious, and the pious pious?

Euth. I remember.

Soc. Tell me what is the nature of this idea, and then I shall have a standard to which I may look, and by which I may measure actions, whether yours or those of any one else, and then I shall be able to say that such and such an action is pious, such another impious.

Euth. I will tell you, if you like.

Soc. I should very much like.

Euth. Piety, then, is that which is dear to the gods, and impiety is that which is not dear to them.

[7] Soc. Very good, Euthyphro; you have now given me the sort of answer which I wanted. But whether what you say is true or not I cannot as yet tell, although I make no doubt that you will prove the truth of your words.

Euth. Of course.

Soc. Come, then, and let us examine what we are saying. That thing or person which is dear to the gods is pious, and that thing or person which is hateful to the gods is impious, these two being the extreme opposites of one another. Was not that said?

Euth. It was.

Soc. And well said?

Euth. Yes, Socrates, I thought so; it was certainly said.

Soc. And further, Euthyphro, the gods were admitted to have enmities and hatreds and differences?

Euth. Yes, that was also said.

Soc. And what sort of difference creates enmity and anger? Suppose for example that you and I, my good friend, differ about a number; do differences of this sort make us enemies and set us at variance with one another? Do we not go at once to arithmetic, and put an end to them by a sum?

Euth. True.

Soc. Or suppose that we differ about magnitudes, do we not quickly end the differences by measuring?

Euth. Very true.

Soc. And we end a controversy about heavy and light by resorting to a weighing machine?

Euth. To be sure.

Soc. But what differences are there which cannot be thus decided, and which therefore make us angry and set us at enmity with one another? I dare say the answer does not occur to you at the moment, and therefore I will suggest that these enmities arise when the matters of difference are the just and unjust, good and evil, honourable and dishonourable. Are not these the points about which men differ, and about which when we are unable satisfactorily to decide our differences, you and I and all of us quarrel, when we do quarrel?

Euth. Yes, Socrates, the nature of the differences about which we quarrel is such as you describe.

Soc. And the quarrels of the gods, noble Euthyphro, when they occur, are of a like nature?

Euth. Certainly they are.

Soc. They have differences of opinion, as you say, about good and evil, just and unjust, honourable and dishonourable: there would have been no quarrels among them, if there had been no such differences—would there now?

Euth. You are quite right.

Soc. Does not every man love that which he deems noble and just and good, and hate the opposite of them?

Euth. Very true.

Soc. But, as you say, people regard the same things, some as just and others as unjust,—about these they dispute; and so there arise wars and fightings among them. [8]

Euth. Very true.

Soc. Then the same things are hated by the gods and loved by the gods, and are both hateful and dear to them?

Euth. True.

Soc. And upon this view the same things, Euthyphro, will be pious and also impious?

Euth. So I should suppose.

Soc. Then, my friend, I remark with surprise that you have not answered the question which I asked. For I certainly did not ask you to tell me what action is both pious and impious: but now it would seem that what is loved by the gods is also hated by them. And therefore, Euthyphro, in thus chastising your father you may very likely be doing what is agreeable to Zeus but disagreeable to Cronos or Uranus, and what is acceptable to Hephaestus but unacceptable to Herè, and there may be other gods who have similar differences of opinion.

Euth. But I believe, Socrates, that all the gods would be agreed as to the propriety of punishing a murderer: there would be no difference of opinion about that.

Soc. Well, but speaking of men, Euthyphro, did you ever hear any one arguing that a murderer or any sort of evil-doer ought to be let off?

Euth. I should rather say that these are the questions which they are always arguing, especially in courts of law: they commit all sorts of crimes, and there is nothing which they will not do or say in their own defence.

Soc. But do they admit their guilt, Euthyphro, and yet say that they ought not to be punished?

Euth. No; they do not.

Soc. Then there are some things which they do not venture to say and do: for they do not venture to argue that the guilty are to be unpunished, but they deny their guilt, do they not?

Euth. Yes.

Soc. Then they do not argue that the evil-doer should not be punished, but they argue about the fact of who the evil-doer is, and what he did and when?

Euth. True.

Soc. And the gods are in the same case, if as you assert they quarrel about just and unjust, and some of them say while others deny that injustice is done among them. For surely neither God nor man will ever venture to say that the doer of injustice is not to be punished?

Euth. That is true, Socrates, in the main.

Soc. But they join issue about the particulars—gods and men alike; and, if they dispute at all, they dispute about some act which is called in question, and which by some is affirmed to be just, by others to be unjust. Is not that true?

Euth. Quite true.

[9] Soc. Well then, my dear friend Euthyphro, do tell me, for my better instruction and information, what proof have you that in the opinion of all the gods a servant who is guilty of murder, and is put in chains by the master of the dead man, and dies because he is put in chains before he who bound him can learn from the interpreters of the gods what he ought to do with him, dies unjustly; and that on behalf of such an one a son ought to proceed against his father and accuse him of murder. How would

you show that all the gods absolutely agree in approving of his act? Prove to me that they do, and I will applaud your wisdom as long as I live.

Euth. It will be a difficult task; but I could make the matter very clear indeed to you.

Soc. I understand; you mean to say that I am not so quick of apprehension as the judges: for to them you will be sure to prove that the act is unjust, and hateful to the gods.

Euth. Yes indeed, Socrates; at least if they will listen to me.

Soc. But they will be sure to listen if they find that you are a good speaker. There was a notion that came into my mind while you were speaking; I said to myself: "Well, and what if Euthyphro does prove to me that all the gods regarded the death of the serf as unjust, how do I know anything more of the nature of piety and impiety? for granting that this action may be hateful to the gods, still piety and impiety are not adequately defined by these distinctions, for that which is hateful to the gods has been shown to be also pleasing and dear to them." And therefore, Euthyphro, I do not ask you to prove this; I will suppose, if you like, that all the gods condemn and abominate such an action. But I will amend the definition so far as to say that what all the gods hate is impious, and what they love pious or holy; and what some of them love and others hate is both or neither. Shall this be our definition of piety and impiety?

Euth. Why not, Socrates?

Soc. Why not! certainly, as far as I am concerned, Euthyphro, there is no reason why not. But whether this admission will greatly assist you in the task of instructing me as you promised, is a matter for you to consider.

Euth. Yes, I should say that what all the gods love is pious and holy, and the opposite which they all hate, impious.

Soc. Ought we to enquire into the truth of this, Euthyphro, or simply to accept the mere statement on our own authority and that of others? Why do you say?

Euth. We should enquire; and I believe that the statement will stand the test of enquiry.

Soc. We shall know better, my good friend, in a little while. The point which I should first wish to understand is whether the pious or holy is beloved by the gods because it is holy, *[10]* or holy because it is beloved of the gods.

Euth. I do not understand your meaning, Socrates.

Soc. I will endeavour to explain: we speak of carrying and we speak of being carried, of leading and being led, seeing and being seen. You know that in all such cases there is a difference, and you know also in what the difference lies?

Euth. I think that I understand.

Soc. And is not that which is beloved distinct from that which loves?

Euth. Certainly.

Soc. Well; and now tell me, is that which is carried in this state of carrying because it is carried, or for some other reason?

Euth. No; that is the reason.

Soc. And the same is true of what is led and of what is seen?

Euth. True.

Soc. And a thing is not seen because it is visible, but conversely, visible because it is seen; nor is a thing led because it is in the state of being led, or carried because it is in the state of being carried, but the converse of this. And now I think, Euthyphro, that my meaning will be intelligible; and my meaning is, that any state of action or passion implies previous action or passion. It does not become because it is becoming, but it is in a state of becoming because it becomes; neither does it suffer because it is in a state of suffering, but it is in a state of suffering because it suffers. Do you not agree?

Euth. Yes.

Soc. Is not that which is loved in some state either of becoming or suffering?

Euth. Yes.

Soc. And the same holds as in the previous instances; the state of being loved follows the act of being loved, and not the act the state.

Euth. Certainly.

Soc. And what do you say of piety, Euthyphro: is not piety, according to your definition, loved by all the gods?

Euth. Yes.

Soc. Because it is pious or holy, or for some other reason?

Euth. No, that is the reason.

Soc. It is loved because it is holy, not holy because it is loved?

Euth. Yes.

Soc. And that which is dear to the gods is loved by them, and is in a state to be loved of them because it is loved of them?

Euth. Certainly.

Soc. Then that which is dear to the gods, Euthyphro, is not holy, nor is that which is holy loved of God, as you affirm; but they are two different things.

Euth. How do you mean, Socrates?

Soc. I mean to say that the holy has been acknowledged by us to be loved of God because it is holy, not to be holy because it is loved.

Euth. Yes.

Soc. But that which is dear to the gods is dear to them because it is loved by them, not loved by them because it is dear to them.

Euth. True.

Soc. But, friend Euthyphro, if that which is holy is the same with that which is dear to God, and is loved because it is holy, then that which is dear to God would have been loved as being *[11]* dear to God; but if that which is dear to God is dear to him because loved by him, then that which is holy would have been holy because loved by him. But now you see that the reverse is the case, and that they are quite different from one another. For one ($\theta\epsilon o\phi\iota\lambda\grave{\epsilon}s$) is of a kind to be loved because it is loved, and the other (*o* $\sigma\iota o\nu$) is loved because it is of a kind to be loved. Thus you appear to me, Euthyphro, when I ask you what is the essence of holiness, to offer an attribute only, and not the essence—the attribute of being loved by all

the gods. But you still refuse to explain to me the nature of holiness. And therefore, if you please, I will ask you not to hide your treasure, but to tell me once more what holiness or piety really is, whether dear to the gods or not (for that is a matter about which we will not quarrel); and what is impiety?

Euth. I really do not know, Socrates, how to express what I mean. For somehow or other our arguments, on whatever ground we rest them, seem to turn round and walk away from us.

Soc. Your words, Euthyphro, are like the handiwork of my ancestor Daedalus; and if I were the sayer or propounder of them, you might say that my arguments walk away and will not remain fixed where they are placed because I am a descendant of his. But now, since these notions are your own, you must find some other gibe, for they certainly, as you yourself allow, show an inclination to be on the move.

Euth. Nay, Socrates, I shall still say that you are the Daedalos who sets arguments in motion; not I, certainly, but you make them move or go round, for they would never have stirred, as far as I am concerned.

Soc. Then I must be a greater than Daedalus: for whereas he only made his own inventions to move, I move those of other people as well. And the beauty of it is, that I would rather not. For I would give the wisdom of Daedalus, and the wealth of Tantalus, to be able to detain them and keep them fixed. But enough of this. As I perceive that you are lazy, I will myself endeavor to show you how you might instruct me in the nature of piety; and I hope that you will not grudge your labour. Tell me, then,—Is not that which is pious necessarily just?

Euth. Yes.

Soc. And is, then, all which is just pious? or, is that which is pious all just, *[12]* but that which is just, only in part and not all, pious?

Euth. I do not understand you, Socrates.

Soc. And yet I know that you are as much wiser than I am, as you are younger. But, as I was saying, revered friend, the abundance of your wisdom makes you lazy. Please to exert yourself, for there is no real difficulty in understanding me. What I mean I may explain by an illustration of what I do not mean. The poet (Stasinus) sings—

Of Zeus, the author and creator of all these things,
You will not tell: for where there is fear there is also reverence.

Now I disagree with this poet. Shall I tell you in what respect?

Euth. By all means.

Soc. I should not say that where there is fear there is also reverence; for I am sure that many persons fear poverty and disease, and the like evils, but I do not perceive that they reverence the objects of their fear.

Euth. Very true.

Soc. But where reverence is, there is fear; for he who has a feeling of reverence and shame about the commission of any action, fears and is afraid of an ill reputation.

Euth. No doubt.

Soc. Then we are wrong in saying that where there is fear there is also reverence; and we should say, where there is reverence there is also fear. But there is not always reverence where there is fear; for fear is a more extended notion, and reverence is a part of fear, just as the odd is a part of number, and number is a more extended notion than the odd. I suppose that you follow me now?

Euth. Quite well.

Soc. That was the sort of question which I meant to raise when I asked whether the just is always the pious, or the pious always the just; and whether there may not be justice where there is not piety; for justice is the more extended notion of which piety is only a part. Do you dissent?

Euth. No, I think that you are quite right.

Soc. Then, if piety is a part of justice, I suppose that we should enquire what part? If you had pursued the enquiry in the previous cases; for instance, if you had asked me

what is an even number, and what part of number the even is, I should have had no difficulty in replying, a number which represents a figure having two equal sides. Do you not agree?

Euth. Yes, I quite agree.

Soc. In like manner, I want you to tell me what part of justice is piety or holiness, that I may be able to tell Meletus not to do me injustice, or indict me for impiety, as I am now adequately instructed by you in the nature of piety or holiness, and their opposites.

Euth. Piety or holiness, Socrates, appears to me to be that part of justice which attends to the gods, as there is the other part of justice which attends to men.

[13] Soc. That is good, Euthyphro; yet still there is a little point about which I should like to have further information, What is the meaning of "attention"? For attention can hardly be used in the same sense when applied to the gods as when applied to other things. For instance, horses are said to require attention, and not every person is able to attend to them, but only a person skilled in horsemanship. Is it not so?

Euth. Certainly.

Soc. I should suppose that the art of horsemanship is the art of attending to horses?

Euth. Yes.

Soc. Nor is every one qualified to attend to dogs, but only the huntsman?

Euth. True.

Soc. And I should also conceive that the art of the huntsman is the art of attending to dogs?

Euth. Yes.

Soc. As the art of the oxherd is the art of attending to oxen?

Euth. Very true.

Soc. In like manner holiness or piety is the art of attending to the gods?—that would be your meaning, Euthyphro?

Euth. Yes.

Soc. And is not attention always designed for the good or benefit of that to which the attention is given? As in the case of horses, you may observe that when attended to by the horseman's art they are benefited and improved, are they not?

Euth. True.

Soc. As the dogs are benefited by the huntsman's art, and the oxen by the art of the oxherd, and all other things are tended or attended for their good and not for their hurt?

Euth. Certainly, not for their hurt.

Soc. But for their good?

Euth. Of course.

Soc. And does piety or holiness, which has been defined to be the art of attending to the gods, benefit or improve them? Would you say that when you do a holy act you make any of the gods better?

Euth. No, no; that was certainly not what I meant.

Soc. And I, Euthyphro, never supposed that you did. I asked you the question about the nature of the attention, because I thought that you did not.

Euth. You do me justice, Socrates; that is not the sort of attention which I mean.

Soc. Good: but I must still ask what is this attention to the gods which is called piety?

Euth. It is such, Socrates, as servants show to their masters.

Soc. I understand—a sort of ministration to the gods.

Euth. Exactly.

Soc. Medicine is also a sort of ministration or service, having in view the attainment of some object—would you not say of health?

Euth. I should.

Soc. Again, there is an art which ministers to the ship-builder with a view to the attainment of some result?

Euth. Yes, Socrates, with a view to the building of a ship.

Soc. As there is an art which ministers to the housebuilder with a view to the building of a house?

Euth. Yes.

Soc. And now tell me, my good friend, about the art which ministers to the gods: what work does that help to accomplish? For you must surely know if, as you say, you

are of all men living the one who is best instructed in religion.

Euth. And I speak the truth, Socrates.

Soc. Tell me then, oh tell me—what is that fair work which the gods do by the help of our ministrations?

Euth. Many and fair, Socrates, are the works which they do.

[14] *Soc.* Why, my friend, and so are those of a general. But the chief of them is easily told. Would you not say that victory in war is the chief of them?

Euth. Certainly.

Soc. Many and fair, too, are the works of the husbandman, if I am not mistaken; but his chief work is the production of food from the earth?

Euth. Exactly.

Soc. And of the many and fair things done by the gods, which is the chief or principal one?

Euth. I have told you already, Socrates, that to learn all these things accurately will be very tiresome. Let me simply say that piety or holiness is learning how to please the gods in word and deed, by prayers and sacrifices. Such piety is the salvation of families and states, just as the impious, which is unpleasing to the gods, is their ruin and destruction.

Soc. I think that you could have answered in much fewer words the chief question which I asked, Euthyphro, if you had chosen. But I see plainly that you are not disposed to instruct me—clearly not: else why, when we reached the point, did you turn aside? Had you only answered me I should have truly learned of you by this time the nature of piety. Now, as the asker of a question is necessarily dependent on the answerer, whither he leads I must follow; and can only ask again, what is the pious, and what is piety? Do you mean that they are a sort of science of praying and sacrificing?

Euth. Yes, I do.

Soc. And sacrificing is giving to the gods, and prayer is asking of the gods?

Euth. Yes, Socrates.

Soc. Upon this view, then, piety is a science of asking and giving?

Euth. You understand me capitally, Socrates.

Soc. Yes, my friend; the reason is that I am a votary of your science, and give my mind to it, and therefore nothing which you say will be thrown away upon me. Please then to tell me, what is the nature of this service to the gods? Do you mean that we prefer requests and give gifts to them?

Euth. Yes, I do.

Soc. Is not the right way of asking to ask of them what we want?

Euth. Certainly.

Soc. And the right way of giving is to give to them in return what they want of us. There would be no meaning in an art which gives to any one that which he does not want.

Euth. Very true, Socrates.

Soc. Then piety, Euthyphro, is an art which gods and men have of doing business with one another.

Euth. That is an expression which you may use, if you like.

Soc. But I have no particular liking for anything but the truth. I wish, however, that you would tell me what benefit accrues to the gods from our gifts. There is no doubt about what they give to us; *[15]* for there is no good thing which they do not give; but how we can give any good thing to them in return is far from being equally clear. If they give everything and we give nothing, that must be an affair of business in which we have very greatly the advantage of them.

Euth. And do you imagine, Socrates, that any benefit accrues to the gods from our gifts?

Soc. But if not, Euthyphro, what is the meaning of gifts which are conferred by us upon the gods?

Euth. What else, but tributes of honour; and, as I was just now saying, what pleases them?

Soc. Piety, then, is pleasing to the gods, but not beneficial or dear to them?

Euth. I should say that nothing could be dearer.

Soc. Then once more the assertion is repeated that piety is dear to the gods?

Euth. Certainly.

Soc. And when you say this, can you wonder at your words not standing firm, but walking away? Will you accuse me of being the Daedalus who makes them walk away, not perceiving that there is another and far greater artist than Daedalus who makes them go round in a circle, and he is yourself; for the argument, as you will perceive, comes round to the same point. Were we not saying that the holy or pious was not the same with that which is loved of the gods? Have you forgotten?

Euth. I quite remember.

Soc. And are you not saying that what is loved of the gods is holy; and is not this the same as what is dear to them—do you see?

Euth. True.

Soc. Then either we were wrong in our former assertion; or, if we were right then, we are wrong now.

Euth. One of the two must be true.

Soc. Then we must begin again and ask, What is piety? That is an enquiry which I shall never be weary of pursuing as far as in me lies; and I entreat you not to scorn me, but to apply your mind to the utmost, and tell me the truth. For, if any man knows, you are he; and therefore I must detain you, like Proteus, until you tell. If you had not certainly known the nature of piety and impiety, I am confident that you would never, on behalf of a serf, have charged your aged father with murder. You would not have run such a risk of doing wrong in the sight of the gods, and you would have had too much respect for the opinions of men. I am sure, therefore, that you know the nature of piety and impiety. Speak out then, my dear Euthyphro, and do not hide your knowledge.

Euth. Another time, Socrates; for I am in a hurry, and must go now.

Soc. Alas! my companion, and will you leave me in despair? I was hoping that you would instruct me in the nature of piety and impiety; and then I might have cleared myself of Meletus and his indictment. *[16]* I

would have told him that I had been en-
lightened by Euthyphro, and had given up
rash innovations and speculations, in which
I indulged only through ignorance, and
that now I am about to lead a better life.

Questions

1. What kind of character do Euthyphro's
words and actions display? What concerns caused
these words and actions?

2. Consider Socrates' questions as a tactic.
When he asks for a definition, he is indirectly asking for something else. What could this be? In what
kind of conflict is he involved? Is this method of
questioning a wise tactic? What is he trying to accomplish with this tactic?

3. Consider Euthyphro's words:

> The real question is whether the murdered man
> has been justly slain. If justly, then your duty is
> to let the matter alone; but if unjustly, then even
> if the murderer lives under the same roof with
> you and eats at the same table, proceed against
> him.

The first sentence would seem to beg the question.
Explain how this occurs. Is Euthyphro right about
this? Explain. Could we say that *what* he says is
right, but there is something wrong with *his* saying
it? Explain.

2

Trying to Persuade
the Crowd

Apology

[17] How you, O Athenians, have been affected by my accusers, I cannot tell; but I know that they almost made me forget who I was—so persuasively did they speak; and yet they have hardly uttered a word of truth. But of the many falsehoods told by them, there was one which quite amazed me;—I mean when they said that you should be upon your guard and not allow yourselves to be deceived by the force of my eloquence. To say this, when they were certain to be detected as soon as I opened my lips and proved myself to be anything but a great speaker, did indeed appear to me most shameless—unless by the force of eloquence they mean the force of truth; for if such is their meaning, I admit that I am eloquent. But in how different a way from theirs! Well, as I was saying, they have scarcely spoken the truth at all; but from me you shall hear the whole truth: not, however, delivered after their manner in a

Reprinted from *The Dialogues of Plato* translated by Benjamin Jowett, third edition, (London: Oxford University Press, 1892).

set oration duly ornamented with words and phrases. No, by heaven! but I shall use the words and arguments which occur to me at the moment; for I am confident in the justice of my cause: at my time of life I ought not to be appearing before you, O men of Athens, in the character of a juvenile orator—let no one expect it of me. And I must beg of you to grant me a favour:— If I defend myself in my accustomed manner, and you hear me using the words which I have been in the habit of using in the agora, at the tables of the money-changers, or anywhere else, I would ask you not to be surprised, and not to interrupt me on this account. For I am more than seventy years of age, and appearing now for the first time in a court of law, I am quite a stranger to the language of the place; and therefore I would have you regard me as if I were really a stranger, [18] whom you would excuse if he spoke in his native tongue, and after the fashion of his country: —Am I making an unfair request of you? Never mind the manner, which may or may not be good; but think only of the truth of my words, and give heed to that: let the speaker speak truly and the judge decide justly.

And first, I have to reply to the older charges and to my first accusers, and then I will go on to the later ones. For of old I have had many accusers, who have accused me falsely to you during many years; and I am more afraid of them than of Anytus and his associates, who are dangerous, too, in their own way. But far more dangerous are the others, who began when you were children, and took possession of your minds with their falsehoods, telling of one Socrates, a wise man, who speculated about the heaven above, and searched into the earth beneath, and made the worse appear the better cause. The disseminators of this tale are the accusers whom I dread; for their hearers are apt to fancy that such enquirers do not believe in the existence of the gods. And they are many and their charges against me are of ancient date and they were made by them in the days when you were more impressible than you are now— in childhood, or it may have been in youth —and the cause when heard went by default, for there was none to answer. And hardest of all, I do not know and cannot tell the names of my accusers; unless in the chance case of a Comic poet. All who from envy and malice have persuaded you— some of them having first convinced themselves—all this class of men are most difficult to deal with; for I cannot have them up here, and cross-examine them, and therefore I must simply fight with shadows in my own defence, and argue when there is no one who answers. I will ask you then to assume with me, as I was saying, that my opponents are of two kinds; one recent, the other ancient: and I hope that you will see the propriety of my answering the latter first, for these accusations you heard long before the others and much oftener.

[19] Well, then, I must make my defence, and endeavor to clear away in a short time, a slander which has lasted a long time. May I succeed, if to succeed be for my good and yours, or likely to avail me in my cause! The task is not an easy one; I quite understand the nature of it. And so leaving the event with God, in obedience to the law I will now make my defence.

I will begin at the beginning, and ask what is the accusation which has given rise to the slander of me, and in fact has encouraged Meletus to prefer this charge against me. Well, what do the slanderers say? They shall be my prosecutors, and I will sum up their words in an affidavit: "Socrates is an evil-doer, and a curious person, who searches into things under the earth and in heaven, and he makes the worse appear the better cause; and he teaches the aforesaid doctrines to others." Such is the nature of the accusation: it is just what you have yourselves seen in the comedy of Aristophanes who has introduced a man whom he calls Socrates, going about and saying that he walks in air, and talking a deal of nonsense concerning matters of which I do not pretend to know either much or little—not that I mean to speak disparagingly of any one who is a student of natural philosophy. I should be very sorry if Meletus could bring so grave a charge against me. But the simple truth is, O Athenians, that I have nothing to do with physical speculations. Very many of those here present are witnesses to the truth of this, and to them I appeal. Speak then, you who have heard me, and tell your neighbours whether any of you have ever known me hold forth in few words or in many upon such matters. . . . You hear their answer. And from what they say of this part of the charge you will be able to judge of the truth of the rest.

As little foundation is there for the report that I am a teacher, and take money; this accusation has no more truth in it than the other. Although, if a man were really able to instruct mankind, to receive money for giving instruction would, in my opinion, be an honour to him. There is Gorgias of Leontium, and Prodicus of Ceos, and Hippias of Elis, who go the round of the cities, and are able to persuade the young men to leave their own citizens by whom they might be taught for nothing, *[20]* and come to them whom they not only pay, but are thankful if they may be allowed to pay them. There is at this time a Parian philosopher residing in Athens, of whom I have heard; and I came to hear of him in this way:—I came across a man who has spent a world of money on the Sophists, Callias, the son of Hipponicus, and knowing that he had sons, I asked him: Callias," I said "if your two sons were foals or calves, there would be no difficulty in finding some one to put over them; we should hire a trainer of horses, or a farmer probably, who would improve and perfect them in their own proper virtue and excellence; but as they are human beings, whom are you thinking of placing over them? Is there any one who understands human and political virtue? You must have thought about the matter, for you have sons; is there any one?" "There is," he said. "Who is he?" said I; "and of what country? and what does he charge?" "Evenus the Parian," he replied; "he is the man, and his charge is five minae." Happy is Evenus, I said to myself, if he really has this wisdom, and teaches at such a moderate charge. Had I the same, I should have been very proud and conceited; but the truth is that I have no knowledge of the kind.

I dare say, Athenians, that some one among you will reply, "Yes, Socrates, but what is the origin of these accusations which are brought against you; there must have been something strange which you have been doing? All these rumours and this talk about you would never have arisen if you had been like other men: tell us, then, what is the cause of them, for we should be sorry to judge hastily of you." Now I regard this as a fair challenge, and I will endeavour to explain to you the reason why I am called wise and have such an evil fame. Please to attend then. And although some of you may think that I am joking, I declare that I will tell you the entire truth. Men of Athens, this reputation of mine has come of a certain sort of wisdom which I possess. If you ask me what kind of wisdom, I reply, wisdom such as may perhaps be attained by

man, for to that extent I am inclined to believe that I am wise; whereas the persons of whom I was speaking have a superhuman wisdom, which I may fail to describe, because I have it not myself; and he who says that I have, speaks falsely, and is taking away my character. And here, O men of Athens, I must beg you not to interrupt me, even if I seem to say something extravagant. For the word which I will speak is not mine. I will refer you to a witness who is worthy of credit; that witness shall be the God of Delphi—he will tell you about my wisdom, if I have any, and of what sort it is. You must have known Chaerephon; he was early a friend of mine, and also a friend of yours, [21] for he shared in the recent exile of the people, and returned with you. Well, Chaerephon, as you know, was very impetuous in all his doings, and he went to Delphi and boldly asked the oracle to tell him whether—as I was saying, I must beg you not to interrupt—he asked the oracle to tell him whether any one was wiser than I was, and the Pythian prophetess answered, that there was no man wiser. Chaerephon is dead himself; but his brother, who is in court, will confirm the truth of what I am saying.

Why do I mention this? Because I am going to explain to you why I have such an evil name. When I heard the answer, I said to myself, What can the god mean? and what is the interpretation of his riddle? for I know that I have no wisdom, small or great. What then can he mean when he says that I am the wisest of men? And yet he is a god, and cannot lie; that would be against his nature. After long consideration, I thought of a method of trying the question. I reflected that if I could only find a man wiser than myself, then I might go to the god with a refutation in my hand. I should say to him, "Here is a man who is wiser than I am; but you said that I was the wisest." Accordingly I went to one who had the reputation of wisdom, and observed him—his name I need not mention; he was a politician whom I selected for examination—and the result was as follows: When I began to talk with him, I could not help thinking that he was not really wise, although he was thought wise by many, and still wiser by himself; and thereupon I tried to explain to him that he thought himself wise, but was not really wise; and the consequence was that he hated me, and his enmity was shared by several who were present and heard me. So I left him, saying to myself, as I went away: Well, although I do not suppose that either of us knows anything really beautiful and good, I am better off than he is,—for he knows nothing, and thinks that he knows; I neither know nor think that I know. In this latter particular, then, I seem to have slightly the advantage of him. Then I went to another who had still higher pretensions to wisdom, and my conclusion was exactly the same. Whereupon I made another enemy of him, and of many others besides him.

Then I went to one man after another, being not unconscious of the enmity which I provoked, and I lamented and feared this: But necessity was laid upon me,—the word of God, I thought, ought to be considered first. And I said to myself, Go I must to all who appear to know, *[22]* and find out the meaning of the oracle. And I swear to you, Athenians, by the dog I swear! for I must tell you the truth—the result of my mission was just this: I found that the men most in repute were all but the most foolish and that others less esteemed were really wiser and better. I will tell you the tale of my wanderings and of the "Herculean" labours, as I may call them, which I endured only to find at last the oracle irrefutable. After the politicians, I went to the poets; tragic, dithyrambic, and all sorts. And there, I said to myself, you will be instantly detected; now you will find out that you are more ignorant than they are. Accordingly, I took them some of the most elaborate passages in their own writings, and asked what was the meaning of them—thinking that they would teach me something. Will you believe me? I am almost ashamed to confess the truth, but I must say that there is hardly a person present who would not

have talked better about their poetry than they did themselves. Then I knew that not by wisdom do poets write poetry but by a sort of genius and inspiration; they are like diviners or soothsayers who also say many fine things, but do not understand the meaning of them. The poets appeared to me to be much in the same case; and I further observed that upon the strength of their poetry they believed themselves to be the wisest of men in other things in which they were not wise. So I departed, conceiving myself to be superior to them for the same reason that I was superior to the politicans.

At last I went to the artisans, for I was conscious that I knew nothing at all, as I may say, and I was sure that they knew many fine things; and here I was not mistaken, for they did know many things of which I was ignorant, and in this they certainly were wiser than I was. But I observed that even the good artisans fell into the same error as the poets;—because they were good workmen they thought that they also knew all sorts of high matters, and this defect in them overshadowed their wisdom: and therefore I asked myself on behalf of the oracle, whether I would like to be as I was, neither having their knowledge nor their ignorance, or be like them in both; and I made answer to myself and to the oracle that I was better off as I was.

This inquisition has led to my having many enemies of the worst and most dangerous kind, *[23]* and has given occasion also to many calumnies. And I am called wise, for my hearers always imagine that I myself possess the wisdom which I find wanting in others: but the truth is, O men of Athens, that God only is wise: and by his answer he intends to show that the wisdom of men is worth little or nothing; he is not speaking of Socrates, he is only using my name by way of illustration, as if he said, He, O men, is the wisest, who, like Socrates, knows that his wisdom is in truth worth nothing. And so I go about the world, obedient to the god, and search and make enquiry into the wisdom of any one, whether citizen or stranger, who appears to be wise; and if he is not wise; then in vindication of the oracle I show him that he is not wise; and my occupation quite absorbs me, and I have no time to give either to any public matter of interest or to any concern of my own, but I am in utter poverty by reason of my devotion to the god.

There is another thing:—young men of the richer classes, who have not much to do, come about me of their own accord; they like to hear the pretenders examined, and they often imitate me, and proceed to examine others; there are plenty of persons, as they quickly discover, who think that they know something, but really know little or nothing; and then those who are examined by them instead of being angry with themselves are angry with me: This confounded Socrates, they say; this villainous misleader of youth!—and then if somebody asks them, Why, what evil does he practise or teach? they do not know, and cannot tell; but in order that they may not appear to be at a loss, they repeat the ready-made charges which are used against all philosophers about teaching things up in the clouds and under the earth, and having no gods, and making the worse appear the better cause; for they do not like to confess that their pretence of knowledge has been detected—which is the truth; and as they are numerous and ambitious and energetic, and are drawn up in battle array and have persuasive tongues, they have filled your ears with their loud and inveterate calumnies. And this is the reason why my three accusers, Meletus and Anytus and Lycon, have set upon me; Meletus, who has a quarrel with me on behalf of the poets; Anytus, on behalf of the craftsmen and politicans; *[24]* Lycon, on behalf of the rhetoricians: and as I said at the beginning, I cannot expect to get rid of such a mass of calumny all in a moment. And this, O men of Athens, is the truth and the whole truth; I have concealed nothing, I have dissembled nothing. And yet, I know that my plainness of speech makes them hate me, and what is their hatred but a proof that I

am speaking the truth?—Hence has arisen the prejudice against me; and this is the reason of it, as you will find out either in this or in any future enquiry.

I have said enough in my defence against the first class of my accusers; I turn to the second class. They are headed by Meletus, that good man and true lover of his country, as he calls himself. Against these, too, I must try to make a defence:—Let their affidavit be read: it contains something of this kind: It says that Socrates is a doer of evil, who corrupts the youth; and who does not believe in the gods of the state, but has other new divinities of his own. Such is the charge; and now let us examine the particular counts. He says that I am a doer of evil, and corrupt the youth; but I say, O men of Athens that Meletus is a doer of evil, in that he pretends to be in earnest when he is only in jest, and is so eager to bring men to trial from a pretended zeal and interest about matters in which he really never had the smallest interest. And the truth of this I will endeavour to prove to you.

Come hither, Meletus, and let me ask a question of you. You think a great deal about the improvement of youth?

Yes, I do.

Tell the judges, then, who is their improver; for you must know, as you have taken the pains to discover their corrupter, and are citing and accusing me before them. Speak, then, and tell the judges who their improver is.—Observe, Meletus, that you are silent, and have nothing to say. But is not this rather disgraceful, and a very considerable proof of what I was saying, that you have no interest in the matter? Speak up, friend, and tell us who their improver is.

The laws.

But that, my good sir, is not my meaning. I want to know who the person is, who, in the first place, knows the laws.

The judges, Socrates, who are present in court.

What, do you mean to say, Meletus, that they are able to instruct and improve youth?

Certainly they are.

What, all of them, or some only and not others?

All of them.

By the goddess Herè, that is good news! There are plenty of improvers, *[25]* then. And what do you say of the audience,—do they improve them?

Yes, they do.

And the senators?

Yes, the senators improve them.

But perhaps the members of the assembly corrupt them?—or do they too improve them?

They improve them.

Then every Athenian improves and elevates them; all with the exception of myself; and I alone am their corrupter? Is that what you affirm?

That is what I stoutly affirm.

I am very unfortunate if you are right. But suppose I ask you a question: How about horses? Does one man do them harm and all the world good? Is not the exact opposite the truth? One man is able to do them good, or at least not many;—the trainer of horses, that is to say, does them good, and others who have to do with them rather injure them? Is not that true, Meletus, of horses, or of any other animals? Most assuredly it is; whether you and Anytus say yes or no. Happy indeed would be the condition of youth if they had one corrupter only, and all the rest of the world were their improvers. But you, Meletus, have sufficiently shown that you never had a thought about the young: your carelessness is seen in your not caring about the very things which you bring against me.

And now, Meletus, I will ask you another question—by Zeus I will: Which is better, to live among bad citizens, or among good ones? Answer, friend, I say; the question is one which may be easily answered. Do not the good do their neighbours good, and the bad do them evil?

Certainly.

And is there any one who would rather be injured than benefited by those who live with him? Answer, my good friend, the law requires you to answer—does any one like to be injured?

Certainly not.

And when you accuse me of corrupting and deteriorating the youth, do you allege that I corrupt them intentionally or unintentionally?

Intentionally, I say.

But you have just admitted that the good do their neighbours good, and evil do them evil. Now, is that a truth which your superior wisdom has recognized thus early in life, and am I, at my age, in such darkness and ignorance as not to know that if a man with whom I have to live is corrupted by me, I am very likely to be harmed by him; and yet I corrupt him, and intentionally, too—so you say, although neither I nor any other human being is ever likely to be convinced by you. *[26]* But either I do not corrupt them, or I corrupt them unintentionally, and on either view of the case you lie. If my offense is unintentional, the law has no cognizance of unintentional offences: you ought to have taken me privately, and warned and admonished me; for if I had been better advised I should have left off doing what I only did untentionally—no doubt I should; but you would have nothing to say to me and refused to teach me. And now you bring me up in this court, which is a place not of instruction, but of punishment.

It will be very clear to you, Athenians, as I was saying, that Meletus has no care at all, great or small, about the matter. But still I should like to know, Meletus, in what I am affirmed to corrupt the young. I suppose you mean, as I infer from your indictment, that I teach them not to acknowledge the gods which the state acknowledges, but some other new divinities or spiritual agencies in their stead. These are the lessons by which I corrupt the youth, as you say.

Yes, that I say emphatically.

Then, by the gods, Meletus, of whom we are speaking, tell me and the court, in somewhat plainer terms, what you mean! for I do not as yet understand whether you affirm that I teach other men to acknowledge some gods, and therefore that I do believe in gods, and am not an entire atheist—this you do not lay to my charge,—but only you say that they are not the same gods which the city recognizes—the charge is that they are different gods. Or, do you mean that I am an atheist simply, and a teacher of atheism?

I mean the latter—that you are a complete atheist.

What an extraordinary statement! Why do you think so, Meletus? Do you mean that I do not believe in the godhead of the sun or moon, like other men?

I assure you, judges, that he does not: for he says that the sun is stone, and the moon earth.

Friend Meletus, you think that you are accusing Anaxagoras: and you have but a bad opinion of the judges, if you fancy them illiterate to such a degree as not to know that these doctrines are found in the books of Anaxagoras the Clazomenian, which are full of them. And so, forsooth, the youth are said to be taught them by Socrates, when there are not unfrequently exhibitions of them at the theatre (price of admission one drachma at the most); and they might pay their money, and laugh at Socrates if he pretends to father these extraordinary views. And so, Meletus, you really think that I do not believe in any god?

I swear by Zeus that you believe absolutely in none at all.

Nobody will believe you, Meletus, and I am pretty sure that you do not believe yourself. I cannot help thinking, men of Athens, that Meletus is reckless and impudent, and that he has written this indictment in a spirit of mere wantonness and youthful bravado. [27] Has he not compounded a riddle, thinking to try me? He said to himself:—I shall see whether the wise Socrates will discover my facetious contradiction, or whether I shall be able to deceive him and the rest of them. For he certainly does appear to me to contradict himself in the indictment as much as if he said that Socrates is guilty of not believing in the gods, and yet of believing in them—but this is not like a person who is in earnest.

I should like you, O men of Athens, to join me in examining what I conceive to be his inconsistency; and do you, Meletus, answer. And I must remind the audience of my request that they would not make a disturbance if I speak in my accustomed manner:

Did ever man, Meletus, believe in the existence of human things, and not of human beings? . . . I wish, men of Athens, that he would answer, and not be always trying to get up an interruption. Did ever any man believe in horsemanship, and not in horses? or in flute-playing, and not in flute-players? No, my friend; I will answer to you and to the court, as you refuse to answer for yourself. There is no man who ever did. But now please to answer the next question: Can a man believe in spiritual and divine agencies, and not in spirits or demigods?

He cannot.

How lucky I am to have extracted that answer, by the assistance of the court! But then you swear in the indictment that I teach and believe in divine or spiritual agencies (new or old, no matter for that); at any rate, I believe in spiritual agencies,—so you say and swear in the affidavit; and yet if I believe in divine beings, how can I help believing in spirits or demigods;—must I not? To be sure I must; and therefore I may assume that your silence gives consent. Now what are spirits or demigods? are they not either gods or the sons of gods?

Certainly they are.

But this is what I call the facetious riddle invented by you: the demigods or spirits are gods, and you say first that I do not believe in gods, and then again that I do believe in gods; that is, if I believe in demigods. For if the demigods are the illegitimate sons of gods, whether by the nymphs or by any other mothers, of whom they are said to be the sons—what human being will ever believe that there are no gods if they are the sons of gods? You might as well affirm the existence of mules, and deny that of horses and asses. Such nonsense, Meletus, could only have been intended by you to make trial of me. You have put this into the indictment because you had nothing real of which to accuse me. But no one who has a particle of understanding will ever be convinced by you that the same men can believe in divine and superhuman things, and yet not believe that there are gods and demigods and heroes. *[28]*

I have said enough in answer to the charge of Meletus: any elaborate defence is unnecessary; but I know only too well how many are the enmities which I have incurred, and this is what will be my destruction if I am destroyed;—not Meletus, nor yet Anytus, but the envy and detraction of the world, which has been the death of many good men, and will probably be the death of many more; there is no danger of my being the last of them.

Some one will say: And are you not ashamed, Socrates, of a course of life which is likely to bring you to an untimely end? To him I may fairly answer: There you are mistaken: a man who is good for anything ought not to calculate the chance of living or dying; he ought only to consider whether in doing anything he is doing right or wrong—acting the part of a good man or of a bad. Whereas, upon your view, the heroes who fell at Troy were not good for much, and the son of Thetis above all, who altogether despised danger in comparison with disgrace; and when he was so eager to slay Hector, his goddess mother said to him, that if he avenged his companion Patroclus, and slew Hector, he would die himself—"Fate," she said, in these or the like words, "waits for you next after Hector"; he, receiving this warning, utterly despised danger and death, and instead of fearing them, feared rather to live in dishonour, and not to avenge his friend. "Let me die forthwith," he replies, "and be avenged of my enemy, rather than abide here by the beaked ships, a laughing-stock and a burden of the earth." Had Achilles any thought of death and danger? For wherever a man's place is, whether the place which he has chosen or that in which he has been placed by a commander, there he ought to remain in the hour of danger; he should not think of death or of anything but of disgrace. And this, O men of Athens, is a true saying.

Strange, indeed, would be my conduct, O men of Athens, if I who, when I was ordered by the generals whom you chose to command me at Potidaea and Amphipolis and Delium, remained where they placed me, like any other man, facing death—if now, when, as I conceive and imagine, God orders me to fulfil the philosopher's mission of searching into myself and other men, I were to desert my post through fear of death, *[29]* or any other fear; that would indeed be strange, and I might justly be arraigned in court for denying the existence of the gods, if I disobeyed the oracle because I was afraid of death, fancying that I was wise when I was not wise. For the fear of death is indeed the pretence of wisdom, and not real wisdom, being a pretence of knowing the unknown; and no one knows whether death, which men in their fear apprehend to be the greatest evil, may not be the greatest good. Is not this ignorance of a disgraceful sort, the ignorance which is the conceit that man knows what he does not know? And in this respect only I believe myself to differ from men in general, and may perhaps claim to be wiser than they are:—that whereas I know but little of the world below, I do not suppose that I know: but I do know that injustice and disobedience to a better, whether God or man, is evil and dishonourable, and I will never fear or avoid a possible good rather than a certain evil. And therefore if you let me go now, and are not convinced by Anytus, who said that since I had been prosecuted I must be put to death (or if not that I ought never to have been prosecuted at all); and that if I escape now, your sons will all be utterly ruined by listening to my words—if you say to me, Socrates, this time we will not mind Anytus, and you shall be let off, but upon one condition, that you are not to enquire and speculate in this way any more, and that if you are caught doing so again you shall die;—if this was the condition on which you let me go, I should reply: Men of Athens, I honour and love you; but I shall obey God rather than you, and while I have life and strength I shall never cease from the practice and teaching of philosophy, exhorting any one whom I meet and saying to him after my manner: You, my friend,—a citizen of the great and mighty and wise city of Athens,—are you not ashamed of heaping up the greatest amount of money and honour and reputation, and caring so little about wisdom and truth and the greatest improvement of the soul, which you never regard or heed at all? And if the person with whom I am arguing, says: Yes, but I do care; then I do not leave him or let him go at once; but I proceed to interrogate and examine and cross-examine him, and if I think that he has no virtue in him, but only says that he has, I reproach him with undervaluing the greater, and overvaluing the less. [30] And I shall repeat the same words to every one whom I meet, young and old, citizen and alien, but especially to the citizens, inasmuch as they are my brethren. For know that this is the command of God, and I believe that no greater good has ever happened in the state than my service to the God. For I do nothing but go about persuading you all, old and young alike, not to take thought for your persons or your properties, but first and chiefly to care about the greatest improvement of the soul. I tell you that virtue is not given by money, but that from virtue comes money and every other good of man, public as well as private. This is my teaching, and if this is the doctrine which corrupts the youth, I am a mischievous person. But if any one says that this is not my teaching, he is speaking an untruth. Wherefore, O men of Athens, I say to you, do as Anytus bids or not as Anytus bids, and either acquit me or not; but whichever you do, understand that I shall never alter my ways, not even if I have to die many times.

Men of Athens, do not interrupt, but hear me; there was an understanding between us, that you should hear me to the end: I have something more to say, at which you may be inclined to cry out; but I believe that to hear me will be good for you, and therefore I beg that you will not cry out. I would have you know, that if you kill such an one as I am, you will injure yourselves more than you will injure me. Nothing will injure me, not Meletus nor yet Anytus—they cannot, for a bad man is not permitted to injure a better than himself. I do not deny that Anytus may, perhaps, kill him, or drive him into exile, or deprive him of civil rights; and he may imagine, and others may imagine, that he is inflicting a great injury upon him: but there I do not agree. For the evil of doing as he is doing—the evil of unjustly taking away the life of another—is greater far.

And now, Athenians, I am not going to argue for my own sake, as you may think, but for yours, that you may not sin against the God by condemning me, who am his gift to you. For if you kill me you will not easily find a successor to me, who, if I may use such a ludicrous figure of speech, am a sort of gadfly, given to the state by God; and the state is a great and noble steed who is tardy in his motions owing to his very size, and requires to be stirred into life. [31] I am that gadfly which God has attached to the state, and all day long and in all places am always fastening upon you, arousing and persuading and reproaching you. You will not easily find another like me, and therefore I would advise you to spare me. I dare say that you may feel out of temper (like a person who is suddenly awakened from sleep), and you think that you might easily strike me dead as Anytus advises, and then you would sleep on for the remainder of your lives, unless God in his care of you sent you another gadfly. When I say that I am given to you by God, the proof of my mission is this:—if I had been like other men, I should not have neglected all my own concerns or patiently seen the neglect of them during all these years, and have been doing yours, coming to you individually like a father or elder brother, exhorting you to regard virtue; such conduct, I say, would be unlike human nature. If I had gained anything, or if my exhortations had been paid, there would have been some sense in my doing so; but now, as you will perceive, not even the impudence of my accusers dares to say that I have ever exacted or sought pay of any one; of that they have no witness. And I have a sufficient witness to the truth of what I say—my poverty.

Some one may wonder why I go about in private giving advice and busying myself with the concerns of others, but do not venture to come forward in public and advise the state. I will tell you why. You have heard me speak at sundry times and in divers places of an oracle or sign which comes to me, and is the divinity which Meletus ridicules in the indictment. This sign, which is a kind of voice, first began to come to me when I was a child; it always forbids but never commands me to do anything which I am going to do. This is what deters me from being a politican. And rightly, as I think. For I am certain, O men of Athens, that if I had engaged in politics, I should have perished long ago, and done no good either to you or to myself. And do not be offended at my telling you the truth: for the truth is, that no man who goes to war with you or any other multitude, honestly striving against the many lawless and unrighteous deeds which are done in a state, *[32]* will save his life; he who will fight for the right, if he would live even for a brief space, must have a private station and not a public one.

I can give you convincing evidence of what I say, not words only, but what you value far more—actions. Let me relate to you a passage of my own life which will prove to you that I should never have yielded to injustice from any fear of death, and that "as I should have refused to yield" I must have died at once. I will tell you a tale of the courts, not very interesting perhaps, but nevertheless true. The only office of state which I ever held, O men of Athens, was that of senator: the tribe Antiochis, which is my tribe, had the presidency at the trial of the generals who had not taken up the bodies of the slain after the battle of Arginusae; and you proposed to try them in a body, contrary to law, as you all thought afterwards; but at the time I was the only one of the Prytanes who was opposed to the illegality, and I gave my vote against you;

and when the orators threatened to impeach and arrest me, and you called and shouted, I made up my mind that I would run the risk, having law and justice with me, rather than take part in your injustice because I feared imprisonment and death. This happened in the days of the democracy. But when the oligarchy of the Thirty was in power, they sent for me and four others into the rotunda, and bade us bring Leon the Salaminian from Salamis, as they wanted to put him to death. This was a specimen of the sort of commands which they were always giving with the view of implicating as many as possible in their crimes; and then I showed, not in word only but in deed, that, if I may be allowed to use such an expression, I cared not a straw for death, and that my great and only care was lest I should do an unrighteous or unholy thing. For the strong arm of that oppressive power did not frighten me into doing wrong; and when we came out of the rotunda the other four went to Salamis and fetched Leon, but I went quietly home. For which I might have lost my life, had not the power of the Thirty shortly afterwards come to an end. And many will witness to my words.

Now do you really imagine that I could have survived all these years, if I had led a public life, supposing that like a good man I had always maintained the right and had made justice, as I ought, the first thing? No indeed, men of Athens, neither I nor any other man. *[33]* But I have been always the same in all my actions, public as well as private, and never have I yielded any base compliance to those who are slanderously termed my disciples, or to any other. Not that I have any regular disciples. But if any one likes to come and hear me while I am pursuing my mission, whether he be young or old, he is not excluded. Nor do I converse only with those who pay; but any one, whether he be rich or poor, may ask and answer me and listen to my words; and whether he turns out to be a bad man or a good one, neither result can be justly imputed to me; for I never taught or pro-

92020

College of St. Francis Library
Joliet, Illinois

fessed to teach him anything. And if any one says that he has ever learned or heard anything from me in private which all the world has not heard, let me tell you that he is lying.

But I shall be asked, Why do people delight in continually conversing with you? I have told you already, Athenians, the whole truth about this matter: they like to hear the cross-examination of the pretenders to wisdom; there is amusement in it. Now this duty of cross-examining other men has been imposed upon me by God; and has been signified to me by oracles, visions, and in every way in which the will of divine power was ever intimated to any one. This is true, O Athenians; or, if not true, would be soon refuted. If I am or have been corrupting the youth, those of them who are now grown up and become sensible that I gave them bad advice in the days of their youth should come forward as accusers, and take their revenge; or if they do not like to come themselves, some of their relatives, fathers, brothers, or other kinsmen, should say what evil their families have suffered at my hands. Now is their time. Many of them I see in the court. There is Crito, who is of the same age and of the same deme with myself, and there is Critobulus his son, whom I also see. Then again there is Lysanias of Sphettus, who is the father of Aeschines—he is present; and also there is Antiphon of Cephisus, who is the father of Epigenes; and there are the brothers of several who have associated with me. There is Nicostratus the son of Theosdotides, and the brother [of] Theodotus (now Theodotus himself is dead, and therefore he, at any rate, will not seek to stop him), and there is Paralus the son of Demodocus, who had a brother Theages; and Adeimantus the son of Ariston, *[34]* whose brother Plato is present; and Aeantodorus, who is the brother of Apollodorus, whom I also see. I might mention a great many others, some of whom Meletus should have produced as witnesses in the course of his speech; and let him still produce them, if he has forgotten—I will make way for him. And let him

say, if he has any testimony of the sort which he can produce. Nay, Athenians, the very opposite is the truth. For all these are ready to witness on behalf of the corrupter, of the injurer of their kindred, as Meletus and Anytus call me; not the corrupted youth only—there might have been a motive for that—but their uncorrupted elder relatives. Why should they too support me with their testimony? Why, indeed, except for the sake of truth and justice, and because they know that I am speaking the truth, and that Meletus is a liar.

Well, Athenians, this and the like of this is all the defence which I have to offer. Yet a word more. Perhaps there may be some one who is offended at me, when he calls to mind how he himself on a similar, or even a less serious occasion, prayed and entreated the judges with many tears, and how he produced his children in court, which was a moving spectacle, together with a host of relations and friends; whereas I, who am probably in danger of my life will do none of these things. The contrast may occur to his mind, and he may be set against me, and vote in anger because he is displeased at me on this account. Now if there be such a person among you,—mind, I do not say that there is,—to him I may fairly reply: My friend, I am a man, and like other men, a creature of flesh and blood, and not "of wood or stone," as Homer says; and I have a family, yes, and sons, O Athenians, three in number, one almost a man, and two others who are still young; and yet I will not bring any of them hither in order to petition you for an acquittal. And why not? Not from any self-assertion or want of respect for you. Whether I am or am not afraid of death is another question, of which I will not now speak. But, having regard to public opinion, I feel that such conduct would be discreditable to myself, and to you, and to the whole state. One who has reached my years, and who has a name for wisdom, ought not to demean himself. Whether this opinion of me be deserved or not, at any rate the world has decided that Socrates is in some way superior to other men. *[35]* And if those among you who are said to be superior in wisdom and courage, and any other virtue, demean themselves in this way, how shameful is their conduct! I have seen men of reputation, when they have been condemned behaving in the strangest manner: they seem to fancy that they were going to suffer something dreadful if they died, and that they could be immortal if you only allowed them to live; and I think that such are a dishonour to the state, and that any stranger coming in would have said of them that the most eminent men of Athens, to whom the Athenians themselves give honour and command, are no better than women. And I say that these things ought not to be done by those of us who have a reputation; and if they are done, you ought not to permit them; you ought rather to show that you are far more disposed to condemn the man who gets up a doleful scene and makes the city ridiculous, than him who holds his peace.

But, setting aside the question of public opinion, there seems to be something wrong in asking a favour of a judge, and thus procuring an acquittal, instead of informing and convincing him. For his duty is, not to make a present of justice, but to give judgment; and he has sworn that he will judge according to the laws, and not according to his own good pleasure; and we ought not to encourage you, nor should you allow yourself to be encouraged, in this habit of perjury—there can be no piety in that. Do not then require me to do what I consider dishonourable and impious and wrong, especially now, when I am being tried for impiety on the indictment of Meletus. For if, O men of Athens, by force of persuasion and entreaty I could overpower your oaths, then I should be teaching you to believe that there are no gods, and in defending should simply convict myself of the charge of not believing in them. But that is not so—far otherwise. For I do believe that there are gods, and in a sense higher than that in which any of my accusers believe in them. And to you and to God

I commit my cause, to be determined by you as is best for you and me.

[Socrates was found guilty by a vote of 281 to 220.]

There are many reasons why I am not grieved, O men of Athens, at the vote of condemnation. *[36]* I expected it, and am only surprised that the votes are so nearly equal; for I had thought that the majority against me would have been far larger; but now, had thirty votes gone over to the other side, I should have been acquitted. And I may say, I think, that I have escaped Meletus. I may say more; for without the assistance of Anytus and Lycon, any one may see that he would not have had a fifth part of the votes, as the law requires, in which case he would have incurred a fine of a thousand drachmae.

And so he proposes death as the penalty. And what shall I propose on my part, O men of Athens? Clearly that which is my due. And what is my due? What return shall be made to the man who has never had the wit to be idle during his whole life; but has been careless of what the many care for—wealth, and family interests, and military offices, and speaking in the assembly, and magistracies, and plots, and parties. Reflecting that I was really too honest a man to be a politican and live, I did not go where I could do no good to you or to myself; but where I could do the greatest good privately to every one of you, thither I went, and sought to persuade every man among you that he must look to himself, and seek virtue and wisdom before he looks to his private interests, and look to the state before he looks to the interests of the state; and that this should be the order which he observes in all his actions. What shall be done to such an one? Doubtless some good thing, O men of Athens, if he has his reward; and the good should be of a kind suitable to him. What would be a reward suitable to a poor man who is your benefactor, and who desires leisure that he may instruct you? There can be no reward so fitting as maintenance in the Prytaneum, O men of Athens, a reward which he deserves far more than the citizen who has won the prize at Olympia in the horse or chariot race, whether the chariots were drawn by two horses or by many. For I am in want, and he has enough; and he only gives you the appearance of happiness, and I give you the reality. And if I am to estimate the penalty fairly, I should say that maintenance in the Prytaneum is the just return. *[37]*

Perhaps you think that I am braving you in what I am saying now, as in what I said before about the tears and prayers. But this is not so. I speak rather because I am convinced that I never intentionally wronged any one, although I cannot convince you—the time has been too short; if there were a law at Athens, as there is in other cities, that a capital cause should not be decided in one day, then I believe that I should have convinced you. But I cannot in a moment refute great slanders; and, as I am convinced that I never wronged another, I will assuredly not wrong myself. I will not say of myself that I deserve any evil, or propose any penalty. Why should I? Because I am afraid of the penalty of death which Meletus proposes? When I do not know whether death is a good or an evil, why should I propose a penalty which would certainly be an evil? Shall I say imprisonment? And why should I live in prison, and be the slave of the magistrates of the year—of the Eleven? Or shall the penalty be a fine, and imprisonment until the fine is paid? There is the same objection. I should have to lie in prison, for money I have none, and cannot pay. And if I say exile (and this may possibly be the penalty which you will affix), I must indeed be blinded by the love of life, if I am so irrational as to expect that when you, who are my own citizens, cannot endure my discourses and words, and have found them so grievous and odious that you will have no more of them, others are likely to endure me. No indeed, men of Athens, that is not very likely. And what a life should I lead, at my age, wandering from city to city, ever changing my place of exile, and always

being driven out! For I am quite sure that wherever I go, there, as here, the young men will flock to me; and if I drive them away, their elders will drive me out at their request; and if I let them come, their fathers and friends will drive me out for their sakes.

Some one will say: Yes, Socrates, but cannot you hold your tongue, and then you may go into a foreign city, and no one will interfere with you? Now I have great difficulty in making you understand my answer to this. For if I tell you that to do as you say would be a disobedience to the God, and therefore that I cannot hold my tongue, *[38]* you will not believe that I am serious; and if I say again that daily to discourse about virtue, and of those other things about which you hear me examining myself and others, is the greatest good of man, and that the unexamined life is not worth living, you are still less likely to believe me. Yet I say what is true, although a thing of which it is hard for me to persuade you. Also, I have never been accustomed to think that I deserve to suffer any harm. Had I money I might have estimated the offence at what I was able to pay, and not have been much the worse. But I have none, and therefore I must ask you to proportion the fine to my means. Well, perhaps I could afford a mina, and therefore I propose that penalty: Plato, Crito, Critobulus, and Apollodorus, my friends here, bid me say thirty minae, and they will be the sureties. Let thirty minae be the penalty; for which sum they will be ample security to you.

[Socrates was condemned to death.]

Not much time will be gained, O Athenians, in return for the evil name which you will get from the detractors of the city, who will say that you killed Socrates, a wise man; for they will call me wise, even although I am not wise, when they want to reproach you. If you had waited a little while, your desire would have been fulfilled in the course of nature. For I am far advanced in years, as you may perceive, and not far from death. I am speaking now not to all of you, but only to those who have condemned me to death. And I have another thing to say to them: You think that I was convicted because I had no words of the sort which would have procured my acquittal—I mean, if I had thought fit to leave nothing undone or unsaid. Not so, the deficiency which led to my conviction was not of words—certainly not. But I had not the boldness or impudence or inclination to address you as you would have liked me to do, weeping and wailing and lamenting, and saying and doing many things which you have been accustomed to hear from others, and which, as I maintain, are unworthy of me. I thought at the time that I ought not to do anything common or mean when in danger: nor do I now repent of the style of my defence; I would rather die, having spoken after my manner, than speak in your manner and live. For neither in war nor yet at law ought I or any man to use every way of escaping death. *[39]* Often in battle there can be no doubt that if a man will throw away his arms, and fall on his knees before his pursuers, he may escape death; and in other dangers there are other ways of escaping death, if a man is willing to say and do anything. The difficulty, my friends, is not to avoid death, but to avoid unrighteousness; for that runs faster than death. I am old and move slowly, and the slower runner has overtaken me, and my accusers are keen and quick, and the faster runner, who is unrighteousness, has overtaken them. And now I depart hence condemned by you to suffer the penalty of death,—they too go their ways condemned by the truth to suffer the penalty of villainy and wrong; and I must abide by my award —let them abide by theirs. I suppose that these things may be regarded as fated,—and I think that they are well.

And now, O men who have condemned me, I would fain prophesy to you; for I am about to die, and in the hour of death men are gifted with prophetic power. And I prophesy to you who are my murderers, that immediately after my departure punishment far heavier than you have inflicted on me will surely await you. Me you have killed because you wanted to escape the accuser, and not to give an account of your lives. But that will not be as you suppose: far otherwise. For I say that there will be more accusers of you than there are now; accusers whom hitherto I have restrained: and as they are younger they will be more inconsiderate with you, and you will be more offended at them. If you think that by killing men you can prevent some one from censuring your evil lives, you are mistaken; that is not a way of escape which is either possible or honourable; the easiest and the noblest way is not to be disabling others, but to be improving yourselves. This is the prophecy which I utter before my departure to the judges who have condemned me.

Friends, who would have acquitted me, I would like also to talk with you about the thing which has come to pass, while the magistrates are busy, and before I go to the place at which I must die. Stay then a little, for we may as well talk with one another while there is time. *[40]* You are my friends, and I should like to show you the meaning of this event which has happened to me. O my judges—for you I may truly call judges—I should like to tell you of a wonderful circumstance. Hitherto the divine faculty of which the internal oracle is the source has constantly been in the habit of opposing me even about trifles, if I was going to make a slip or error in any matter; and now as you see there has come upon me that which may be thought, and is generally believed to be, the last and worst evil. But the oracle made no sign of opposition, either when I was leaving my house in the morning, or when I was on my way to the court, or while I was speaking, at anything which I was going to say; and yet I have often been stopped in the middle of a speech, but now in nothing I either said or did touching the matter in hand has the oracle opposed me. What do I take to be the explanation of this silence? I will tell you. It is an intimation that what has happened to me is a good, and that those of us who think that death is an evil are in error. For the customary sign would surely have opposed me had I been going to evil and not to good.

Let us reflect in another way, and we shall see that there is great reason to hope that death is a good; for one of two things —either death is a state of nothingness and utter unconsciousness, or, as men say, there is a change and migration of the soul from this world to another. Now if you suppose that there is no consciousness, but a sleep like the sleep of him who is undisturbed even by dreams, death will be an unspeakable gain. For if a person were to select the night in which his sleep was undisturbed even by dreams, and were to compare with this the other days and nights of his life, and then were to tell us how many days and nights he had passed in the course of his life better and more pleasantly than this one, I think that any man, I will not say a private man, but even the great king will not find many such days or nights, when compared with the others. Now if death be of such a nature, I say that to die is gain; for eternity is then only a single night. But if death is the journey to another place, and there, as men say, all the dead abide, what good, O my friends and judges, can be greater than this? If indeed when the pilgrim arrives in the world below, *[41]* he is delivered from the professors of justice in this world, and finds the true judges who are said to give judgment there, Minos and Rhadamanthus and Aeacus and Triptolemus, and other sons of God who were righteous in their own life, that pilgrimage will be worth making. What would not a man give if he might converse with Orpheus and Musaeus and Hesiod and Homer? Nay, if this be true, let me die again and again. I myself, too, shall have a wonderful interest in there meeting and conversing with Palamedes, and Ajax the son of Telamon, and any other ancient hero who has suffered death through an unjust judgment; and there will be no small

pleasure, as I think, in comparing my own sufferings with theirs. Above all, I shall then be able to continue my search into true and false knowledge; as in this world, so also in the next; and I shall find out who is wise, and who pretends to be wise, and is not. What would not a man give, O judges, to be able to examine the leader of the great Trojan expedition; or Odysseus or Sysyphus, or numberless others, men and women too! What infinite delight would there be in conversing with them and asking them questions! In another world they do not put a man to death for asking questions: assuredly not. For besides being happier than we are, they will be immortal, if what is said is true.

Wherefore, O judges, be of good cheer about death, and know of a certainty, that no evil can happen to a good man, either in life or after death. He and his are not neglected by the gods; nor has my own approaching end happened by mere chance. But I see clearly that the time had arrived when it was better for me to die and be released from trouble; wherefore the oracle gave no sign. For which reason, also, I am not angry with my condemners, or with my accusers; they have done me no harm, although they did not mean to do me any good; and for this I may gently blame them.

Still I have a favour to ask of them. When my sons are grown up, I would ask you, O my friends, to punish them; and I would have you trouble them, as I have troubled you, if they seem to care about riches, or anything, more than about virtue; or if they pretend to be something when they are really nothing—then reprove them, as I have reproved you, for not caring about that for which they ought to care and thinking that they are something when they are really nothing. *[42]* And if you do this, both I and my sons will have received justice at your hands.

The hour of departure has arrived, and we go our ways—I to die, and you to live. Which is better God only knows.

Questions

1. Notice that Socrates, while repeatedly speaking of the difficulty of making himself clear to his hearers, does not appeal to definitions. Why is this?

2. Socrates is concerned with giving a defense against both kinds of charges. How well does he do? If he does well, why isn't he acquitted? If he does not do well, how could he do better?

3. Consider yourself a member of the jury. How would you vote? (No doubt this is a difficult question. *None* of the difficulty, however, is faced by saying that this took place a long time ago and in a different culture. By all means inform yourself concerning the Athenian *polis* and its legal system.) What reasons can you give for your decision? What kind of reasons are they?

4. Callias "has spent a world of money on the Sophists." What was he trying to buy? How is truth regarded in Sophistry? Contrast Callias' quest with the charge that Socrates gives to his friends at the close of the dialogue. Who cares better for his sons? Explain.

5. Socrates scorns "a man [who] is willing to do and say anything" in order to remain alive. Many people seem to claim that life itself is the highest value. Does Socrates disagree with this view? If so, how so? If there is a disagreement, what is it about? How can it be settled?

3

Talking to a Friend

Crito

Persons of the Dialogue: Socrates; Crito. Scene: The Prison of Socrates

[43] Socrates. Why have you come at this hour, Crito? it must be quite early?

Crito. Yes, certainly.

Soc. What is the exact time?

Cr. The dawn is breaking.

Soc. I wonder that the keeper of the prison would let you in.

Cr. He knows me, because I often come, Socrates; moreover, I have done him a kindness.

Soc. And are you only just arrived?

Cr. No, I came some time ago.

Soc. Then why did you sit and say nothing, instead of at once awakening me?

Cr. I should not have liked myself, Socrates, to be in such great trouble and unrest as you are—indeed I should not: I have been watching with amazement your peaceful slumbers; and for that reason I did not awake you, because I wished to minimize the pain. I have always thought you to be of a happy disposition; but never did I see anything like the easy, tranquil manner in which you bear this calamity.

Soc. Why, Crito, when a man has reached my age he ought not to be repining at the approach of death.

Cr. And yet other old men find themselves in similar misfortunes, and age does not prevent them from repining.

Soc. That is true. But you have not told me why you come at this early hour.

Cr. I come to bring you a message which is sad and painful; not, as I believe, to yourself, but to all of us who are your friends, and saddest of all to me.

Soc. What? Has the ship come from Delos, on the arrival of which I am to die?

Cr. No, the ship has not actually arrived, but she will probably be here to-day, as persons who have come from Sunium tell me that they left her there; and therefore to-morrow, Socrates, will be the last day of your life.

Soc. Very well, Crito; if such is the will of God, I am willing; but my belief is that there will be a delay of a day.

[44] Cr. Why do you think so?

Reprinted from *The Dialogues of Plato* translated by Benjamin Jowett, third edition, (London: Oxford University Press, 1892).

Soc. I will tell you. I am to die on the day after the arrival of the ship.

Cr. Yes; that is what the authorities say.

Soc. But I do not think that the ship will be here until to-morrow; this I infer from a vision which I had last night, or rather only just now, when you fortunately allowed me to sleep.

Cr. And what was the nature of the vision?

Soc. There appeared to me the likeness of a woman, fair and comely, clothed in bright raiment, who called to me and said: O Socrates,

> *The third day hence to fertile Phthia shalt thou go.*

Cr. What a singular dream, Socrates!

Soc. There can be no doubt about the meaning, Crito, I think.

Cr. Yes; the meaning is only too clear. But, oh! my beloved Socrates, let me entreat you once more to take my advice and escape. For if you die I shall not only lose a friend who can never be replaced, but there is another evil: people who do not know you and me will believe that I might have saved you if I had been willing to give money, but that I did not care. Now, can there be a worse disgrace than this—that I should be thought to value money more than the life of a friend? For the many will not be persuaded that I wanted you to escape, and that you refused.

Soc. But why, my dear Crito, should we care about the opinion of the many? Good men, and they are the only persons who are worth considering, will think of these things truly as they occurred.

Cr. But you see, Socrates, that the opinion of the many must be regarded, for what is now happening shows that they can do the greatest evil to any one who has lost their good opinion.

Soc. I only wish it were so, Crito; and that the many could do the greatest evil; for then they would also be able to do the greatest good—and what a fine thing this would be! But in reality they can do neither; for they cannot make a man either wise or foolish; and whatever they do is the result of chance.

Cr. Well, I will not dispute with you; but please to tell me, Socrates, whether you are not acting out of regard to me and your other friends: are you not afraid that if you escape from prison we may get into trouble with the informers for having stolen you away, and lose either the whole or a great part of our property; or that even a worse evil may happen to us? *[45]* Now, if you fear on our account, be at ease; for in order to save you, we ought surely to run this, or even a greater risk; be persuaded, then, and do as I say.

Soc. Yes, Crito, that is one fear which you mention, but by no means the only one.

Cr. Fear not—there are persons who are willing to get you out of prison at no great cost; and as for the informers, they are far from being exorbitant in their demands—a little money will satisfy them. My means, which are certainly ample, are at your service, and if you have a scruple about spending all mine, here are strangers who will give you the use of theirs; and one of them, Simmias the Theban, has brought a large sum of money for this very purpose; and Cebes and many others are prepared to spend their money in helping you to escape. I say, therefore, do not hesitate on our account, and do not say, as you did in the court, that you will have a difficulty in knowing what to do with yourself anywhere else. For men will love you in other places to which you may go, and not in Athens only; there are friends of mine in Thessaly, if you like to go to them, who will value and protect you, and no Thessalian will give you any trouble. Nor can I think that you are at all justified, Socrates, in betraying your own life when you might be saved; in acting thus you are playing into the hands of your enemies, who are hurrying on your destruction. And further I should say that you are deserting your own children; for you might bring them up and educate them; instead of which you go away and leave them, and they will have to take their chance; and if they do not meet with the usual fate of orphans, there will be small thanks to you. No man should bring children into the world who is unwilling to persevere to the end in their nurture and education. But you appear to be choosing the easier part, not the better and manlier, which would have been more becoming in one who professes to care for virtue in all his actions, like yourself. And indeed, I am ashamed not only of you, but of us who are your friends, when I reflect that the whole business will be attributed entirely to our want of courage. The trial need never have come on, or might have been managed differently; and this last act, or crowning folly, will seem to have occurred through our negligence and cowardice, who might have saved you, *[46]* if we had been good for anything; and you might have saved yourself, for there was no difficulty at all. See now, Socrates, how sad and discreditable are the consequences, both to us and you. Make up your mind then, or rather have your mind already made up, for the time of deliberation is over, and there is only one thing to be done, which must be done this very night, and if we delay at all will be no longer practicable or possible; I beseech you therefore, Socrates, be persuaded by me, and do as I say.

Soc. Dear Crito, your zeal is invaluable, if a right one; but if wrong, the greater the zeal the greater the danger; and therefore we ought to consider whether I shall or shall not do as you say. For I am and always have been one of those natures who must be guided by reason, whatever the reason may be which upon reflection appears to me to be the best; and now that this chance has befallen me, I cannot repudiate my own words: the principles which I have hitherto honoured and revered I still honour, and unless we can at once find other and better principles, I am certain not to agree with you; no, not even if the power of the multitude could inflict many more imprisonments, confiscations, deaths, frightening us like children with hobgoblin terrors. What will be the fairest way of considering the question? Shall I return to your old argument about the opinions of men?—we were

saying that some of them are to be regarded, and others not. Now were we right in maintaining this before I was condemned? And has the argument which was once good now proved to be talk for the sake of talking—mere childish nonsense? That is what I want to consider with your help, Crito:—whether, under my present circumstances, the argument appears to be in any way different or not; and is to be allowed by me or disallowed. That argument, which, as I believe, is maintained by many persons of authority, was to the effect, as I was saying, that the opinions of some men are to be regarded, and of other men not to be regarded. Now you, Crito, are not going to die to-morrow—at least, *[47]* there is no human probability of this— and therefore you are disinterested and not liable to be deceived by the circumstances in which you are placed. Tell me then, whether I am right in saying that some opinions, and the opinions of some men only, are to be valued, and that other opinions, and the opinions of other men, are not to be valued. I ask you whether I was right in maintaining this?

Cr. Certainly.

Soc. The good are to be regarded, and not the bad?

Cr. Yes.

Soc. And the opinions of the wise are good, and the opinions of the unwise are evil?

Cr. Certainly.

Soc. And what was said about another matter? Is the pupil who devotes himself to the practice of gymnastics supposed to attend to the praise and blame and opinion of every man, or of one man only—his physician or trainer, whoever he may be?

Cr. Of one man only.

Soc. And he ought to fear the censure and welcome the praise of that one only, and not of the many?

Cr. Clearly so.

Soc. And he ought to act and train, and eat and drink in the way which seems good to his single master who has understanding, rather than according to the opinion of all other men put together?

Cr. True.

Soc. And if he disobeys and disregards the opinion and approval of the one, and regards the opinion of the many who have no understanding, will he not suffer evil?

Cr. Certainly he will.

Soc. And what will the evil be, whither tending and what affecting, in the disobedient person?

Cr. Clearly, affecting the body; that is what is destroyed by the evil.

Soc. Very good; and is not this true, Crito, of other things which we need not separately enumerate? In questions of just and unjust, fair and foul, good and evil, which are the subjects of our present consultation, ought we to follow the opinion of the many and to fear them; or the opinion of the one man who has understanding? ought we not to fear and reverence him more than all the rest of the world: and if we desert him shall we not destroy and injure that principle in us which may be assumed to be improved by justice and deteriorated by injustice;—there is such a principle?

Cr. Certainly there is, Socrates.

Soc. Take a parallel instance:—if, acting under the advice of those who have no understanding, we destroy that which is improved by health and is deteriorated by disease, would life be worth having? And that which has been destroyed is—the body?

Cr. Yes.

Soc. Could we live, having an evil and corrupted body?

Cr. Certainly not.

Soc. And will life be worth having, if that higher part of man be destroyed, which is improved by justice and depraved by injustice? Do we suppose that principle, *[48]* whatever it may be in man, which has to do with justice and injustice, to be inferior to the body?

Cr. Certainly not.

Soc. More honourable than the body?

Cr. Far more.

Soc. Then, my friend, we must not regard what the many say of us: but what he, the one man who has understanding of just and unjust, will say, and what the truth will say.

And therefore you begin in error when you advise that we should regard the opinion of the many about just and unjust, good and evil, honourable and dishonourable.—"Well," some one will say, "but the many can kill us."

Cr. Yes, Socrates; that will clearly be the answer.

Soc. And it is true: but still I find with surprise that the old argument is unshaken as ever. And I should like to know whether I may say the same of another proposition —that not life, but a good life, is to be chiefly valued?

Cr. Yes, that also remains unshaken.

Soc. And a good life is equivalent to a just and honourable one—that holds also?

Cr. Yes, it does.

Soc. From these premises I proceed to argue the question whether I ought or ought not to try and escape without the consent of the Athenians: and if I am clearly right in escaping, then I will make the attempt; but if not, I will abstain. The other considerations which you mention, of money and loss of character and the duty of educating one's children, are, I fear, only the doctrines of the multitude, who would be as ready to restore people to life, if they were able, as they are to put them to death —and with as little reason. But now, since the argument has thus far prevailed, the only question which remains to be considered is, whether we shall do rightly either in escaping or in suffering others to aid in our escape and paying them in money and thanks, or whether in reality we shall not do rightly; and if the latter, then death or any other calamity which may ensue on my remaining here must not be allowed to enter into the calculation.

Cr. I think that you are right, Socrates; how then shall we proceed?

Soc. Let us consider the matter together, and do you either refute me if you can, and I will be convinced; or else cease, my dear friend, from repeating to me that I ought to escape against the wishes of the Athenians: for I highly value your attempts to persuade me to do so, but I may not be persuaded against my own better judgment. *[49]* And now please to consider my first position, and try how you can best answer me.

Cr. I will.

Soc. Are we to say that we are never intentionally to do wrong, or that in one way we ought and in another we ought not to do wrong, or is doing wrong always evil and dishonourable, as I was just now saying, and as has been already acknowledged by us? Are all our former admissions which were made within a few days to be thrown away? And have we, at our age, been earnestly discoursing with one another all our life long only to discover that we are no better than children? Or, in spite of the opinion of the many, and in spite of consequences whether better or worse, shall we insist on the truth of what was then said, that injustice is always an evil and dishonour to him who acts unjustly? Shall we say so or not?

Cr. Yes.

Soc. Then we must do no wrong?

Cr. Certainly not.

Soc. Nor when injured injure in return, as the many imagine; for we must injure no one at all?

Cr. Clearly not.

Soc. Again, Crito, may we do evil?

Cr. Surely not, Socrates.

Soc. And what of doing evil in return for evil, which is the morality of the many—is that just or not?

Cr. Not just.

Soc. For doing evil to another is the same as injuring him?

Cr. Very true.

Soc. Then we ought not to retaliate or render evil for evil to any one, whatever evil we may have suffered from him. But I would have you consider, Crito, whether you really mean what you are saying. For this opinion has never been held, and never will be held, by any considerable number of persons; and those who are agreed and those who are not agreed upon this point have no common ground, and can only despise one another when they see how widely they differ. Tell me, then, whether you agree with and assent to my first principle, that neither injury nor retaliation nor warding off evil by evil is ever right. And shall that be the premiss of our argument? Or do you decline and dissent from this? For so I have ever thought, and continue to think; but, if you are of another opinion, let me hear what you have to say. If, however, you remain of the same mind as formerly, I will proceed to the next step.

Cr. You may proceed, for I have not changed my mind.

Soc. Then I will go on to the next point, which may be put in the form of a question: —Ought a man to do what he admits to be right, or ought he to betray the right?

Cr. He ought to do what he thinks right.

Soc. But if this is true, what is the application? In leaving the prison against the will of the Athenians, *[50]* do I wrong any? or rather do I not wrong those whom I ought least to wrong? Do I not desert the principles which were acknowledged by us to be just—what do you say?

Cr. I cannot tell, Socrates; for I do not know.

Soc. Then consider the matter in this way:—Imagine that I am about to play truant (you may call the proceeding by any name which you like), and the laws and the government come and interrogate me: "Tell us, Socrates," they say; "what are you about? are you not going by an act of yours to overturn us—the laws, and the whole state, as far as in you lies? Do you imagine that a state can subsist and not be overthrown, in which the decisions of law have no power, but are set aside and trampled upon by individuals?" What will be our answer, Crito, to these and the like words? Any one and especially a rhetorician, will have a good deal to say on behalf of the law which requires a sentence to be carried out. He will argue that this law should not be set aside; and shall we reply, "Yes; but the state has injured us and given an unjust sentence." Suppose I say that?

Cr. Very good, Socrates.

Soc. "And was that our agreement with you?" the law would answer; "or were you to abide by the sentence of the state?" And if I were to express my astonishment at their words, the law would probably add: "Answer, Socrates, instead of opening your eyes—you are in the habit of asking and answering questions. Tell us,—What complaint have you to make against us which justifies you in attempting to destroy us and the state? In the first place did we not bring you into existence? Your father married your mother by our aid and begat you. Say whether you have any objection to urge against those of us who regulate marriage?" None, I should reply. "Or against those of us who after birth regulate the nurture and education of children, in which you also were trained? Were not the laws, which have the charge of education, right in commanding your father to train you in music and gymnastic?" Right, I should reply. "Well then, since you were brought into the world and nurtured and educated by us, can you deny in the first place that you are our child and slave, as your fathers were before you? And if this is true you are not on equal terms with us; nor can you think that you have a right to do to us what we are doing to you. Would you have any right to strike or revile or do any other evil to your father or your master, if you had one, because you have been struck or reviled by him, or received some other evil at his hands?—you would not say this? *[51]* And because we think right to destroy you, do you think that you have any right to destroy us in return, and your country as far as in you lies? Will you, O professor of true virtue, pretend that you are justified in this? Has a philosopher like you failed to discover that our country is more to be valued and higher and holier far than mother or father or any ancestor, and more to be regarded in the eyes of the gods and of men of understanding? also to be soothed, and gently and reverently entreated when angry, even more than a father, and either to be persuaded, or if not persuaded, to be obeyed? And when we are punished by her, whether with imprisonment or stripes, the punishment is to be endured in silence: and if she leads us to

wounds or death in battle, thither we follow as is right; neither may any one yield or retreat or leave his rank, but whether in battle or in a court of law, or in any other place, he must do what his city and his country order him; or he must change their view of what is just: and if he may do no violence to his father or mother, much less may he do violence to his country." What answer shall we make to this, Crito? Do the laws speak truly, or do they not?

Cr. I think that they do.

Soc. Then the laws will say, "Consider, Socrates, if we are speaking truly that in your present attempt you are going to do us an injury. For, having brought you into the world, and nurtured and educated you, and given you and every other citizen a share in every good which we had to give, we further proclaim to any Athenian by the liberty which we allow him, that if he does not like us when he has become of age and has seen the ways of the city, and made our acquaintance, he may go where he pleases and take his goods with him. None of us laws will forbid him or interfere with him. Any one who does not like us and the city, and who wants to emigrate to a colony or to any other city, may go where he likes, retaining his property. But he who has experience of the manner in which we order justice and administer the state, and still remains, has entered into an implied contract that he will do as we command him. And he who disobeys us is, as we maintain, thrice wrong; first, because in disobeying us he is disobeying his parents; secondly, because we are the authors of his education; thirdly, because he has made an agreement with us that he will duly obey our commands; *[52]* and he neither obeys them nor convinces us that our commands are unjust; and we do not rudely impose them, but give him the alternative of obeying or convincing us;— that is what we offer, and he does neither.

"These are the sort of accusations to which, as we were saying, you, Socrates, will be exposed if you accomplish your intentions; you above all other Athenians." Suppose now I ask, why I rather than anybody else? they will justly retort upon me that I above all other men have acknowledged the agreement. "There is clear proof," they will say, "Socrates, that we and the city were not displeasing to you. Of all Athenians you have been the most constant resident in the city, which, as you never leave, you may be supposed to love. For you never went out of the city either to see the games, except once when you went to the Isthmus, or to any other place unless when you were on military service; nor did you travel as other men do. Nor had you any curiosity to know other states or their laws: your affections did not go beyond us and our state; we were your special favourites, and you acquiesced in our government of you; and here in this city you begat your children, which is a proof of your satisfaction. Moreover, you might in the course of the trial, if you had liked, have fixed the penalty at banishment; the state which refuses to let you go now would have let you go then. But you pretended that you preferred death to exile, and that you were not unwilling to die. And now you have forgotten these fine sentiments, and pay no respect to us the laws, of whom you are the destroyer; and are doing what only a miserable slave would do, running away and turning your back upon the compacts and agreements which you made as a citizen. And first of all this very question: Are we right in saying that you agreed to be governed according to us in deed, and not in word only? Is that true or not?" How shall we answer, Crito? Must we not assent?

Cr. We cannot help it, Socrates.

Soc. Then will they not say: "You, Socrates, are breaking the covenants and agreements which you made with us at your leisure, not in any haste or under any compulsion or deception, but after you have had seventy years to think of them, during which time you were at liberty to leave the city, if we were not to your mind, or if our covenants appeared to you to be unfair. You had your choice, and might have gone either to Lacedaemon or Crete, both which states are often praised by you for their good government, *[53]* or to some other Hellenic or foreign state. Whereas you, above all other Athenians, seemed to be so fond of the state, or, in other words, of us her laws (and who would care about a state which has no laws?), that you never stirred out of her; the halt, the blind, the maimed were not more stationary in her than you were. And now you run away and forsake your agreements. Not so, Socrates, if you will take our advice; do not make yourself ridiculous by escaping out of the city.

"For just consider, if you transgress and err in this sort of way, what good will you do either to yourself or to your friends? That your friends will be driven into exile and deprived of citizenship, or will lose their property, is tolerably certain; and you yourself, if you fly to one of the neighbouring cities, as, for example, Thebes or Megara, both of which are well governed, will come to them as an enemy, Socrates, and their government will be against you, and all patriotic citizens will cast an evil eye upon you as a subverter of the laws, and you will confirm in the minds of the judges the justice of their own condemnation of you. For he who is a corrupter of the laws is more than likely to be a corrupter of the young and foolish portion of mankind. Will you then flee from well-ordered cities and virtuous men? and is existence worth having on these terms? Or will you go to them without shame, and talk to them, Socrates? And what will you say to them? What you say here about virtue and justice and institutions and laws being the best things among men? Would that be decent of you? Surely not. But if you go away from well-governed states to Crito's friends in Thessaly, where there is great disorder and license, they will be charmed to hear the tale of your escape from prison, set off with ludicrous particulars of the manner in which you were wrapped in a goatskin or some other disguise, and metamorphosed as the manner is of runaways; but will there be no one to remind you that in your old age you were not ashamed to violate the most sacred laws from a miserable desire of a little more life? Perhaps not, if you keep them in a good temper; but if they are out of temper you will hear many degrading things; you will live, but how?—as the flatterer of all men, and the servant of all men; and doing what?—eating and drinking in Thessaly having gone abroad in order that you may get a dinner. And where will be your fine sentiments about justice and virtue? *[54]* Say that you wish to live for the sake of your children—you want to bring them up and educate them—will you take them into Thessaly and deprive them of Athenian citizenship? Is this the benefit which you will confer upon them? Or are you under the impression that they will be better cared for and educated here if you are still alive, although absent from them; for your friends will take care of them? Do you fancy that if you are an inhabitant of Thessaly they will take care of them, and if you are an inhabitant of the other world that they will not take care of them? Nay; but if they who call themselves friends are good for anything, they will—to be sure they will.

"Listen, then, Socrates, to us who have brought you up. Think not of life and children first, and of justice afterwards, but of justice first, that you may be justified before the princes of the world below. For neither will you nor any that belong to you be happier or holier or juster in this life, or happier in another, if you do as Crito bids. Now you depart in innocence, a sufferer and not a doer of evil; a victim, not of the laws but of men. But if you go forth, returning evil for evil, and injury for injury, breaking the covenants and agreements which you have made with us, and wronging those whom you ought least of all to wrong, that is to say, yourself, your friends, your country, and us, we shall be angry with you while you live, and our brethren, the laws in the world below, will receive you as an enemy; for they will know that you have done your best to destroy us. Listen, then, to us and not to Crito."

This, dear Crito, is the voice which I seem to hear murmuring in my ears, like the sound of the flute in the ears of the mystic; that voice, I say, is humming in my ears, and prevents me from hearing any other. And I know that anything more which you may say will be vain. Yet speak, if you have anything to say.

Cr. I have nothing to say, Socrates.

Soc. Leave me, then, Crito, to fulfil the will of God, and to follow whither he leads.

Questions

1. Suppose someone says, "If I were in Socrates' place, I would escape." So far this is philosophically uninteresting. It may reveal much about the speaker, but it does not prescribe what one *ought* to do; it does not illuminate the moral right and wrong of the matter. But what if the speaker claims that escaping is morally right? The reasoning employed might be of the following form: X is what I would do; (of course) I do what is moral; therefore X is moral. This *form* may be valid, but does it show any insight into and understanding of the nature of morality? Socrates argues and thinks in order to discover his duty so that he might submit to it. He does not consult his inclinations and assume that they are the standard of morality. Contrast these forms of thought. Is submission a necessary element of morality?

2. Notice the paradoxical nature of Socrates' thought. What he decides will determine whether he lives or dies, whether his life has meant anything or not. Yet, he seems quite impersonal; he seems to leave himself out of the thought. Can you explain this?

3. What has Socrates' life meant? Given what he says in "Apology" as well as this dialogue, describe what his concerns have been throughout his life. Are these concerns possible for us? Can we develop a Socratic character?

4. Suppose Dietrich Bonhoeffer had been given a chance to escape before he was hung by the Nazis. Would he have responded as did Socrates? How would the analogy between parents and laws apply to Bonhoeffer's situation?

4

Concerning Death and the Soul

Phaedo

Persons of the Dialogue: Phaedo, who is the narrator of the Dialogue to Echecrates of Phlius; Socrates; Apollodorus; Simmias; Cebes; Crito; Attendant of the Prison. Scene: The Prison of Socrates; Place of the Narration: Phlius

[57] Echecrates. Were you yourself, Phaedo, in the prison with Socrates on the day when he drank the poison?

Phaedo. Yes, Echecrates, I was.

Ech. I should so like to hear about his death. What did he say in his last hours? We were informed that he died by taking poison, but no one knew anything more; for no Phliasian ever goes to Athens now, and it is a long time since any stranger from Athens has found his way hither; so that we had no clear account.

[58] Phaed. Did you not hear of the proceedings at the trial?

Ech. Yes; some one told us about the trial, and we could not understand why, having been condemned, he should have been put to death, not at the time, but long afterwards. What was the reason of this?

Phaed. An accident, Echecrates: the stern of the ship which the Athenians send to Delos happened to have been crowned on the day before he was tried.

Ech. What is this ship?

Phaed. It is the ship in which, according to Athenian tradition, Theseus went to Crete when he took with him the fourteen youths, and was the saviour of them and of himself. And they are said to have vowed to Apollo at the time, that if they were saved they would send a yearly mission to Delos. Now this custom still continues, and the whole period of the voyage to and from Delos, beginning when the priest of Apollo crowns the stern of the ship, is a holy season, during which the city is not allowed to be polluted by public executions; and when the vessel is detained by contrary winds, the time spent in going and returning is very considerable. As I was saying, the ship was crowned on the day before the trial, and this was the reason why Socrates lay in prison and was not put to death until long after he was condemned.

Ech. What was the manner of his death, Phaedo? What was said or done? And

Reprinted from *The Dialogues of Plato* translated by Benjamin Jowett, third edition, (London: Oxford University Press, 1892).

which of his friends were with him? Or did the authorities forbid them to be present—so that he had no friends near him when he died?

Phaed. No; there were several of them with him.

Ech. If you have nothing to do, I wish that you would tell me what passed, as exactly as you can.

Phaed. I have nothing at all to do, and will try to gratify your wish. To be reminded of Socrates is always the greatest delight to me, whether I speak myself or hear another speak of him.

Ech. You will have listeners who are of the same mind with you, and I hope that you will be as exact as you can.

Phaed. I had a singular feeling at being in his company. For I could hardly believe that I was present at the death of a friend, and therefore I did not pity him, Echecrates; he died so fearlessly, and his words and bearing were so noble and gracious, that to me he appeared blessed. I thought that in going to the other world he could not be without a divine call, *[59]* and that he would be happy, if any man ever was, when he arrived there; and therefore I did not pity him as might have seemed natural at such an hour. But I had not the pleasure which I usually feel in philosophical discourse (for philosophy was the theme of which we spoke). I was pleased, but in the pleasure there was also a strange admixture of pain; for I reflected that he was soon to die, and this double feeling was shared by us all; we were laughing and weeping by turns, especially the excitable Apollodorus—you know the sort of man?

Ech. Yes.

Phaed. He was quite beside himself; and I and all of us were greatly moved.

Ech. Who were present?

Phaed. Of native Athenians there were, besides Apollodorus, Critobulus and his father Crito, Hermogenes, Epigenes, Aeschines, Antisthenes; likewise Ctesippus of the deme of Paeania, Menexenus, and some others; Plato, if I am not mistaken, was ill.

Ech. Were there any strangers?

Phaed. Yes, there were; Simmias the Theban, and Cebes, and Phaedondes; Euclid and Terpsion, who came from Megara.

Ech. And was Aristippus there, and Cleombrotus?

Phaed. No, they were said to be in Aegina.

Ech. Any one else?

Phaed. I think that these were nearly all.

Ech. Well, and what did you talk about?

Phaed. I will begin at the beginning, and endeavour to repeat the entire conversation. On the previous days we had been in the habit of assembling early in the morning at the court in which the trial took place, and which is not far from the prison. There we used to wait talking with one another until the opening of the doors (for they were not opened very early); then we went in and generally passed the day with Socrates. On the last morning we assembled sooner than usual, having heard on the day before when we quitted the prison in the evening that the sacred ship had come from Delos; and so we arranged to meet very early at the accustomed place. On our arrival the jailer who answered the door, instead of admitting us, came out and told us to stay until he called us "For the Eleven," he said, "are now with Socrates; they are taking off his chains, and giving orders that he is to die today." He soon returned and said that we might come in. *[60]* On entering we found Socrates just released from chains, and Xanthippè, whom you know, sitting by him, and holding his child in her arms. When she saw us she uttered a cry and said, as women will: "O Socrates, this is the last time that either you will converse with your friends, or they with you." Socrates turned to Crito and said: "Crito, let some one take her home." Some of Crito's people accordingly led her away, crying out and beating herself. And when she was gone, Socrates, sitting up on the couch, bent and rubbed his leg, saying, as he was rubbing: How singular is the thing called pleasure, and how curiously related to pain, which might be thought to be the opposite of it; for they are never present to a man at the same instant, and yet he who pursues either is generally compelled to take the other; their bodies are two, but they are joined by a single head. And I cannot help thinking that if Aesop had remembered them, he would have made a fable about God trying to reconcile their strife, and how, when he could not, he fastened their heads together; and this is the reason why when one comes the other follows: as I know by my own experience now, when after the pain in my leg which was caused by the chain, pleasure appears to succeed.

Upon this Cebes said: I am glad, Socrates, that you have mentioned the name of Aesop. For it reminds me of a question which has been asked by many, and was asked of me only the day before yesterday by Evenus the poet—he will be sure to ask it again, and therefore if you would like me to have an answer ready for him, you may as well tell me what I should say to him:— he wanted to know why you, who never before wrote a line of poetry, now that you are in prison are turning Aesop's fables into verse, and also composing that hymn in honour of Apollo.

Tell him, Cebes, he replied, what is the truth—that I had no idea of rivalling him or his poems; to do so, as I knew, would be no easy task. But I wanted to see whether I could purge away a scruple which I felt about the meaning of certain dreams. In the course of my life I have often had intimations in dreams "that I should compose music." The same dream came to me sometimes in one form, and sometimes in another, but always saying the same or nearly the same words: "Cultivate and make music," said the dream. And hitherto I had imagined that this was only intended to exhort and encourage me in the study of philosophy, which has been the pursuit of my life, [61] and is the noblest and best of music. The dream was bidding me do what I was already doing, in the same way that the competitor in a race is bidden by the spectators to run when he is already running.

But I was not certain of this; for the dream might have meant music in the popular sense of the word, and being under sentence of death, and the festival giving me a respite, I thought that it would be safer for me to satisfy the scruple, and, in obedience to the dream, to compose a few verses before I departed. And first I made a hymn in honour of the god of the festival, and then considering that a poet, if he is really to be a poet, should not only put together words, but should invent stories, and that I have no invention, I took some fables of Aesop, which I had ready at hand and which I knew —they were the first I came upon—and turned them into verse. Tell this to Evenus, Cebes, and bid him be of good cheer; say that I would have him come after me if he be a wise man, and not tarry; and that today I am likely to be going, for the Athenians say that I must.

Simmias said: What a message for such a man! having been a frequent companion of his I should say that, as far as I know him, he will never take your advice unless he is obliged.

Why, said Socrates,—is not Evenus a philosopher?

I think that he is, said Simmias.

Then he, or any man who has the spirit of philosophy, will be willing to die; but he will not take his own life, for that is held to be unlawful.

Here he changed his position, and put his legs off the couch on to the ground, and during the rest of the conversation he remained sitting.

Why do you say, enquired Cebes, that a man ought not to take his own life, but that the philsopher will be ready to follow the dying?

Socrates replied: And have you, Cebes and Simmias, who are the disciples of Philolaus, never heard him speak of this?

Yes, but his language was obscure, Socrates.

My words, too, are only an echo; but there is no reason why I should not repeat what I have heard: and indeed, as I am going to another place, it is very meet for me to be thinking and talking of the nature of the pilgrimage which I am about to make. What can I do better in the interval between this and the setting of the sun?

Then tell me, Socrates, why is suicide held to be unlawful? as I have certainly heard Philolaus, about whom you were just now asking, affirm when he was staying with us at Thebes; and there are others who say the same, although I have never understood what was meant by any of them.

[62] Do not lose heart, replied Socrates, and the day may come when you will understand. I suppose that you wonder why, when other things which are evil may be good at certain times and to certain persons, death is to be the only exception, and why, when a man is better dead, he is not permitted to be his own benefactor, but must wait for the hand of another.

Very true, said Cebes, laughing gently and speaking in his native Boeotian.

I admit the appearance of inconsistency in what I am saying; but there may not be any real inconsistency after all. There is a doctrine whispered in secret that man is a prisoner who has no right to open the door and run away; this is a great mystery which I do not quite understand. Yet I too believe that the gods are our guardians, and that we men are a possession of theirs. Do you not agree?

Yes, I quite agree, said Cebes.

And if one of your own possessions, an ox or an ass, for example, took the liberty of putting himself out of the way when you had given no intimation of your wish that he should die, would you not be angry with him, and would you not punish him if you could?

Certainly, replied Cebes.

Then, if we look at the matter thus, there may be reason in saying that a man should wait, and not take his own life until God summons him, as he is now summoning me.

Yes, Socrates, said Cebes, there seems to be truth in what you say. And yet how can you reconcile this seemingly true belief that God is our guardian and we his possessions, with the willingness to die which you were just now attributing to the philosopher? That the wisest of men should be willing to leave a service in which they are ruled by the gods who are the best of rulers, is not reasonable; for surely no wise man thinks that when set at liberty he can take better care of himself than the gods take of him. A fool may perhaps think so—he may argue that he had better run away from his master, not considering that his duty is to remain to the end, and not to run away from the good, and that there would be no sense in his running away. The wise man will want to be ever with him who is better than himself. Now this, Socrates, is the reverse of what was just now said; for upon this view the wise man should sorrow and the fool rejoice at passing out of life.

[63] The earnestness of Cebes seemed to please Socrates. Here, said he, turning to us, is a man who is always enquiring, and is not so easily convinced by the first thing which he hears.

And certainly, added Simmias, the objection which he is now making does appear to me to have some force. For what can be the meaning of a truly wise man wanting to fly away and lightly leave a master who is better than himself? And I rather imagine that Cebes is referring to you: he thinks that you are too ready to leave us, and too ready to leave the gods whom you acknowledge to be our good masters.

Yes, replied Socrates; there is reason in what you say. And so you think that I ought to answer your indictment as if I were in a court?

We should like you to do so, said Simmias.

Then I must try to make a more successful defence before you than I did before the judges. For I am quite ready to admit, Simmias and Cebes, that I ought to be grieved at death, if I were not persuaded in the first place that I am going to other gods who are wise and good (of which I am as certain as I can be of any such matters), and secondly (though I am not so sure of this last) to men departed, better than those whom I leave behind; and therefore I do not grieve as I might have done, for I have good hope that there is yet something remaining for the dead, and as has been said of old, some far better thing for the good than for the evil.

But do you mean to take away your thoughts with you, Socrates? said Simmias. Will you not impart them to us?—for they are a benefit in which we too are entitled to share. Moreover, if you succeed in convincing us, that will be an answer to the charge against yourself.

I will do my best, replied Socrates. But you must first let me hear what Crito wants; he has long been wishing to say something to me.

Only this, Socrates, replied Crito:—the attendant who is to give you the poison has been telling me, and he wants me to tell you, that you are not to talk much; talking, he says, increases heat, and this is apt to interfere with the action of the poison; persons who excite themselves are sometimes obliged to take a second or even a third dose.

Then, said Socrates, let him mind his business and be prepared to give the poison twice or even thrice if necessary; that is all.

I knew quite well what you would say, replied Crito; but I was obliged to satisfy him.

Never mind him, he said.

And now, O my judges, I desire to prove to you that the real philosopher has reason to be of good cheer when he is about to die, and that after death he may hope to obtain the greatest good in the [64] other world. And how this may be, Simmias and Cebes, I will endeavour to explain. For I deem that the true votary of philosophy is likely to be misunderstood by other men; they do not perceive that he is always pursuing death and dying; and if this be so, and he has had the desire of death all his life long, why when his time comes should he repine at that which he has been always pursuing and desiring?

Simmias said laughingly: Though not in a laughing humour, you have made me laugh, Socrates; for I cannot help thinking that the many when they hear your words will say how truly you have described philosophers, and our people at home will likewise say that the life which philosophers desire is in reality death, and that they have found them out to be deserving of the death which they desire.

And they are right, Simmias, in thinking so, with the exception of the words "they have found them out"; for they have not found out either what is the nature of that death which the true philosopher deserves, or how he deserves or desires death. But enough of them:—let us discuss the matter among ourselves. Do we believe that there is such a thing as death?

To be sure, replied Simmias.

Is it not the separation of soul and body? And to be dead is the completion of this; when the soul exists in herself, and is released from the body and the body is released from the soul, what is this but death?

Just so, he replied.

There is another question, which will probably throw light on our present enquiry if you and I can agree about it:— Ought the philosopher to care about the pleasures—if they are to be called pleasures—of eating and drinking?

Certainly not, answered Simmias.

And what about the pleasures of love— should he care for them?

By no means.

And will he think much of the other ways of indulging the body, for example, the acquisition of costly raiment, or sandals, or other adornments of the body? Instead of caring about them, does he not rather despise anything more than nature needs? What do you say?

I should say that the true philosopher would despise them.

Would you not say that he is entirely concerned with the soul and not with the body? He would like, as far as he can, to get away from the body and to turn to the soul.

Quite true.

In matters of this sort philosophers, above all other men, may be observed in every sort of way to dissever the soul from the communion *[65]* of the body.

Very true.

Whereas, Simmias, the rest of the world are of opinion that to him who has no sense of pleasure and no part in bodily pleasure, life is not worth having; and that he who is indifferent about them is as good as dead.

That is also true.

What again shall we say of the actual acquirement of knowledge?—is the body, if invited to share in the enquiry, a hinderer or a helper? I mean to say, have sight and hearing any truth in them? Are they not, as the poets are always telling us, inaccurate witnesses? and yet, if even they are inaccurate and indistinct, what is to be said of the other senses?—for you will allow that they are the best of them?

Certainly, he replied.

Then when does the soul attain truth?—for in attempting to consider anything in company with the body she is obviously deceived.

True.

Then must not true existence be revealed to her in thought, if at all?

Yes.

And thought is best when the mind is gathered into herself and none of these things trouble her—neither sounds nor sights nor pain nor any pleasure,—when she takes leave of the body, and has as little as possible to do with it, when she has no bodily sense or desire, but is aspiring after true being?

Certainly.

And in this the philosopher dishonours the body; his soul runs away from his body and desires to be alone and by herself?

That is true.

Well, but there is another thing, Simmias: Is there or is there not an absolute justice?

Assuredly there is.

And an absolute beauty and absolute good?

Of course.

But did you ever behold any of them with your eyes?

Certainly not.

Or did you ever reach them with any other bodily sense?—and I speak not of these alone, but of absolute greatness, and health, and strength, and of the essence or true nature of everything. Has the reality of them ever been perceived by you through the bodily organs? or rather, is not the nearest approach to the knowledge of their several natures made by him who so orders his intellectual vision as to have the most exact conception of the essence of each thing which he considers?

Certainly.

And he attains to the purest knowledge of them who goes to each with the mind alone, not introducing or intruding in the act of thought, sight or any other sense together with reason, but with the very light of the mind in her own clearness searches into the very *[66]* truth of each; he who has got rid, as far as he can, of eyes and ears and, so to speak, of the whole body, these being in his opinion distracting elements which when they infect the soul hinder her from acquiring truth and knowledge—who, if not he, is likely to attain to the knowledge of true being?

What you say has a wonderful truth in it, Socrates, replied Simmias.

And when real philosophers consider all these things, will they not be led to make a reflection which they will express in words something like the following? "Have we not found," they will say, "a path of thought which seems to bring us and our argument to the conclusion, that while we are in the body, and while the soul is infected with the evils of the body, our desire will not be satisfied? and our desire is of the truth. For the body is a source of endless trouble to us by reason of the mere requirement of food; and is liable also to diseases which overtake and impede us in the search after true being: it fills us full of loves, and lusts, and fears, and fancies of all kinds, and endless foolery, and in fact, as men say, takes away from us the power of thinking at all. Whence come wars, and fightings, and factions? whence but from the body and the lusts of the body? Wars are occasioned by the love of money, and money has to be acquired for the sake and in the service of the body; and by reason of all these impediments we have no time to give to philosophy; and, last and worst of all, even if we are at leisure and betake ourselves to some speculation, the body is always breaking in upon us, causing turmoil and confusion in our enquiries, and so amazing us that we are prevented from seeing the truth. It has been proved to us by experience that if we would have pure knowledge of anything we must be quit of the body—the soul in herself must behold things in themselves: and then we shall attain the wisdom which we desire, and of which we say that we are lovers; not while we live, but after death; for if while in company with the body, the soul cannot have pure knowledge, one of two things follows—either knowledge is not to be attained at all, or, if at all, [67] after death. For then, and not till then, the soul will be parted from the body and exist in herself alone. In this present life, I reckon that we make the nearest approach to knowledge when we have the least possible intercourse or communion with the body, and are not surfeited with the bodily nature, but keep ourselves pure until the hour when God himself is pleased to release us. And thus having got rid of the foolishness of the body we shall be pure and hold converse with the pure, and know of ourselves the clear light everywhere, which is no other than the light of truth." For the impure are not permitted to approach the pure. These are the sort of words, Simmias, which the true lovers of knowledge cannot help saying to one another, and thinking. You would agree; would you not?

Undoubtedly, Socrates.

But, O my friend, if this be true, there is great reason to hope that, going whither I go, when I have come to the end of my journey, I shall attain that which has been the pursuit of my life. And therefore I go on my way rejoicing, and not I only, but every other man who believes that his mind has been made ready and that he is in a manner purified.

Certainly, replied Simmias.

And what is purification but the separation of the soul from the body, as I was saying before; the habit of the soul gathering and collecting herself into herself from all sides out of the body; the dwelling in her own place alone, as in another life, so also in this, as far as she can;—the release of the soul from the chains of the body?

Very true, he said.

And this separation and release of the soul from the body is termed death?

To be sure, he said.

And the true philosophers, and they only, are ever seeking to release the soul. Is not the separation and release of the soul from the body their especial study?

That is true.

And, as I was saying at first, there would be a ridiculous contradition in men studying to live as nearly as they can in a state of death, and yet repining when it comes upon them.

Clearly.

And the true philosophers, Simmias, are always occupied in the practice of dying, wherefore also to them least of all men is death terrible. Look at the matter thus:—if they have been in every way the enemies of the body, and are wanting to be alone with the soul, when this desire of theirs is granted, how inconsistent would they be if they trembled and repined, instead of rejoicing at their departure to that place where, when they arrive, they hope to gain that which in life they desired—and this was wisdom—and at the [68] same time to be rid of the company of their enemy. Many a man has been willing to go to the world below animated by the hope of seeing there an earthly love, or wife, or son, and conversing with them. And will he who is a true lover of wisdom, and is strongly persuaded in like manner that only in the world below he can worthily enjoy her, still repine at death? Will he not depart with joy? Surely he will, O my friend, if he be a true philosopher. For he will have a firm conviction that there, and there only, he can find wisdom in her purity. And if this be true, he would be very absurd, as I was saying, if he were afraid of death.

He would indeed, replied Simmias.

And when you see a man who is repining at the approach of death, is not his reluctance a sufficient proof that he is not a lover of wisdom, but a lover of the body, and probably at the same time a lover of either money or power, or both?

Quite so, he replied.

And is not courage, Simmias, a quality which is specially characteristic of the philosopher?

Certainly.

There is temperance again, which even by the vulgar is supposed to consist in the control and regulation of the passions, and in the sense of superiority to them—is not temperance a virtue belonging to those only who despise the body, and who pass their lives in philosophy?

Most assuredly.

For the courage and temperance of other men, if you will consider them, are really a contradiction.

How so?

Well, he said, you are aware that death is regarded by men in general as a great evil.

Very true, he said.

And do not courageous men face death because they are afraid of yet greater evils?

That is quite true.

Then all but the philosophers are courageous only from fear, and because they are afraid: and yet that a man should be courageous from fear, and because he is a coward, is surely a strange thing.

Very true.

And are not the temperate exactly in the same case? They are temperate because they are intemperate—which might seem to be a contradiction, but is nevertheless the sort of thing which happens with this foolish temperance. For there are pleasures which they are afraid of losing; and in their desire to keep them, they abstain from some pleasures, because they are overcome by others; and although to be conquered by pleasure is called by men intemperance, [69] to them the conquest of pleasure consists in being conquered by pleasure. And that is what I mean by saying that, in a sense, they are made temperate through intemperance.

Such appears to be the case.

Yet the exchange of one fear or pleasure or pain for another fear or pleasure or pain, and of the greater for the less, as if they were coins, is not the exchange of virtue. O my blessed Simmias, is there not one true coin for which all things ought to be exchanged?—and that is wisdom; and only in exchange for this, and in company with this, is anything truly bought or sold, whether courage or temperance or justice. And is not all true virtue the companion of wisdom, no matter what fears or pleasures or other similar goods or evils may or may not attend her? But the virtue which is made up of these goods, when they are severed from wisdom and exchanged with one another, is a shadow of virtue only, nor is there any freedom or health or truth in her; but in the true exchange there is a purging away of all these things, and temperance, and justice, and courage, and wisdom herself are the purgation of them. The founders of the mysteries would appear to have had a real meaning, and were not talking nonsense when they intimated in a figure long ago that he who passes unsanctified and uninitiated into the world below will lie in a slough, but that he who arrives there after initiation and purification will dwell with the gods. For "many," as they say in the mysteries, "are the thyrsus-bearers, but few are the mystics,"—meaning, as I interpret the words, "the true philosophers." In the number of whom, during my whole life, I have been seeking, according to my ability, to find a place;—whether I have sought in a right way or not, and whether I have succeeded or not, I shall truly know in a little while, if God will, when I myself arrive in the other world—such is my belief. And therefore I maintain that I am right, Simmias and Cebes, in not grieving or repining at parting from you and my masters in this world, for I believe that I shall equally find good masters and friends in another world. But most men do not believe this saying; if then I succeed in convincing you by my defence better than I did the Athenian judges, it will be well.

Cebes answered: I agree, Socrates, in the greater part of what you say. [70] But in what concerns the soul, men are apt to be incredulous; they fear that when she has left the body her place may be nowhere, and that on the very day of death she may perish and come to an end—immediately on her release from the body, issuing forth dispersed like smoke or air and in her flight vanishing away into nothingness. If she could only be collected into herself after she has obtained release from the evils of which you were speaking, there would be good reason to hope, Socrates, that what you say is true. But surely it requires a great deal of argument and many proofs to show that when the man is dead his soul yet exists, and has any force or intelligence.

True, Cebes, said Socrates; and shall I suggest that we converse a little of the probabilities of these things?

I am sure, said Cebes, that I should greatly like to know your opinion about them.

I reckon, said Socrates, that no one who heard me now, not even if he were one of my old enemies, the Comic poets, could accuse me of idle talking about matters in which I have no concern:—If you please, then, we will proceed with the enquiry.

Suppose we consider the question whether the souls of men after death are or are not in the world below. There comes into my mind an ancient doctrine which affirms that they go from hence into the other world, and returning hither, are born again from the dead. Now if it be true that the living come from the dead, then our souls must exist in the other world, for if

not, how could they have been born again? And this would be conclusive, if there were any real evidence that the living are only born from the dead; but if this is not so, then other arguments will have to be adduced.

Very true, replied Cebes.

Then let us consider the whole question, not in relation to man only, but in relation to animals generally, and to plants, and to everything of which there is generation, and the proof will be easier. Are not all things which have opposites generated out of their opposites? I mean such things as good and evil, just and unjust—and there are innumerable other opposites which are generated out of opposites. And I want to show that in all opposites there is of necessity a similar alternation; I mean to say, for example, that anything which becomes greater must become greater after being less.

True.

And that which becomes less must have been once greater and then have become less. [71]

Yes.

And the weaker is generated from the stronger, and the swifter from the slower.

Very true.

And the worse is from the better, and the more just is from the more unjust.

Of course.

And is this true of all opposites? and are we convinced that all of them are generated out of opposites?

Yes.

And in this universal opposition of all things, are there not also two intermediate processes which are ever going on, from one to the other opposite, and back again; where there is a greater and a less there is also an intermediate process of increase and diminution, and that which grows is said to wax, and that which decays to wane?

Yes, he said.

And there are many other processes, such as division and composition, cooling and heating, which equally involve a passage into and out of one another. And this necessarily holds of all opposites, even though not always expressed in words—they are really generated out of one another, and there is a passing or process from one to the other of them?

Very true, he replied.

Well, and is there not an opposite of life, as sleep is the opposite of waking?

True, he said.

And what is it?

Death, he answered.

And these, if they are opposites, are generated the one from the other, and have their two intermediate processes also?

Of course.

Now, said Socrates, I will analyze one of the two pairs of opposites which I have mentioned to you, and also its intermediate processes, and you shall analyze the other to me. One of them I term sleep, the other waking. The state of sleep is opposed to the state of waking, and out of sleeping waking is generated, and out of waking, sleeping; and the process of generation is in the one case falling asleep, and in the other waking up. Do you agree?

I entirely agree.

Then, suppose that you analyze life and death to me in the same manner. Is not death opposed to life?

Yes.

And they are generated one from the other?

Yes.

What is generated from the living?

The dead.

And what from the dead?

I can only say in answer—the living.

Then the living, whether things or persons, Cebes, are generated from the dead?

That is clear, he replied.

Then the inference is that our souls exist in the world below?

That is true.

And one of the two processes or generations is visible—for surely the act of dying is visible?

Surely, he said.

What then is to be the result? Shall we exclude the opposite process? and shall we

suppose nature to walk on one leg only? Must we not rather assign to death some corresponding process of generation?

Certainly, he replied.

And what is that process?

Return to life.

And return to life, if there be such a thing, is the birth of the dead into the world of the living? [72]

Quite true.

Then here is a new way by which we arrive at the conclusion that the living come from the dead, just as the dead come from the living; and this, if true, affords a most certain proof that the souls of the dead exist in some place out of which they come again.

Yes, Socrates, he said; the conclusion seems to flow necessarily out of our previous admissions.

And that these admissions were not unfair, Cebes, he said, may be shown, I think, as follows: If generation were in a straight line only, and there were no compensation or circle in nature, no turn or return of elements into their opposites, then you know that all things would at last have the same form and pass into the same state, and there would be no more generation of them.

What do you mean? he said.

A simple thing enough, which I will illustrate by the case of sleep, he replied. You know that if there were no alternation of sleeping and waking, the tale of the sleeping Endymion would in the end have no meaning, because all other things would be asleep too, and he would not be distinguishable from the rest. Or if there were composition only, and no division of substances, then the chaos of Anaxagoras would come again. And in like manner, my dear Cebes, if all things which partook of life were to die, and after they were dead remained in the form of death, and did not come to life again, all would at last die, and nothing would be alive—what other result could there be? For if the living spring from any other things, and they too die, must not all things at last be swallowed up in death?

There is no escape, Socrates, said Cebes; and to me your argument seems to be absolutely true.

Yes, he said, Cebes, it is and must be so, in my opinion; and we have not been deluded in making these admissions; but I am confident that there truly is such a thing as living again, and that the living spring from the dead, and that the souls of the dead are in existence, and that the good souls have a better portion than the evil.

Cebes added: Your favourite doctrine, Socrates, that knowledge is simply recollection, if true, also necessarily implies a previous time in which we have learned that which we now recollect. But this would be impossible unless our soul had been in some place [73] before existing in the form of man; here then is another proof of the soul's immortality.

But tell me, Cebes, said Simmias, interposing, what arguments are urged in favour of this doctrine of recollection. I am not very sure at the moment that I remember them.

One excellent proof, said Cebes, is afforded by questions. If you put a question to a person in a right way, he will give a true answer of himself, but how could he do this unless there were knowledge and right reason already in him? And this is most clearly shown when he is taken to a diagram or to anything of that sort.

But if, said Socrates, you are still incredulous, Simmias, I would ask you whether you may not agree with me when you look at the matter in another way;—I mean, if you are still incredulous as to whether knowledge is recollection?

Incredulous I am not, said Simmias; but I want to have this doctrine of recollection brought to my own recollection, and, from what Cebes has said, I am beginning to recollect and be convinced: but I should still like to hear what you were going to say.

This is what I would say, he replied:—We should agree, if I am not mistaken, that what a man recollects he must have known at some previous time.

Very true.

And what is the nature of this knowledge or recollection? I mean to ask, Whether a person who, having seen or heard or in any way perceived anything, knows not only that, but has a conception of something else which is the subject, not of the same but of some other kind of knowledge, may not be fairly said to recollect that of which he has the conception?

What do you mean?

I mean what I may illustrate by the following instance:—The knowledge of a lyre is not the same as the knowledge of a man?

True.

And yet what is the feeling of lovers when they recognize a lyre, or a garment, or anything else which the beloved has been in the habit of using? Do not they, from knowing the lyre, form in the mind's eye an image of the youth to whom the lyre belongs? And this is recollection. In like manner any one who sees Simmias may remember Cebes; and there are endless examples of the same thing.

Endless, indeed, replied Simmias.

And recollection is most commonly a process of recovering that which has been already forgotten through time and inattention.

Very true, he said.

Well; and may you not also from seeing the picture of a house or a lyre remember a man? and from the picture of Simmias, you may be led to remember Cebes;

True.

Or you may also be led to the recollection of Simmias himself?

[74] Quite so.

And in all these cases, the recollection may be derived from things either like or unlike?

It may be.

And when the recollection is derived from like things, then another consideration is sure to arise, which is—whether the likeness in any degree falls short or not of that which is recollected?

Very true, he said.

And shall we proceed a step further, and affirm that there is such a thing as equality, not of one piece of wood or stone with another, but that, over and above this, there is absolute equality? Shall we say so?

Say so, yes, replied Simmias, and swear to it, with all the confidence in life.

And do we know the nature of this absolute essence?

To be sure, he said.

And whence did we obtain our knowledge? Did we not see equalities of material things, such as pieces of wood and stones, and gather from them the idea of an equality which is different from them? For you will acknowledge that there is a difference. Or look at the matter in another way:—Do not the same pieces of wood or stone appear at one time equal, and at another time unequal?

That is certain.

But are real equals ever equal? or is the idea of equality the same as of inequality?

Impossible, Socrates.

Then these (so-called) equals are not the same with the idea of equality?

I should say, clearly not, Socrates.

And yet from these equals, although differing from the idea of equality, you conceived and attained that idea?

Very true, he said.

Which might be like, or might be unlike them?

Yes.

But that makes no difference: whenever from seeing one thing you conceived another, whether like or unlike, there must surely have been an act of recollection?

Very true.

But what would you say of equal portions of wood and stone, or other material equals? and what is the impression produced by them? Are they equals in the same sense in which absolute equality is equal? or do they fall short of this perfect equality in a measure?

Yes, he said, in a very great measure too.

And must we not allow, that when I or any one, looking at any object, observes that the thing which he sees aims at being some other thing, but falls short of, and cannot be, that other thing, but is inferior,

he who makes this observation must have had a previous knowledge of that to which the other, although similar, was inferior.

Certainly.

And has not this been our own case in the matter of equals and of absolute equality?

Precisely.

Then we must have known equality previously to the time when we first saw the material equals, *[75]* and reflected that all these apparent equals strive to attain absolute equality, but fall short of it?

Very true.

And we recognize also that this absolute equality has only been known, and can only be known, through the medium of sight or touch, or of some other of the senses, which are all alike in this respect?

Yes, Socrates, as far as the argument is concerned, one of them is the same as the other.

From the senses then is derived the knowledge that all sensible things aim at an absolute equality of which they fall short?

Yes.

Then before we began to see or hear or perceive in any way, we must have had a knowledge of absolute equality, or we could not have referred to that standard the equals which are derived from the senses? —for to that they all aspire, and of that they fall short.

No other inference can be drawn from the previous statements.

And did we not see and hear and have the use of our other senses as soon as we were born?

Certainly.

Then we must have acquired the knowledge of equality at some previous time?

Yes.

That is to say, before we were born, I suppose?

True.

And if we acquired this knowledge before we were born, and were born having the use of it, then we also knew before we were born and at the instant of birth not only the equal or the greater or the less, but all other ideas; for we are not speaking only of equality, but of beauty, goodness, justice, holiness, and of all which we stamp with the name of essence in the dialectical process, both when we ask and when we answer questions. Of all this we may certainly affirm that we acquired the knowledge before birth?

We may.

But if, after having acquired, we have not forgotten what in each case we acquired, then we must always have come into life having knowledge, and shall always continue to know as long as life lasts—for knowing is the acquiring and retaining knowledge and not forgetting. Is not forgetting, Simmias, just the losing of knowledge?

Quite true, Socrates.

But if the knowledge which we acquired before birth was lost by us at birth, and if afterwards by the use of the senses we recovered what we previously knew, will not the process which we call learning be a recovering of the knowledge which is natural to us, and may not this be rightly termed recollection?

Very true.

[76] So much is clear—that when we perceive something, either by the help of sight, or hearing, or some other sense, from that perception we are able to obtain a notion of some other thing like or unlike which is associated with it but has been forgotten. Whence, as I was saying, one of two alternatives follows:—either we had this knowledge at birth, and continued to know through life; or, after birth, those who are said to learn only remember, and learning is simply recollection.

Yes, that is quite true, Socrates.

And which alternative, Simmias, do you prefer? Had we the knowledge at our birth, or did we recollect the things which we knew previously to our birth?

I cannot decide at the moment.

At any rate you can decide whether he who has knowledge will or will not be able to render an account of his knowledge? What do you say?

Certainly, he will.

But do you think that every man is able to give an account of these very matters about which we are speaking?

Would that they could, Socrates, but I rather fear that tomorrow, at this time, there will no longer be any one alive who is able to give an account of them such as ought to be given.

Then you are not of opinion, Simmias, that all men know these things?

Certainly not.

They are in process of recollecting that which they learned before?

Certainly.

But when did our souls acquire this knowledge?—not since we were born as men?

Certainly not.

And therefore, previously?

Yes.

Then, Simmias, our souls must also have existed without bodies before they were in the form of man, and must have had intelligence.

Unless indeed you suppose, Socrates, that these notions are given us at the very moment of birth; for this is the only time which remains.

Yes, my friend, but if so, when do we lose them? for they are not in us when we are born—this is admitted. Do we lose them at the moment of receiving them, or if not at what other time?

No, Socrates, I perceive that I was unconsciously talking nonsense.

Then may we not say, Simmias, that if, as we are always repeating, there is an absolute beauty, and goodness, and an absolute essence of all things; and if to this, which is now discovered to have existed in our former state, we refer all our sensations, and with this compare them, finding these ideas to be pre-existent and our inborn possession—then our souls must have had a prior existence, but if not, there would be no force in the argument? There is the same proof that these ideas must have existed before we were born, as that our souls existed before we were born; and if not the ideas, then not the souls.

Yes, Socrates; I am convinced that there is precisely the same necessity for the one as for the other; and the argument retreats successfully to the position that the existence of the soul before *[77]* birth cannot be separated from the existence of the essence of which you speak. For there is nothing which to my mind is so patent as that beauty, goodness, and the other notions of which you were just now speaking, have a most real and absolute existence; and I am satisfied with the proof.

Well, but is Cebes equally satisfied? for I must convince him too.

I think, said Simmias, that Cebes is satisfied: although he is the most incredulous of mortals, yet I believe that he is sufficiently convinced of the existence of the soul before birth. But that after death the soul will continue to exist is not yet proven even to my own satisfaction. I cannot get rid of the feeling of the many to which Cebes was referring—the feeling that when the man dies the soul will be dispersed, and that this may be the extinction of her. For admitting that she may have been born elsewhere, and framed out of other elements, and was in existence before entering the human body, why after having intered in and gone out again may she not herself be destroyed and come to an end?

Very true, Simmias, said Cebes; about half of what was required has been proven; to wit, that our souls existed before we were born:—that the soul will exist after death as well as before birth is the other half of which the proof is still wanting, and has to be supplied; when that is given the demonstration will be complete.

But that proof, Simmias and Cebes, has been already given, said Socrates, if you put the two arguments together—I mean this and the former one, in which we admitted that everything living is born of the dead. For if the soul exists before birth, and in coming to life and being born can be born only from death and dying, must she not after death continue to exist, since she has to be born again?—Surely the proof which you desire has been already furnished. Still

I suspect that you and Simmias would be glad to probe the argument further. Like children, you are haunted with a fear that when the soul leaves the body, the wind may really blow her away and scatter her; especially if a man should happen to die in a great storm and not when the sky is calm.

Cebes answered with a smile: Then, Socrates, you must argue us out of our fears—and yet, strictly speaking, they are not our fears, but there is a child within us to whom death is a sort of hobgoblin: him too we must persuade not to be afraid when he is alone in the dark.

Socrates said: Let the voice of the charmer be applied daily until you have charmed away the fear.

[78] And where shall we find a good charmer of our fears, Socrates, when you are gone?

Hellas, he replied, is a large place, Cebes, and has many good men, and there are barbarous races not a few: seek for him among them all, far and wide, sparing neither pains nor money; for there is no better way of spending your money. And you must seek among yourselves too; for you will not find others better able to make the search.

The search, replied Cebes, shall certainly be made. And now, if you please, let us return to the point of the argument at which we digressed.

By all means, replied Socrates; what else should I please?

Very good.

Must we not, said Socrates, ask ourselves what that is which, as we imagine, is liable to be scattered, and about which we fear? and what again is that about which we have no fear? And then we may proceed further to enquire whether that which suffers dispersion is or is not of the nature of soul—our hopes and fears as to our own souls will turn upon the answers to these questions.

Very true, he said.

Now the compound or composite may be supposed to be naturally capable, as of being compounded, so also of being dissolved; but that which is uncompounded, and that only, must be, if anything is, indissoluble.

Yes; I should imagine so, said Cebes.

And the uncompounded may be assumed to be the same and unchanging, whereas the compound is always changing and never the same.

I agree, he said.

Then now let us return to the previous discussion. Is that idea or essence, which in the dialectical process we define as essence or true existence—whether essence of equality, beauty, or anything else—are these essences, I say, liable at times to some degree of change? or are they each of them always what they are, having the same simple self-existent and unchanging forms, not admitting of variation at all, or in any way, or at any time?

They must be always the same, Socrates, replied Cebes.

And what would you say of the many beautiful—whether men or horses or garments or any other things which are named by the same names and may be called equal or beautiful,—are they all unchanging and the same always, or quite the reverse? May they not rather be described as almost always changing and hardly ever the same, either with themselves or with one another?

The latter, replied Cebes; they are always in a state of change.

[79] And these you can touch and see and perceive with the senses, but the unchanging things you can only perceive with the mind—they are invisible and are not seen?

That is very true, he said.

Well then, added Socrates, let us suppose that there are two sorts of existences—one seen, the other unseen.

Let us suppose them.

The seen is the changing, and the unseen is the unchanging?

That may be also supposed.

And, further, is not one part of us body, another part soul?

To be sure.

And to which class is the body more alike and akin?

Clearly to the seen—no one can doubt that.

And is the soul seen or not seen?

Not by man, Socrates.

And what we mean by "seen" and "not seen" is that which is or is not visible to the eye of man?

Yes, to the eye of man.

And is the soul seen or not seen?

Not seen.

Unseen then?

Yes.

Then the soul is more like to the unseen, and the body to the seen?

That follows necessarily, Socrates.

And were we not saying long ago that the soul when using the body as an instrument of perception, that is to say, when using the sense of sight or hearing or some other sense (for the meaning of perceiving through the body is perceiving through the senses)—were we not saying that the soul too is then dragged by the body into the region of the changeable, and wanders and is confused; the world spins round her, and she is like a drunkard, when she touches change?

Very true.

But when returning into herself she reflects, then she passes into the other world, the region of purity, and eternity, and immortality, and unchangeableness, which are her kindred, and with them she ever lives, when she is by herself and is not let or hindered; then she ceases from her erring ways, and being in communion with the unchanging is unchanging. And this state of the soul is called wisdom?

That is well and truly said, Socrates, he replied.

And to which class is the soul more nearly alike and akin, as far as may be inferred from this argument, as well as from the preceding one?

I think, Socrates, that, in the opinion of every one who follows the argument, the soul will be infinitely more like the unchangeable—even the most stupid person will not deny that.

And the body is more like the changing?

Yes.

Yet once more consider the matter in another light: When the soul and the body are united, *[80]* then nature orders the soul to rule and govern, and the body to obey and serve. Now which of these two functions is akin to the divine? and which to the mortal? Does not the divine appear to you to be that which naturally orders and rules, and the mortal to be that which is subject and servant?

True.

And which does the soul resemble?

The soul resembles the divine, and the body the mortal—there can be no doubt of that, Socrates.

Then reflect, Cebes: of all which has been said is not this the conclusion?—that the soul is in the very likeness of the divine, and immortal, and intellectual, and uniform, and indissoluble, and unchangeable; and that the body is in the very likeness of the human, and mortal, and unintellectual, and multiform, and dissoluble, and changeable. Can this, my dear Cebes, be denied?

It cannot.

But if it be true, then is not the body liable to speedy dissolution? and is not the soul almost or altogether indissoluble?

Certainly.

And do you further observe, that after a man is dead, the body, or visible part of him, which is lying in the visible world, and is called a corpse, and would naturally be dissolved and decomposed and dissipated, is not dissolved or decomposed at once, but may remain for some time, nay even for a long time, if the constitution be sound at the time of death, and the season of the year favourable? For the body when shrunk and embalmed, as the manner is in Egypt, may remain almost entire through infinite ages; and even in decay, there are still some portions, such as the bones and ligaments, which are practically indestructible:—Do you agree?

Yes.

And is it likely that the soul, which is invisible, in passing to the place of the true Hades, which like her is invisible, and pure, and noble, and on her way to the good and wise God, whither, if God will, my soul is also soon to go,—that the soul, I repeat, if this be her nature and origin, will be blown away and destroyed immediately on quitting the body, as the many say? That can never be, my dear Simmias and Cebes. The truth rather is, that the soul which is pure at departing and draws after her no bodily taint, having never voluntarily during life had connection with the body, which she is ever avoiding, herself gathered into herself;—and making such abstraction her perpetual study—which means that she has been a true disciple of philosophy; *[81]* and therefore has in fact been always engaged in the practice of dying? For is not philosophy the study of death?—

Certainly—

That soul, I say, herself invisible, departs to the invisible world—to the divine and immortal and rational; thither arriving, she is secure of bliss and is released from the error and folly of men, their fears and wild passions and all other human ills, and for ever dwells, as they say of the initiated, in company with the gods. Is not this true, Cebes?

Yes, said Cebes, beyond a doubt.

But the soul which has been polluted, and is impure at the time of her departure, and is the companion and servant of the body always, and is in love with and fascinated by the body and by the desires and pleasures of the body, until she is led to believe that the truth only exists in a bodily form, which a man may touch and see and taste, and use for the purposes of his lusts, —the soul, I mean, accustomed to hate and fear and avoid the intellectual principle, which to the bodily eye is dark and invisible, and can be attained only by philosophy;—do you suppose that such a soul will depart pure and unalloyed?

Impossible, he replied.

She is held fast by the corporeal, which the continual association and constant care of the body have wrought into her nature.

Very true.

And this corporeal element, my friend, is heavy and weighty and earthy, and is that element of sight by which a soul is depressed and dragged down again into the visible world, because she is afraid of the invisible and of the world below—prowling about tombs and sepulchres, near which, as they tell us, are seen certain ghostly apparitions of souls which have not departed pure, but are cloyed with sight and therefore visible.

That is very likely, Socrates.

Yes, that is very likely, Cebes; and these must be the souls, not of the good, but of the evil, which are compelled to wander about such places in payment of the penalty of their former evil way of life; and they continue to wander until through the craving after the corporeal which never leaves them, they are imprisoned finally in another body. And they may be supposed to find their prisons in the same natures which they have had in their former lives.

What natures do you mean, Socrates?

What I mean is that men who have followed after gluttony, and wantonness, and drunkenness, and have had no thought of avoiding them, *[82]* would pass into asses and animals of that sort. What do you think?

I think such an opinion to be exceedingly probable.

And those who have chosen the portion of injustice, and tyranny, and violence, will pass into wolves, or into hawks and kites;—whither else can we suppose them to go?

Yes, said Cebes; with such natures, beyond question.

And there is no difficulty, he said, in assigning to all of them places answering to their several natures and propensities?

There is not, he said.

Some are happier than others; and the happiest both in themselves and in the place to which they go are those who have practised the civil and social virtues which

are called temperance and justice, and are acquired by habit and attention without philosophy and mind.

Why are they the happiest?

Because they may be expected to pass into some gentle and social kind which is like their own, such as bees or wasps or ants, or back again into the form of man, and just and moderate men may be supposed to spring from them.

Very likely.

No one who has not studied philosophy and who is not entirely pure at the time of his departure is allowed to enter the company of the Gods, but the lover of knowledge only. And this is the reason, Simmias and Cebes, why the true votaries of philosophy abstain from all fleshy lusts, and hold out against them and refuse to give themselves up to them,—not because they fear poverty or the ruin of their families, like the lovers of money, and the world in general; nor like the lovers of power and honour, because they dread the dishonour or disgrace of evil deeds.

No, Socrates, that would not become them, said Cebes.

No indeed, he replied; and therefore they who have any care of their own souls, and do not merely live moulding and fashioning the body, say farewell to all this; they will not walk in the ways of the blind: and when philosophy offers them purification and release from evil, they feel that they ought not to resist her influence, and whither she leads they turn and follow.

What do you mean, Socrates?

I will tell you, he said. The lovers of knowledge are conscious that the soul was simply fastened and glued to the body—until philosophy received her, she could only view real existence through the bars of a prison, not in and through herself; she was wallowing in the mire of every sort of ignorance, and by reason of lust had become the principal accomplice in her own captivity. *[83]* This was her original state; and then, as I was saying, and as the lovers of knowledge are well aware, philosophy, seeing how terrible was her confinement, of which she was to herself the cause, received and gently comforted her and sought to release her, pointing out that the eye and the ear and the other senses are full of deception, and persuading her to retire from them, and abstain from all but the necessary use of them, and be gathered up and collected into herself, bidding her trust in herself and her own pure apprehension of pure existence, and to mistrust whatever comes to her through other channels and is subject to variation; for such things are visible and tangible, but what she sees in her own nature is intelligible and invisible. And the soul of the true philosopher thinks that she ought not to resist this deliverance, and therefore abstains from pleasures and desires and pains and fears, as far as she is able; reflecting that when a man has great joys or sorrows or fears or desires, he suffers from them, not merely the sort of evil which might be anticipated—as for example, the loss of his health or property which he has sacrificed to his lusts—but an evil greater far, which is the greatest and worst of all evils, and one of which he never thinks.

What is it, Socrates? said Cebes.

The evil is that when the feeling of pleasure or pain is most intense, every soul of man imagines the objects of this intense feeling to be then plainest and truest: but this is not so, they are really the things of sight.

Very true.

And is not this the state in which the soul is most enthralled by the body?

How so?

Why, because each pleasure and pain is a sort of nail which nails and rivets the soul to the body, until she becomes like the body, and believes that to be true which the body affirms to be true; and from agreeing with the body and having the same delights she is obliged to have the same habits and haunts, and is not likely ever to be pure at her departure to the world below, but is always infected by the body; and so she sinks into another body and there germinates and grows, and has therefore no part

in the communion of the divine and pure and simple.

Most true, Socrates, answered Cebes.

And this, Cebes, is the reason why the true lovers of knowledge are temperate and brave; and not for the reason which the world gives.

[84] Certainly not.

Certainly not! The soul of a philosopher will reason in quite another way; she will not ask philosophy to release her in order that when released she may deliver herself up again to the thraldom of pleasures and pains, doing a work only to be undone again, weaving instead of unweaving her Penelope's web. But she will calm passion, and follow reason, and dwell in the contemplation of her, beholding the true and divine (which is not matter of opinion), and thence deriving nourishment. Thus she seeks to live while she lives, and after death she hopes to go to her own kindred and to that which is like her, and to be freed from human ills. Never fear, Simmias and Cebes, that a soul which has been thus nurtured and has had these pursuits, will at her departure from the body be scattered and blown away by the winds and be nowhere and nothing.

When Socrates had done speaking, for a considerable time there was silence; he himself appeared to be meditating, as most of us were, on what had been said; only Cebes and Simmias spoke a few words to one another. And Socrates observing them asked what they thought of the argument, and whether there was anything wanting? For, said he, there are many points still open to suspicion and attack, if any one were disposed to sift the matter thoroughly. Should you be considering some other matter I say no more, but if you are still in doubt do not hesitate to say exactly what you think, and let us have anything better which you can suggest; and if you think that I can be of any use, allow me to help you.

Simmias said: I must confess, Socrates, that doubts did arise in our minds, and each of us was urging and inciting the other to put the question which we wanted to have answered but which neither of us liked to ask, fearing that our importunity might be troublesome at such a time.

Socrates replied with a smile: O Simmias, what are you saying? I am not very likely to persuade other men that I do not regard my present situation as a misfortune, if I cannot even persuade you that I am no worse off now than at any other time in my life. Will you not allow that I have as much of the spirit of prophecy in me as the swans? For they, when they perceive that they must die, having sung all their life long, do then sing more lustily than ever, rejoicing in the thought that they are about to go away to the god *[85]* whose ministers they are. But men, because they are themselves afraid of death, slanderously affirm of the swans that they sing a lament at the last, not considering that no bird sings when cold, or hungry, or in pain, not even the nightingale, nor the swallow, nor yet the hoopoe; which are said indeed to tune a lay of sorrow, although I do not believe this to be true of them any more than of the swans. But because they are sacred to Apollo, they have the gift of prophecy, and anticipate the good things of another world; wherefore they sing and rejoice in that day more than ever they did before. And I too, believing myself to be the consecrated servant of the same God, and the fellow-servant of the swans, and thinking that I have received from my master gifts of prophecy which are not inferior to theirs, would not go out of life less merrily than the swans. Never mind then, if this be your only objection, but speak and ask anything which you like, while the eleven magistrates of Athens allow.

Very good, Socrates, said Simmias; then I will tell you my difficulty, and Cebes will tell you his. I feel myself (and I dare say that you have the same feeling), how hard or rather impossible is the attainment of any certainty about questions such as these in the present life. And yet I should deem him a coward who did not prove what is said about them to the uttermost, or whose heart failed him before he had examined them on every side. For he should persevere until he has achieved one of two things: either he should discover, or be taught the truth about them; or, if this be impossible, I would have him take the best and most irrefragable of human theories, and let this be the raft upon which he sails through life—not without risk, as I admit, if he cannot find some word of God which will more surely and safely carry him. And now, as you bid me, I will venture to question you, and then I shall not have to reproach myself hereafter with not having said at the time what I think. For when I consider the matter, either alone or with Cebes, the argument does certainly appear to me, Socrates, to be not sufficient.

Socrates answered: I dare say, my friend, that you may be right, but I should like to know in what respect the argument is insufficient.

In this respect, replied Simmias:—Suppose a person to use the same argument about harmony and the lyre—might he not say that harmony is a thing invisible, *[86]* incorporeal, perfect, divine, existing in the lyre which is harmonized, but that the lyre and the strings are matter and material, composite, earthy, and akin to mortality? And when some one breaks the lyre, or cuts and rends the strings, then he who takes this view would argue as you do, and on the same analogy, that the harmony survives and has not perished—you cannot imagine, he would say, that the lyre without the strings, and the broken strings themselves which are mortal remain, and yet that the harmony, which is of heavenly and immortal nature and kindred, has perished—perished before the mortal. The harmony must still be somewhere, and the wood and strings will decay before anything can happen to that. The thought, Socrates, must have occurred to your own mind that such is our conception of the soul; and that when the body is in a manner strung and held together by the elements of hot and cold, wet and dry, then the soul is the harmony or due proportionate admixture of them.

But if so, whenever the strings of the body are unduly loosened or overstrained through disease or other injury, then the soul, though most divine, like other harmonies of music or of works of art, of course perishes at once; although the material remains of the body may last for a considerable time, until they are either decayed or burnt. And if any one maintains that the soul, being the harmony of the elements of the body, is first to perish in that which is called death, how shall we answer him?

Socrates looked fixedly at us as his manner was, and said with a smile: Simmias has reason on his side; and why does not some one of you who is better able than myself answer him? for there is force in his attack upon me. But perhaps, before we answer him, we had better also hear what Cebes has to say that we may gain time for reflection, and when they have both spoken, we may either assent to them, if there is truth in what they say, or if not, we will maintain our position. Please to tell me then, Cebes, he said, what was the difficulty which troubled you?

Cebes said: I will tell you. My feeling is that the argument is where it was, and open to the same objections which were urged before; [87] for I am ready to admit that the existence of the soul before entering into the bodily form has been very ingeniously, and, if I may say so, quite sufficiently proven; but the existence of the soul after death is still, in my judgment, unproven. Now my objection is not the same as that of Simmias; for I am not disposed to deny that the soul is stronger and more lasting than the body, being of opinion that in all such respects the soul very far excels the body. Well then, says the argument to me, why do you remain unconvinced?—When you see that the weaker continues in existence after the man is dead, will you not admit that the more lasting must also survive during the same period of time? Now I will ask you to consider whether the objection, which, like Simmias, I will express in a figure, is of any weight. The analogy which I will adduce is that of an old weaver, who dies, and after

his death somebody says:—He is not dead, he must be alive;—see, there is the coat which he himself wove and wore, and which remains whole and undecayed. And then he proceeds to ask of some one who is incredulous, whether a man lasts longer, or the coat which is in use and wear; and when he is answered that a man lasts far longer, thinks that he has thus certainly demonstrated the survival of the man, who is the more lasting, because the less lasting remains. But that, Simmias, as I would beg you to remark, is a mistake; any one can see that he who talks thus is talking nonsense. For the truth is, that the weaver of aforesaid, having woven and worn many such coats, outlived several of them; and was outlived by the last; but a man is not therefore proved to be slighter and weaker than a coat. Now the relation of the body to the soul may be expressed in a similar figure; and any one may very fairly say in like manner that the soul is lasting, and the body weak and shortlived in comparison. He may argue in like manner that every soul wears out many bodies, especially if a man live many years. While he is alive the body deliquesces and decays, and the soul always weaves another garment and repairs the waste. But of course, whenever the soul perishes, she must have on her last garment, and this will survive her; and then at length, when the soul is dead, the body will show its native weakness, and quickly decompose and pass away. I would therefore rather not rely on the argument from superior strength to prove the continued existence of the soul after death. [88] For granting even more than you affirm to be possible, and acknowledging not only that the soul existed before birth, but also that the souls of some exist, and will continue to exist after death, and will be born and die again, and that there is a natural strength in the soul which will hold out and be born many times—nevertheless, we may be still inclined to think that she will weary in the labours of successive births, and may at last succumb in one of her deaths and utterly perish; and this death and dissolution of the body which brings destruction to the soul may be unknown to any of us, for no one of us can have had any experience of it: and if so, then I maintain that he who is confident about death has but a foolish confidence, unless he is able to prove that the soul is altogether immortal and imperishable. But if he cannot prove the soul's immortality, he who is about to die will always have reason to fear that when the body is disunited, the soul also may utterly perish.

All of us, as we afterwards remarked to one another, had an unpleasant feeling at hearing what they said. When we had been so firmly convinced before, now to have our faith shaken seemed to introduce a confusion and uncertainty, not only into the previous argument, but into any future one; either we were incapable of forming a judgment, or there were no grounds of belief.

Ech. There I feel with you—by heaven I do, Phaedo, and when you were speaking, I was beginning to ask myself the same question: What argument can I ever trust again? For what could be more convincing than the argument of Socrates, which has now fallen into discredit? That the soul is a harmony is a doctrine which has always had a wonderful attraction for me, and, when mentioned, came back to me at once, as my own original conviction. And now I must begin again and find another argument which will assure me that when the man is dead the soul survives. Tell me, I implore you, how did Socrates proceed? Did he appear to share the unpleasant feeling which you mention? or did he calmly meet the attack? And did he answer forcibly or feebly? Narrate what passed as exactly as you can.

Phaed. Often, Echecrates, I have wondered at Socrates, but never more than on that occasion. *[89]* That he should be able to answer was nothing, but what astonished me was, first, the gentle and pleasant and approving manner in which he received the words of the young men, and then his quick sense of the wound which had been in-

flicted by the argument, and the readiness with which he healed it. He might be compared to a general rallying his defeated and broken army, urging them to accompany him and return to the field of argument.

Ech. What followed?

Phaed. You shall hear, for I was close to him on his right hand, seated on a sort of stool, and he on a couch which was a good deal higher. He stroked my head, and pressed the hair upon my neck—he had a way of playing with my hair; and then he said: To-morrow, Phaedo, I suppose that these fair locks of yours will be severed.

Yes, Socrates, I suppose that they will, I replied.

Not so, if you will take my advice.

What shall I do with them? I said.

To-day, he replied, and not to-morrow, if this argument dies and we cannot bring it to life again, you and I will both shave our locks: and if I were you, and the argument got away from me, and I could not hold my ground against Simmias and Cebes, I would myself take an oath, like the Argives, not to wear hair any more until I had renewed the conflict and defeated them.

Yes, I said; but Heracles himself is said not to be a match for two.

Summon me then, he said, and I will be your Iolaus until the sun goes down.

I summon you rather, I rejoined, not as Heracles summoning Iolaus, but as Iolaus might summon Heracles.

That will do as well, he said. But first let us take care that we avoid a danger.

Of what nature? I said.

Lest we become misologists, he replied: no worse thing can happen to a man than this. For as there are misanthropists or haters of men, there are also misologists or haters of ideas, and both spring from the same cause, which is ignorance of the world. Misanthropy arises out of the too great confidence of inexperience;—you trust a man and think him altogether true and sound and faithful, and then in a little while he turns out to be false and knavish; and then another and another, and when this has happened several times to a man, especially when it happens among those whom he deems to be his own most trusted and familiar friends, and he has often quarrelled with them, he at last hates all men, and believes that no one has any good in him at all. You must have observed this trait of character?

I have.

And is not the feeling discreditable? Is it not obvious that such an one having to deal with other men, was clearly without any experience of human nature; for experience would have taught him the true state of the case, *[90]* that few are the good and few the evil, and that the great majority are in the interval between them.

What do you mean? I said.

I mean, he replied, as you might say of the very large and very small—that nothing is more uncommon than a very large or very small man; and this applies generally to all extremes, whether of great and small, or swift and slow, or fair and foul, or black and white: and whether the instances you select be men or dogs or anything else, few are the extremes, but many are in the mean between them. Did you never observe this?

Yes, I said, I have.

And do you not imagine, he said, that if there were a competition in evil, the worst would be found to be very few?

Yes, that is very likely, I said.

Yes, that is very likely, he replied; although in this respect arguments are unlike men—there I was led on by you to say more than I had intended; but the point of comparison was, that when a simple man who has no skill in dialectics believes an argument to be true which he afterwards imagines to be false, whether really false or not, and then another and another, he has no longer any faith left, and great disputers, as you know, come to think at last that they have grown to be the wisest of mankind; for they alone perceive the utter unsoundness and instability of all arguments, or indeed, of all things, which, like the currents in the Euripus, are going up and down in never-ceasing ebb and flow.

That is quite true, I said.

Yes, Phaedo, he replied, and how melancholy, if there be such a thing as truth or certainty or possibility of knowledge—that a man should have lighted upon some argument or other which at first seemed true and then turned out to be false, and instead of blaming himself and his own want of wit, because he is annoyed, should at last be too glad to transfer the blame from himself to arguments in general: and for ever afterwards should hate and revile them, and lose truth and the knowledge of realities.

Yes, indeed, I said; that is very melancholy.

Let us then, in the first place, he said, be careful of allowing or of admitting into our souls the notion that there is no health or soundness in any arguments at all. Rather say that we have not yet attained to soundness in ourselves, and that we must struggle manfully and do our best to gain health of mind—you and all other men having regard to the whole of your future life, and I myself in the prospect of death. *[91]* For at this moment I am sensible that I have not the temper of a philosopher; like the vulgar, I am only a partisan. Now the partisan, when he is engaged in a dispute, cares nothing about the rights of the question, but is anxious only to convince his hearers of his own assertions. And the difference between him and me at the present moment is merely this—that whereas he seeks to convince his hearers that what he says is true, I am rather seeking to convince myself; to convince my hearers is a secondary matter with me. And do but see much I gain by the argument. For if what I say is true, then I do well to be persuaded of the truth; but if there be nothing after death, still, during the short time that remains, I shall not distress my friends with lamentations, and my ignorance will not last, but will die with me, and therefore no harm will be done. This is the state of mind, Simmias and Cebes, in which I approach the argument. And I would ask you to be thinking of the truth and not of Socrates: agree with me, if I seem to you to be speaking the truth; or if not, withstand me might and main, that I may not deceive you as well as myself in my enthusiasm, and like the bee, leave my sting in you before I die.

And now let us proceed, he said. And first of all let me be sure that I have in my mind what you were saying. Simmias, if I remember rightly, has fears and misgivings whether the soul, although a fairer and diviner thing than the body, being as she is in the form of harmony, may not perish first. On the other hand, Cebes appeared to grant that the soul was more lasting than the body, but he said that no one could know whether the soul, after having worn out many bodies, might not perish herself and leave her last body behind her; and that this is death, which is the destruction not of the body but of the soul, for in the body the work of destruction is ever going on. Are not these, Simmias and Cebes, the points which we have to consider?

They both agreed to this statement of them.

He proceeded: And did you deny the force of the whole preceding argument, or of a part only?

Of a part only, they replied.

And what did you think, he said, of that part of the argument in which we said that knowledge was recollection, and hence inferred that the soul must have previously existed somewhere else *[92]* before she was enclosed in the body?

Cebes said that he had been wonderfully impressed by that part of the argument, and that his conviction remained absolutely unshaken. Simmias agreed, and added that he himself could hardly imagine the possibility of his ever thinking differently.

But, rejoined Socrates, you will have to think differently, my Theban friend, if you still maintain that harmony is a compound, and that the soul is a harmony which is made out of strings set in the frame of the body; for you will surely never allow yourself to say that a harmony is prior to the elements which compose it.

Never, Socrates.

But do you not see that this is what you imply when you say that the soul existed before she took the form and body of man, and was made up of elements which as yet had no existence? For harmony is not like the soul, as you suppose; but first the lyre, and the strings, and the sounds exist in a state of discord, and then harmony is made last of all, and perishes first. And how can such a notion of the soul as this agree with the other?

Not at all, replied Simmias.

And yet, he said, there surely ought to be harmony in a discourse of which harmony is the theme?

There ought, replied Simmias.

But there is no harmony, he said, in the two propositions that knowledge is recollection, and that the soul is a harmony. Which of them will you retain?

I think, he replied, that I have a much stronger faith, Socrates, in the first of the two, which has been fully demonstrated to me, than in the latter, which has not been demonstrated at all, but rests only on probable and plausible grounds; and is therefore believed by the many. I know too well that these arguments from probabilities are imposters, and unless great caution is observed in the use of them, they are apt to be deceptive—in geometry, and in other things too. But the doctrine of knowledge and recollection has been proven to me on trustworthy grounds: and the proof was that the soul must have existed before she came into the body, because to her belongs the essence of which the very name implies existence. Having, as I am convinced, rightly accepted this conclusion, and on sufficient grounds, I must, as I suppose, cease to argue or allow others to argue that the soul is a harmony.

Let me put the matter, Simmias, he said, in another point of view: *[93]* Do you imagine that a harmony or any other composition can be in a state other than that of the elements, out of which it is compounded?

Certainly not.

Or do or suffer anything other than they do or suffer?

He agreed.

Then a harmony does not, properly speaking, lead the parts or elements which make up the harmony, but only follows them.

He assented.

For harmony cannot possibly have any motion, or sound, or other quality which is opposed to its parts.

That would be impossible, he replied.

And does not the nature of every harmony depend upon the manner in which the elements are harmonized?

I do not understand you, he said.

I mean to say that a harmony admits of degrees, and is more of a harmony, and more completely a harmony, when more truly and fully harmonized, to any extent which is possible; and less of a harmony, and less completely a harmony, when less truly and fully harmonized.

True.

But does the soul admit of degrees? or is one soul in the very least degree more or less, or more or less completely, a soul than another?

Not in the least.

Yet surely of two souls, one is said to have intelligence and virtue, and to be good, and the other to have folly and vice, and to be an evil soul: and this is said truly?

Yes, truly.

But what will those who maintain the soul to be a harmony say of this presence of virtue and vice in the soul?—will they say that here is another harmony, and another discord, and that the virtuous soul is harmonized, and herself being a harmony has another harmony within her, and that the vicious soul is inharmonical and has no harmony within her?

I cannot tell, replied Simmias; but I suppose that something of the sort would be asserted by those who say that the soul is a harmony.

And we have already admitted that no soul is more a soul than another; which is equivalent to admitting that harmony is not more or less harmony, or more or less completely a harmony?

Quite true.

And that which is not more or less a harmony is not more or less harmonized?

True.

And that which is not more or less harmonized cannot have more or less of harmony, but only an equal harmony?

Yes, an equal harmony.

Then one soul not being more or less absolutely a soul than another, is not more or less harmonized?

Exactly.

And therefore has neither more nor less of discord, nor yet of harmony?

She has not.

And having neither more nor less of harmony or of discord, one soul has no more vice or virtue than another, if vice be discord and virtue harmony?

Not at all more.

[94] Or speaking more correctly, Simmias, the soul, if she is a harmony, will never have any vice; because a harmony, being absolutely a harmony, has no part in the inharmonical.

No.

And therefore a soul which is absolutely a soul has no vice?

How can she have, if the previous argument holds?

Then, if all souls are equally by their nature souls, all souls of all living creatures will be equally good?

I agree with you, Socrates, he said.

And can all this be true, think you? he said; for these are the consequences which seem to follow from the assumption that the soul is a harmony?

It cannot be true.

Once more, he said, what ruler is there of the elements of human nature other than the soul, and especially the wise soul? Do you know of any?

Indeed, I do not.

And is the soul in agreement with the affections of the body? or is she at variance with them? For example, when the body is hot and thirsty, does not the soul incline us against drinking? and when the body is hungry, against eating? and this is only one instance out of ten thousand of the opposition of the soul to the things of the body.

Very true.

But we have already acknowledged that the soul, being a harmony, can never utter a note at variance with the tensions and relaxations and vibrations and other affections of the strings out of which she is composed; she can only follow, she cannot lead them?

It must be so, he replied.

And yet do we not now discover the soul to be doing the exact opposite—leading the elements of which she is believed to be composed; almost always opposing and coercing them in all sorts of ways throughout life, sometimes more violently with the pains of medicine and gymnastic; then again more gently; now threatening, now admonishing the desires, passions, fears, as if talking to a thing which is not herself, as Homer in the *Odyssey* represents Odysseus doing in the words:

> He beat his breast, and thus reproached his heart
> Endure, my heart; far worse hast thou endured!

Do you think that Homer wrote this under the idea that the soul is a harmony capable of being led by the affections of the body, and not rather of a nature which should lead and master them—herself a far diviner thing than any harmony?

Yes, Socrates, I quite think so.

Then, my friend, we can never be right in saying that the soul is a harmony, *[95]* for we should contradict the divine Homer, and contradict ourselves.

True, he said.

Thus much, said Socrates, of Harmonia, your Theban goddess, who has graciously yielded to us; but what shall I say, Cebes, to her husband Cadmus, and how shall I make peace with him?

I think that you will discover a way of propitiating him, said Cebes; I am sure that

you have put the argument with Harmonia in a manner that I could never have expected. For when Simmias was mentioning his difficulty, I quite imagined that no answer could be given to him, and therefore I was surprised at finding that his argument could not sustain the first onset of yours, and not impossibly the other, whom you call Cadmus, may share a similar fate.

Nay, my good friend, said Socrates, let us not boast, lest some evil eye should put to flight the word which I am about to speak. That, however, may be left in the hands of those above; while I draw near in Homeric fashion, and try the mettle of your words. Here lies the point:—You want to have it proven to you that the soul is imperishable and immortal, and the philosopher who is confident in death appears to you to have but a vain and foolish confidence, if he believes that he will fare better in the world below than one who has led another sort of life, unless he can prove this: and you say that the demonstration of the strength and divinity of the soul, and of her existence prior to our becoming men, does not necessarily imply her immortality. Admitting the soul to be long-lived, and to have known and done much in a former state, still she is not on that account immortal; and her entrance into the human form may be a sort of disease which is the beginning of dissolution, and may at last, after the toils of life are over, end in that which is called death. And whether the soul enters into the body once only or many times, does not, as you say, make any difference in the fears of individuals. For any man, who is not devoid of sense, must fear, if he has no knowledge and can give no account of the soul's immortality. This, or something like this, I suspect to be your notion, Cebes; and I designedly recur to it in order that nothing may escape us, and that you may, if you wish, add or subtract anything.

But, said Cebes, as far as I see at present, I have nothing to add or subtract: I mean what you say that I mean.

Socrates paused awhile, and seemed to be absorbed in reflection. At length he said:

You are raising a tremendous question, Cebes, involving the whole nature of generation and corruption, [96] about which, if you like, I will give you my own experience; and if anything which I say is likely to avail towards the solution of your difficulty you may make use of it.

I should very much like, said Cebes, to hear what you have to say.

Then I will tell you, said Socrates. When I was young, Cebes, I had a prodigious desire to know that department of philosophy which is called the investigation of nature; to know the causes of things, and why a thing is and is created or destroyed appeared to me to be a lofty profession; and I was always agitating myself with the consideration of questions such as these:—Is the growth of animals the result of some decay which the hot and cold principle contracts, as some have said? Is the blood the element with which we think, or the air, or the fire? or perhaps nothing of the kind—but the brain may be the originating power of the perceptions of hearing and sight and smell, and memory and opinion may come from them, and science may be based on memory and opinion when they have attained fixity. And then I went on to examine the corruption of them, and then to the things of heaven and earth, and at last I concluded myself to be utterly and absolutely incapable of these enquiries, as I will satisfactorily prove to you. For I was fascinated by them to such a degree that my eyes grew blind to things which I had seemed to myself, and also to others, to know quite well; I forgot what I had before thought self-evident truths; e.g. such a fact as that the growth of man is the result of eating and drinking; for when by the digestion of food flesh is added to flesh and bone to bone, and whenever there is an aggregation of congenial elements, the lesser bulk becomes larger and the small man great. Was not that a reasonable notion?

Yes, said Cebes, I think so.

Well; but let me tell you something more. There was a time when I thought that I understood the meaning of greater and less pretty well; and when I saw a great man standing by a little one, I fancied that one was taller than the other by a head; or one horse would appear to be greater than another horse: and still more clearly did I seem to perceive that ten is two more than eight, and that two cubits are more than one, because two is the double of one.

And what is now your notion of such matters? said Cebes.

I should be far enough from imagining, he replied, that I knew the cause of any of them, by heaven I should; for I cannot satisfy myself that, [97] when one is added to one, the one to which the addition is made becomes two, or that the two units added together make two by reason of the addition. I cannot understand how, when separated from the other, each of them was one and not two, and now, when they are brought together, the mere juxtaposition or meeting of them should be the cause of their becoming two: neither can I understand how the division of one is the way to make two; for then a different cause would produce the same effect,—as in the former instance the addition and juxtaposition of one to one was the cause of two, in this the separation and subtraction of one from the other would be the cause. Nor am I any longer satisfied that I understand the reason why one or anything else is either generated or destroyed or is at all, but I have in my mind some confused notion of a new method, and can never admit the other.

Then I heard some one reading, as he said, from a book of Anaxagoras, that mind was the disposer and cause of all, and I was delighted at this notion, which appeared quite admirable, and I said to myself: If mind is the disposer, mind will dispose all for the best, and put each particular in the best place; and I argued that if any one desired to find out the cause of the generation or destruction or existence of anything, he must find out what state of being or doing or suffering was best for that thing, and therefore a man had only to consider the best for himself and others, and then he would also know the worse, since the same science comprehended both. And I rejoiced to think that I had found in Anaxagoras a teacher of the causes of existence such as I desired, and I imagined that he would tell me first whether the earth is flat or round; and whichever was true, he would proceed to explain the cause and the necessity of this being so, and then he would teach me the nature of the best and show that this was best; and if he said that the earth was in the centre, he would further explain that this position was the best, and I should be satisfied with the explanation given, and not want any other sort of cause. [98] And I thought that I would then go on and ask him about the sun and moon and stars, and that he would explain to me their comparative swiftness, and their returnings and various states, active and passive, and how all of them were for the best. For I could not imagine that when he spoke of mind as the disposer of them, he would give any other account of their being as they are, except that this was best; and I thought that when he had explained to me in detail the cause of each and the cause of all, he would go on to explain to me what was best for each and what was good for all. These hopes I would not have sold for a large sum of money, and I seized the books and read them as fast as I could in my eagerness to know the better and the worse.

What expectations I had formed, and how grievously was I disappointed! As I proceeded, I found my philosopher altogether forsaking mind or any other principle of order, but having recourse to air, and ether, and water, and other eccentricities. I might compare him to a person who began by maintaining generally that mind is the cause of the actions of Socrates, but who, when he endeavoured to explain the causes of my several actions in detail, went on to show that I sit here because my body is made up of bones and muscles; and the bones, as he would say, are hard and have joints which divide them, and the muscles are elastic, and they cover the bones, which have also a covering or environment of flesh and skin which contains them; and as the bones are lifted at their joints by the contraction or relaxation of the muscles, I am able to bend my limbs, and this is why I am sitting here in a curved posture—that is what he would say; and he would have a similar explanation of my talking to you, which he would attribute to sound, and air, and hearing, and he would assign ten thousand other causes of the same sort, forgetting to mention the true cause, which is, that the Athenians have thought fit to condemn me, and accordingly I have thought it better and more right to remain here and undergo my sentence; [99] for I am inclined to think that these muscles and bones of mine would have gone off long ago to Megara or Boeotia—by the dog, they would, if they had been moved only by their own idea of what was best, and if I had not chosen the better and nobler part, instead of playing truant and running away, of enduring any punishment which the state inflicts. There is surely a strange confusion of causes and conditions in all this. It may be said, indeed, that without bones and muscles and the other parts of the body I cannot execute my purposes. But to say that I do as I do because of them, and that this is the way in which mind acts, and not from choice of the best, is a very careless and idle mode of speaking. I wonder that they cannot distinguish the cause from the condition, which the many, feeling about in the dark, are always mistaking and misnaming. And thus one man makes a vortex all round and steadies the earth by the heaven; another gives the air as a support to the earth, which is a sort of broad trough. Any power which in arranging them as they are arranges them for the best never enters into their minds; and instead of finding any superior strength in it, they rather expect to discover another Atlas of the world who is stronger and more everlasting and more containing than the good;—of the obligatory and containing power of the good they think nothing; and yet this is the principle which I would fain learn if any one would teach me. But as I have failed either to discover myself, or to learn of any one else, the nature of the best, I will exhibit to you, if you like, what I have found to be the second best mode of enquiring into the cause.

I should very much like to hear, he replied.

Socrates proceeded: I thought that as I had failed in the contemplation of true existence, I ought to be careful that I did not lose the eye of my soul; as people may injure their bodily eye by observing and gazing on the sun during an eclipse, unless they take the precaution of only looking at the image reflected in the water, or in some similar medium. So in my own case, I was afraid that my soul might be blinded altogether if I looked at things with my eyes or tried to apprehend them by the help of the senses. And I thought that I had better have recourse to the world of mind and seek there the truth of existence. *[100]* I dare say that the simile is not perfect—for I am very far from admitting that he who contemplates existences through the medium of thought, sees them only "through a glass darkly," any more than he who considers them in action and operation. However, this was the method which I adopted: I first assumed some principle which I judged to be the strongest, and then I affirmed as true whatever seemed to agree with this, whether relating to the cause or to anything else; and that which disagreed I regarded as untrue. But I should like to explain my meaning more clearly, as I do not think that you as yet understand me.

No indeed, replied Cebes, not very well.

There is nothing new, he said, in what I am about to tell you; but only what I have been always and everywhere repeating in the previous discussion and on other occasions: I want to show you the nature of that cause which has occupied my thoughts. I shall have to go back to those familiar words which are in the mouth of every one, and first of all assume that there is an absolute beauty and goodness and greatness, and the like; grant me this, and I hope to be able to show you the nature of the cause, and to prove the immortality of the soul.

Cebes said: You may proceed at once with the proof, for I grant you this.

Well, he said, then I should like to know whether you agree with me in the next step; for I cannot help thinking, if there be anything beautiful other than absolute beauty should there be such, that it can be beautiful only in so far as it partakes of absolute beauty—and I should say the same of everything. Do you agree in this notion of the cause?

Yes, he said, I agree.

He proceeded: I know nothing and can understand nothing of any other of those wise causes which are alleged; and if a person says to me that the bloom of colour, or form, or any such thing is a source of beauty, I leave all that, which is only confusing to me, and simply and singly, and perhaps foolishly, hold and am assured in my own mind that nothing makes a thing beautiful but the presence and participation of beauty in whatever way or manner obtained; for as to the manner I am uncertain, but I stoutly contend that by beauty all beautiful things become beautiful. This appears to me to be the safest answer which I can give, either to myself or to another, and to this I cling, in the persuasion that this principle will never be overthrown, and that to myself or to any one who asks the question, I may safely reply, That by beauty beautiful things become beautiful. Do you not agree with me?

I do.

And that by greatness only great things become great and greater greater, and by smallness the less become less?

True.

Then if a person were to remark that A is taller by a head than B, *[101]* and B less by a head than A, you would refuse to admit his statement, and would stoutly contend that what you mean is only that the greater is greater by, and by reason of, greatness, and the less is less only by, and by reason of, smallness; and thus you would avoid the danger of saying that the greater is greater and the less less by the measure of the head, which is the same in both, and would also avoid the monstrous absurdity of supposing that the greater man is greater by reason of the head, which is small. You would be afraid to draw such an inference, would you not?

Indeed, I should, said Cebes, laughing.

In like manner you would be afraid to say that ten exceeded eight by, and by reason of, two; but would say by, and by reason of, number; or you would say that two cubits exceed one cubit not by a half, but by magnitude?—for there is the same liability to error in all these cases.

Very true, he said.

Again, would you not be cautious of affirming that the addition of one to one, or the division of one, is the cause of two? And you would loudly asseverate that you know of no way in which anything comes into existence except by participation in its own proper essence, and consequently, as far as you know, the only cause of two is the participation in duality—this is the way to make two, and the participation in one is the way to make one. You would say: I will let alone puzzles of division and addition—wiser heads than mine may answer them; inexperienced as I am, and ready to start, as the proverb says, at my own shadow, I cannot afford to give up the sure ground of a principle. And if any one assails you there, you would not mind him, or answer him until you had seen whether the consequences which follow agree with one another or not, and when you are further required to give an explanation of this principle, you would go on to assume a higher principle, and a higher, until you found a resting-place in the best of the higher; but you would not confuse the principle and the consequences in your reasoning, like the Eristics—at least if you wanted to discover real existence. Not that this confusion signifies to them, who never care or think about the matter at all, for they have the wit to be well pleased with themselves however great may be the turmoil of their ideas. *[102]* But you, if you are a philosopher, will certainly do as I say.

What you say is most true, said Simmias and Cebes, both speaking at once.

Ech. Yes, Phaedo; and I do not wonder at their assenting. Any one who has the least sense will acknowledge the wonderful clearness of Socrates' reasoning.

Phaed. Certainly, Echecrates; and such was the feeling of the whole company at the time.

Ech. Yes, and equally of ourselves, who were not of the company, and are now listening to your recital. But what followed?

Phaed. After all this had been admitted, and they had agreed that ideas exist, and that other things participate in them and derive their names from them, Socrates, if I remember rightly, said:—

This is your way of speaking; and yet when you say that Simmias is greater than Socrates and less than Phaedo, do you not predicate of Simmias both greatness and smallness?

Yes, I do.

But still you allow that Simmias does not really exceed Socrates, as the words may seem to imply, because he is Simmias, but by reason of the size which he has; just as Simmias does not exceed Socrates because he is Simmias, any more than because Socrates is Socrates, but because he has smallness when compared with the greatness of Simmias?

True.

And if Phaedo exceeds him in size, this is not because Phaedo is Phaedo, but because Phaedo has greatness relatively to Simmias, who is comparatively smaller?

That is true.

And therefore Simmias is said to be great, and is also said to be small, because he is in a mean between them, exceeding the smallness of the one by his greatness, and allowing the greatness of the other to exceed his smallness. He added, laughing, I am speaking like a book, but I believe that what I am saying is true.

Simmias assented.

I speak as I do because I want you to agree with me in thinking, not only that absolute greatness will never be great and also small, but that greatness in us or in the concrete will never admit the small or admit of being exceeded: instead of this, one of two things will happen, either the greater will fly or retire before the opposite, which is the less, or at the approach of the less has already ceased to exist; but will not, if allowing or admitting of smallness, be changed by that; even as I, having received and admitted smallness when compared with Simmias, remain just as I was, and am the same small person. And as the idea of greatness cannot condescend ever to be or become small, in like manner the smallness in us cannot be or become great; nor can any other opposite which remains the same ever be or become its own opposite, *[103]* but either passes away or perishes in the change.

That, replied Cebes, is quite my notion.

Hereupon one of the company, though I do not exactly remember which of them, said: In heaven's name, is not this the direct contrary of what was admitted before—that out of the greater came the less and out of the less the greater, and that opposites were simply generated from opposites; but now this principle seems to be utterly denied.

Socrates inclined his head to the speaker and listened. I like your courage, he said, in reminding us of this. But you do not observe that there is a difference in the two cases. For then we were speaking of opposites in the concrete, and now of the essential opposite which, as is affirmed, neither in us nor in nature can ever be at variance with itself: then, my friend, we were speaking of things in which opposites are inherent and which are called after them, but now about the opposites which are inherent in them and which give their name to them; and these essential opposites will never, as we maintain, admit of generation into or out of one another. At the same time, turning to Cebes, he said: Are you at all disconcerted, Cebes, at our friend's objection?

No, I do not feel so, said Cebes; and yet I cannot deny that I am often disturbed by objections.

Then we are agreed after all, said Socrates, that the opposite will never in any case be opposed to itself?

To that we are quite agreed, he replied.

Yet once more let me ask you to consider the question from another point of view, and see whether you agree with me:— There is a thing which you term heat, and another thing which you term cold?

Certainly.

But are they the same as fire and snow?

Most assuredly not.

Heat is a thing different from fire, and cold is not the same with snow?

Yes.

And yet you will surely admit, that when snow, as was before said, is under the influence of heat, they will not remain snow and heat; but at the advance of the heat, the snow will either retire or perish?

Very true, he replied.

And the fire too at the advance of the cold will either retire or perish; and when the fire is under the influence of the cold, they will not remain as before, fire and cold.

That is true, he said.

And in some cases the name of the idea is not only attached to the idea in an eternal connection, but anything else which, not being the idea, exists only in the form of the idea, may also lay claim to it. I will try to make this clearer by an example:—The odd number is always called by the name of odd?

Very true.

But is this the only thing which is called odd? Are there not other things which have their own name, *[104]* and yet are called odd, because, although not the same as oddness, they are never without oddness? —that is what I mean to ask—whether numbers such as the number three are not of the class of odd. And there are many other examples: would you not say, for example, that three may be called by its proper name, and also be called odd, which is not the same with three? and this may be said not only of three but also of five, and of every alternate number—each of them without being oddness is odd; and in the same way two and four, and the other series of alternate numbers, has every number even, without being evenness. Do you agree?

Of course.

Then now mark the point at which I am aiming:—not only do essential opposites exclude one another, but also concrete things, which, although not in themselves opposed, contain opposites; these, I say, likewise reject the idea which is opposed to that which is contained in them, and when it approaches them they either perish or withdraw. For example: Will not the number three endure annihilation or anything sooner than be converted into an even number, while remaining three?

Very true, said Cebes.

And yet, he said, the number two is certainly not opposed to the number three?

It is not.

Then not only do opposite ideas repel the advance of one another, but also there are other natures which repel the approach of opposites.

Very true, he said.

Suppose, he said, that we endeavour, if possible, to determine what these are.

By all means.

Are they not, Cebes, such as compel the things of which they have possession, not only to take their own form, but also the form of some opposite?

What do you mean?

I mean, as I was just now saying, and as I am sure that you know, that those things which are possessed by the number three must not only be three in number, but must also be odd.

Quite true.

And on this oddness, of which the number three has the impress, the opposite idea will never intrude?

No.

And this impress was given by the odd principle?

Yes.

And to the odd is opposed the even?

True.

Then the idea of the even number will never arrive at three?

No.

Then three has no part in the even?

None.

Then the triad or number three is uneven?

Very true.

To return then to my distinction of natures which are not opposed, and yet do not admit opposites—as, in the instance given, three, although not opposed to the even, does not any the more admit of the even, but always brings the opposite into play on the other side; [105] or as two does not receive the odd, or fire the cold—from these examples (and there are many more of them) perhaps you may be able to arrive at the general conclusion, that not only opposites will not receive opposites, but also that nothing which brings the opposite will admit the opposite of that which it brings, in that to which it is brought. And here let me recapitulate—for there is no harm in repetition. The number five will not admit the nature of the even, any more than ten, which is the double of five, will admit the nature of the odd. The double has another opposite, and is not strictly opposed to the odd, but nevertheless rejects the odd altogether. Nor again will parts in the ratio 3:2, nor any fraction in which there is a half, nor again in which there is a third, admit the notion of the whole, although they are not opposed to the whole: You will agree?

Yes, he said, I entirely agree and go along with you in that.

And now, he said, let us begin again; and do not you answer my question in the words in which I ask it: let me have not the old safe answer of which I spoke at first, but another equally safe, of which the truth will be inferred by you from what has been just said. I mean that if any one asks you "what that is, of which the inherence makes the body hot," you will reply not heat (this is what I call the safe and stupid answer), but fire, a far superior answer, which we are now in a condition to give. Or if any one asks you "why a body is diseased," you will not say from disease, but from fever; and instead of saying that oddness is the cause of odd numbers, you will say that the monad is the cause of them: and so of things in general, as I dare say that you will understand sufficiently without my adducing any further examples.

Yes, he said, I quite understand you.

Tell me, then, what is that of which the inherence will render the body alive?

The soul, he replied.

And is this always the case?

Yes, he said, of course.

Then whatever the soul possesses, to that she comes bearing life?

Yes, certainly.

And is there any opposite to life?

There is, he said.

And what is that?

Death.

Then the soul, as has been acknowledged, will never receive the opposite of what she brings.

Impossible, replied Cebes.

And now, he said, what did we just now call that principle which repels the even?

The odd.

And that principle which repeals the musical or the just?

The unmusical, he said, and the unjust.

And what do we call that principle which does not admit of death?

The immortal, he said.

And does the soul admit of death?

No.

Then the soul is immortal?

Yes, he said.

And may we say that this has been proven?

Yes, abundantly proven, Socrates, he replied.

[106] Supposing that the odd were imperishable, must not three be imperishable?

Of course.

And if that which is cold were imperishable, when the warm principle came attacking the snow, must not the snow have retired whole and unmelted—for it could never have perished, nor could it have remained and admitted the heat?

True, he said.

Again, if the uncooling or warm principle were imperishable, the fire when assailed by cold would not have perished or have been extinguished, but would have gone away unaffected?

Certainly, he said.

And the same may be said of the immortal: if the immortal is also imperishable, the soul when attacked by death cannot perish; for the preceding argument shows that the soul will not admit of death, or ever be dead, any more than three or the odd number will admit of the even, or fire, or the heat in the fire, of the cold. Yet a person may say: "But although the odd will not become even at the approach of the even, why may not the odd perish and the even take the place of the odd?" Now to him who makes this objection, we cannot answer that the odd principle is imperishable; for this has not been acknowledged, but if this had been acknowledged, there would have been no difficulty in contending that at the approach of the even the odd principle and the number three took their departure; and the same argument would have held good of fire and heat and any other thing.

Very true.

And the same may be said of the immortal: if the immortal is also imperishable, then the soul will be imperishable as well as immortal; but if not, some other proof of her imperishableness will have to be given.

No other proof is needed, he said; for if the immortal, being eternal, is liable to perish, then nothing is imperishable.

Yes, replied Socrates, and yet all men will agree that God, and the essential form of life, and the immortal in general, will never perish.

Yes, all men, he said—that is true; and what is more, gods, if I am not mistaken, as well as men.

Seeing then that the immortal is indestructible, must not the soul, if she is immortal, be also imperishable?

Most certainly.

Then when death attacks a man, the mortal portion of him may be supposed to die, but the immortal retires at the approach of death and is preserved safe and sound?

True.

Then, Cebes, beyond question, the soul is immortal and imperishable, *[107]* and our souls will truly exist in another world!

I am convinced, Socrates, said Cebes, and have nothing more to object; but if my friend Simmias, or any one else, has any further objection to make, he had better speak out, and not keep silence, since I do not know to what other season he can defer the discussion, if there is anything which he wants to say or to have said.

But I have nothing more to say, replied Simmias; nor can I see any reason for doubt after what has been said. But I still feel and cannot help feeling uncertain in my own mind, when I think of the greatness of the subject and the feebleness of man.

Yes, Simmias, replied Socrates, that is well said: and I may add that first principles, even if they appear certain, should be carefully considered; and when they are satisfactorily ascertained, then, with a sort of hesitating confidence in human reason, you may, I think, follow the course of the argument; and if that be plain and clear, there will be no need for any further enquiry.

Very true.

But then, O my friends, he said, if the soul is really immortal, what care should be taken of her, not only in respect of the portion of time which is called life, but of eternity! And the danger of neglecting her from this point of view does indeed appear to be awful. If death had only been the end of all, the wicked would have had a good bargain in dying, for they would have been happily quit not only of their body, but of their own evil together with their souls. But now, inasmuch as the soul is mainifestly immortal, there is no release or salvation from evil except the attainment of the highest virtue and wisdom. For the soul when on her progress to the world below takes nothing with her but nurture and education; and these are said greatly to benefit or greatly to injure the departed, at the very beginning of his journey thither.

For after death, as they say, the genius of each individual, to whom he belonged in life, leads him to a certain place in which the dead are gathered together, whence after judgment has been given they pass into the world below, following the guide, who is appointed to conduct them from this world to the other: and when they have there received their due and remained their time, another guide brings them back again after many revolutions of ages. Now this way to the other world is not, *[108]* as Aeschylus says in the Telephus, a single and straight path—if that were so no guide would be needed, for no one could miss it; but there are many partings of the road, and windings, as I infer from the rites and sacrifices which are offered to the gods below in places where three ways meet on earth. The wise and orderly soul follows in the straight path and is conscious of her surroundings; but the soul which desires the body, and which, as I was relating before, has long been fluttering about the lifeless frame and the world of sight, is after many struggles and many sufferings hardly and with violence carried away by her attendant genius; and when she arrives at the place where the other souls are gathered, if she be impure and have done impure deeds, whether foul murders or other crimes which are the brothers of these, and the works of brothers in crime—from that soul every one flees and turns away; no one will be her companion, no one her guide, but alone she wanders in extremity of evil until certain times are fulfilled, and when they are fulfilled, she is borne irresistibly to her own fitting habitation; as every pure and just soul which has passed through life in the company and under the guidance of the gods has also her own proper home.

Now the earth has divers wonderful regions, and is indeed in nature and extent very unlike the notions of geographers, as I believe on the authority of one who shall be nameless.

What do you mean, Socrates? said Simmias. I have myself heard many descriptions of the earth, but I do not know, and I should very much like to know, in which of these you put faith.

And I, Simmias, replied Socrates, if I had the art of Glaucus would tell you; although I know not that the art of Glaucus could prove the truth of my tale, which I myself should never be able to prove, and even if I could, I fear, Simmias, that my life would come to an end before the argument was completed. I may describe to you, however, the form and regions of the earth according to my conception of them.

That, said Simmias, will be enough.

Well then, he said, my conviction is, that the earth is a round body in the centre of the heavens, and therefore has no need of air or of any similar force to be a support, *[109]* but is kept there and hindered from falling or inclining any way by the equability of the surrounding heaven and by her own equipoise. For that which, being in equipoise, is in the centre of that which is equably diffused, will not incline any way in any degree, but will always remain in the same state and not deviate. And this is my first notion.

Which is surely a correct one, said Simmias.

Also I believe that the earth is very vast, and that we who dwell in the region extending from the river Phasis to the Pillars of Heracles inhabit a small portion only about the sea, like ants or frogs about a marsh, and that there are other inhabitants of many other like places; for everywhere on the face of the earth there are hollows of various forms and sizes, into which the water and the mist and the lower air collect. But the true earth is pure and situated in the pure heaven—there are the stars also; and it is the heaven which is commonly spoken of by us as the ether, and of which our own earth is the sediment gathering in the hollows beneath. But we who live in these hollows are deceived into the notion that we are dwelling above on the surface of the earth; which is just as if a creature who was at the bottom of the sea were to fancy that he was on the surface of the water, and that the sea was the heaven through which he saw the sun and the other stars, he having never come to the surface by reason of

his feebleness and sluggishness, and having never lifted up his head and seen, nor ever heard from one who had seen, how much purer and fairer the world above is than his own. And such is exactly our case: for we are dwelling in a hollow of the earth, and fancy that we are on the surface; and the air we call heaven, in which we imagine that the stars move. But the fact is, that owing to our feebleness and sluggishness we are prevented from reaching the surface of the air: for if any man could arrive at the exterior limit, or take the wings of a bird and come to the top, then like a fish who puts his head out of the water and sees this world, he would see a world beyond; and, if the nature of man could sustain the sight, he would acknowledge that this other world was the place of the true heaven and the true light and the true earth. *[110]* For our earth, and the stones, and the entire region which surrounds us, are spoilt and corroded, as in the sea all things are corroded by the brine, neither is there any noble or perfect growth, but caverns only, and sand, and an endless slough of mud; and even the shore is not to be compared to the fairer sights of this world. And still less is this our world to be compared with the other. Of that upper earth which is under the heaven, I can tell you a charming tale, Simmias, which is well worth hearing.

And we, Socrates, replied Simmias, shall be charmed to listen to you.

The tale, my friend, he said, is as follows: —In the first place, the earth, when looked at from above, is in appearance streaked like one of those balls which have leather coverings in twelve pieces, and is decked with various colours, of which the colours used by painters on earth are in a manner samples. But there the whole earth is made up of them, and they are brighter far and clearer than ours; there is a purple of wonderful lustre, also the radiance of gold, and the white which is in the earth is whiter than any chalk or snow. Of these and other colours the earth is made up, and they are more in number and fairer than the eye of man has ever seen; the very hollows (of which I was speaking) filled with air and water have a colour of their own, and are seen like light gleaming amid the diversity of the other colours, so that the whole presents a single and continuous appearance of variety in unity. And in this fair region everything that grows—trees, and flowers, and fruits—are in a like degree fairer than any here; and there are hills, having stones in them in a like degree smoother, and more transparent, and fairer in colour than our highly-valued emeralds and sardonyxes and jaspers, and other gems, which are but minute fragments of them: for there all the stones are like our precious stones, and fairer still. The reason is, that they are pure, and not, like our precious stones, infected or corroded by the corrupt briny elements which coagulate among us, and which breed foulness and disease both in earth and stones, as well as in animals and plants. They are the jewels of the upper earth, which also shines with gold and silver and the like, *[111]* and they are set in the light of day and are large and abundant and in all places, making the earth a sight to gladden the beholder's eye. And there are animals and men, some in a middle region, others dwelling about the air as we dwell about the sea; others in islands which the air flows round, near the continent; and in a word, the air is used by them as the water and the sea are by us, and the ether is to them what air is to us. Moreover, the temperament of their seasons is such that they have no disease, and live much longer than we do, and have sight and hearing and smell, and all the other senses, in far greater perfection, in the same proportion that air is purer than water or the ether than air. Also they have temples and sacred places in which the gods really dwell, and they hear their voices and receive their answers, and are conscious of them and hold converse with them; and they see the sun, moon, and stars as they truly are, and their other blessedness is of a piece with this.

Such is the nature of the whole earth, and of the things which are around the earth;

and there are divers regions in the hollows on the face of the globe everywhere, some of them deeper and more extended than that which we inhabit, others deeper but with a narrower opening than ours, and some are shallower and also wider. All have numerous perforations, and there are passages broad and narrow in the interior of the earth, connecting them with one another; and there flows out of and into them, as into basins, a vast tide of water, and huge subterranean streams of perennial rivers, and springs hot and cold, and a great fire, and great rivers of fire, and streams of liquid mud, thin or thick (like the rivers of mud in Sicily, and the lava streams which follow them), and the regions about which they happen to flow are filled up with them. And there is a swinging or see-saw in the interior of the earth which moves all this up and down, and is due to the following cause:—There is a chasm which is the vastest of them all, and pierces right through the whole earth; *[112]* this is that chasm which Homer describes in the words:

Far off, where is the inmost depth beneath the earth;

and which he in other places, and many other poets, have called Tartarus. And the see-saw is caused by the streams flowing into and out of this chasm, and they each have the nature of the soil through which they flow. And the reason why the streams are always flowing in and out, is that the watery element has no bed or bottom, but is swinging and surging up and down, and the surrounding wind and air do the same; they follow the water up and down, hither and thither, over the earth—just as in the act of respiration the air is always in process of inhalation and exhalation;—and the wind swinging with the water in and out produces fearful and irresistible blasts: when the waters retire with a rush into the lower parts of the earth, as they are called, they flow through the earth in those regions, and fill them up like water raised by a pump, and then when they leave those regions and rush back hither, they again fill the hollows here, and when these are filled, flow through subterranean channels and find their way to their several places, forming seas, and lakes, and rivers, and springs. Thence they again enter the earth, some of them making a long circuit into many lands, others going to a few places and not so distant; and again fall into Tartarus, some at a point a good deal lower than that at which they rose, and others not much lower, but all in some degree lower than the point from which they came. And some burst forth again on the opposite side, and some on the same side, and some wind round the earth with one or many folds like the coils of a serpent, and descend as far as they can, but always return and fall into the chasm. The rivers flowing in either direction can descend only to the centre and no further, for opposite to the rivers is a precipice.

Now these rivers are many, and mighty, and diverse, and there are four principal ones, of which the greatest and outermost is that called Oceanus, which flows round the earth in a circle; and in the opposite direction flows Acheron, which passes under the earth through desert places into the Acherusian lake: *[113]* this is the lake to the shores of which the souls of many go when they are dead, and after waiting an appointed time, which is to some a longer and to some a shorter time, they are sent back to be born again as animals. The third river passes out between the two, and near the place of outlet pours into a vast region of fire, and forms a lake larger than the Mediterranean Sea, boiling with water and mud; and proceeding muddy and turbid, and winding about the earth, comes, among other places, to the extremities of the Acherusian lake, but mingles not with the waters of the lake, and after making many coils about the earth plunges into Tartarus at a deeper level. This is that Pyriphlegethon, as the stream is called, which throws up jets of fire in different parts of the earth. The fourth river goes out on the opposite side, and falls first of all into a wild and savage region, which is all of a dark blue

colour, like lapis lazuli; and this is that river which is called the Stygian river, and falls into and forms the Lake Styx, and after falling into the lake and receiving strange powers in the waters, passes under the earth, winding round in the opposite direction, and comes near the Acherusian lake from the opposite side to Pyriphlegethon. And the water of this river too mingles with no other, but flows round in a circle and falls into Tartarus over against Pyriphlegethon; and the name of the river, as the poets say, is Cocytus.

Such is the nature of the other world; and when the dead arrive at the place to which the genius of each severally guides them, first of all, they have sentence passed upon them, as they have lived well and piously or not. And those who appear to have lived neither well nor ill, go to the river Acheron, and embarking in any vessels which they may find, are carried in them to the lake, and there they dwell and are purified of their evil deeds, and having suffered the penalty of the wrongs which they have done to others, they are absolved, and receive the rewards of their good deeds, each of them according to his deserts. But those who appear to be incurable by reason of the greatness of their crimes—who have committed many and terrible deeds of sacrilege, murders foul and violent, or the like —such are hurled into Tartarus which is their suitable destiny, and they never come out. Those again who have committed crimes, which, although great, are not irremediable—who in a moment of anger, for example, have done some violence to a father or a mother, *[114]* and have repented for the remainder of their lives, or, who have taken the life of another under the like extenuating circumstances—these are plunged into Tartarus, the pains of which they are compelled to undergo for a year, but at the end of the year the wave casts them forth—mere homicides by way of Cocytus, parricides and matricides by Pyriphlegethon—and they are borne to the Acherusian lake, and there they lift up their voices and call upon the victims whom they have slain or wronged, to have pity on them, and to be kind to them, and let them come out into the lake. And if they prevail, then they come forth and cease from their troubles; but if not, they are carried back again into Tartarus and from thence into the rivers unceasingly, until they obtain mercy from those whom they have wronged: for that is the sentence inflicted upon them by their judges. Those too who have been pre-eminent for holiness of life are released from this earthly prison, and go to their pure home which is above, and dwell in the purer earth; and of these, such as have duly purified themselves with philosophy live henceforth altogether without the body, in mansions fairer still, which may not be described, and of which the time would fail me to tell.

Wherefore, Simmias, seeing all these things, what ought not we to do that we may obtain virtue and wisdom in this life? Fair is the prize, and the hope great!

A man of sense ought not to say, nor will I be very confident, that the description which I have given of the soul and her mansions is exactly true. But I do say that, inasmuch as the soul is shown to be immortal, he may venture to think, not improperly or unworthily, that something of the kind is true. The venture is a glorious one, and he ought to comfort himself with words like these, which is the reason why I lengthen out the tale. Wherefore, I say, let a man be of good cheer about his soul, who having cast away the pleasures and ornaments of the body as alien to him and working harm rather than good, has sought after the pleasures of knowledge; and has arrayed the soul, not in some foreign attire, but in her own proper jewels, temperance, and justice, and courage, and nobility, *[115]* and truth—in these adorned she is ready to go on her journey to the world below, when her hour comes. You, Simmias and Cebes, and all other men, will depart at some time or other. Me already, as a tragic poet would say, the voice of fate calls. Soon I must drink the poison; and I think that I had better repair to the bath first, in order that the women may not have the trouble of washing my body after I am dead.

When he had done speaking, Crito said: And have you any commands for us, Socrates—anything to say about your children, or any other matter in which we can serve you?

Nothing particular, Crito, he replied: only, as I have always told you, take care of yourselves; that is a service which you may be ever rendering to me and mine and to all of us, whether you promise to do so or not. But if you have no thought for yourselves, and care not to walk according to the rule which I have prescribed for you, not now for the first time, however much you may profess or promise at the moment, it will be of no avail.

We will do our best, said Crito: And in what way shall we bury you?

In any way that you like; but you must get hold of me, and take care that I do not run away from you. Then he turned to us, and added with a smile:—I cannot make Crito believe that I am the same Socrates who have been talking and conducting the argument; he fancies that I am the other Socrates whom he will soon see, a dead body—and he asks, How shall he bury me? And though I have spoken many words in the endeavor to show that when I have drunk the poison I shall leave you and go to the joys of the blessed,—these words of mine, with which I was comforting you and myself, have had, as I perceive, no effect upon Crito. And therefore I want you to be surety for me to him now, as at the trial he was surety to the judges for me: but let the promise be of another sort; for he was surety for me to the judges that I would remain, and you must be my surety to him that I shall not remain, but go away and depart; and then he will suffer less at my death, and not be grieved when he sees my body being burned or buried. I would not have him sorrow at my hard lot, or say at the burial, Thus we lay out Socrates, or, Thus we follow him to the grave or bury him; for false words are not only evil in themselves, but they infect the soul with evil. Be of good cheer then, my dear Crito, and say that you are burying my body only, [116] and do with that whatever is usual, and what you think best.

When he had spoken these words, he arose and went into a chamber to bathe; Crito followed him and told us to wait. So we remained behind, talking and thinking of the subject of discourse, and also of the greatness of our sorrow; he was like a father of whom we were being bereaved, and we were about to pass the rest of our lives as orphans. When he had taken the bath his children were brought to him—(he had two young sons and an elder one); and the women of his family also came, and he talked to them and gave them a few directions in the presence of Crito; then he dismissed them and returned to us.

Now the hour of sunset was near, for a good deal of time had passed while he was within. When he came out, he sat down with us again after his bath, but not much was said. Soon the jailer, who was the servant of the Eleven, entered and stood by him, saying:—To you, Socrates, whom I know to be the noblest and gentlest and best of all who ever came to this place, I will not impute the angry feelings of other men, who rage and swear at me, when, in obedience to the authorities, I bid them drink the poison—indeed, I am sure that you will not be angry with me; for others, as you are aware, and not I, are to blame. And so fare you well, and try to bear lightly what must needs be—you know my errand. Then bursting into tears he turned away and went out.

Socrates looked at him and said: I return your good wishes, and will do as you bid. Then turning to us, he said, How charming the man is: since I have been in prison he has always been coming to see me, and at times he would talk to me, and was as good to me as could be, and now see how generously he sorrows on my account. We must do as he says, Crito; and therefore let the cup be brought, if the poison is prepared: if not, let the attendant prepare some.

Yet, said Crito, the sun is still upon the hilltops, and I know that many a one has taken the draught late, and after the announcement has been made to him, he has eaten and drunk, and enjoyed the society of his beloved; do not hurry—there is time enough.

Socrates said: Yes, Crito, and they of whom you speak are right in so acting, for they think that they will be gainers by the delay; but I am right in not following their example, for I do not think that I should gain anything by drinking the poison a little later; [117] I should only be ridiculous in my own eyes for sparing and saving a life which is already forfeit. Please then to do as I say, and not to refuse me.

Crito made a sign to the servant, who was standing by; and he went out, and having been absent for some time, returned with the jailer carrying the cup of poison. Socrates said: You, my good friend, who are experienced in these matters, shall give me directions how I am to proceed. The man answered: You have only to walk about until your legs are heavy, and then to lie down, and the poison will act. At the same time he handed the cup to Socrates, who in the easiest and gentlest manner, without the least fear or change of colour or feature, looking at the man with all his eyes, Echecrates, as his manner was, took the cup and said: What do you say about making a libation out of this cup to any god? May I, or not? The man answered: We only prepare, Socrates, just so much as we deem enough. I understand, he said: but I may and must ask the gods to prosper my journey from this to the other world—even so —and so be it according to my prayer. Then raising the cup to his lips, quite readily and cheerfully he drank off the poison. And hitherto most of us had been able to control our sorrow; but now when we saw him drinking, and saw too that he had finished the draught, we could no longer forbear, and in spite of myself my own tears were flowing fast; so that I covered my face and wept, not for him, but at the thought of my own calamity in having to part from such a friend. Nor was I the first; for Crito, when he found himself unable to restrain his tears, had got up, and I followed; and at that moment, Apollodorus, who had been weeping all the time, broke out in a loud and passionate cry which made cowards of us all. Socrates alone retained his calmness: What is this strange outcry? he said. I sent away the women mainly in order that they might not misbehave in this way, for I have been told that a man should die in peace. Be quiet then, and have patience. When we heard his words we were ashamed, and refrained our tears; and he walked about until, as he said, his legs began to fail, and then he lay on his back, according to the directions, and the man who gave him the poison now and then looked at his feet and legs; and after a while he pressed his foot hard, and asked him if he could feel; and he said, *[118]* No; and then his leg, and so upwards and upwards, and showed us that he was cold and stiff. And he felt them himself, and said: When the poison reaches the heart, that will be the end. He was beginning to grow cold about the groin, when he uncovered his face, for he had covered himself up, and said—they were his last words —he said: Crito, I owe a cock to Asclepius; will you remember to pay the debt? The debt shall be paid, said Crito; is there anything else? There was no answer to this question; but in a minute or two a movement was heard, and the attendants uncovered him; his eyes were set, and Crito closed his eyes and mouth.

Such was the end, Echecrates, of our friend; concerning whom I may truly say, that of all the men of his time whom I have known, he was the wisest and justest and best.

Questions

1. Socrates is about to die and yet, paradoxically, it is he who must comfort his friends. Why?

2. Pascal says:

> It is certain that the mortality or immortality of the soul must make an entire difference to morality. And yet philosphers have constructed their ethics independently of this: They discuss to pass the hour.
> Plato, to incline to Christianity.*

A. Although this dialogue takes place at the end of Socrates' life, it is clear that he has been busy about philosophical concerns throughout his life. Has his belief in immortality made an "entire difference"? Describe what his life might have been like without his belief.
B. What difference *does* "the mortality or immortality of the soul . . . make . . . to morality"? Why?

3. Suppose we ignore Socrates' doctrine of recollection. Can we understand anything about the soul without this doctrine? Is anything of importance left in the dialogue? If Socrates' presuppositions about language that give rise to the doctrine of recollection are denied, what still may be learned from this dialogue?

4. Halfway through the dialogue Simmias says, ". . . how hard or rather impossible is the attainment of any certainty about questions such as these in the present life." Almost at the very end of the dialogue, after all the arguments, Socrates is able to say only that one ". . . may venture to think, not improperly or unworthily, that something of the kind is true." The speakers agree that answers to questions concerning the soul cannot be definite. Contrast this concept with the *kind* of answer that Anaxagoras apparently gave to questions (and that we might give if we viewed the question as one requiring information). Socrates makes his point (indirectly again) by the continual use of analogies, myths, and "mysteries" and warns his hearers not to become "misologists"; so apparently an unscientific kind of reasoning is being suggested. What kind of issues *are* morality and immortality, then, and how are they to be addressed?

---

*W. F. Trotter, trans., *Pascal's Pensées* (New York: E. P. Dutton & Co., Inc., 1958), p. 62.

5

A Socrates Gone Mad

Diogenes (404-323 B.C.)

Diogenes was a native of Sinope, son of Hicesius, a banker. Diocles relates that he went into exile because his father was entrusted with the money of the state and adulterated the coinage. But Eubulides in his book on Diogenes says that Diogenes himself did this and was forced to leave home along with his father. Moreover Diogenes himself actually confesses in his *Pordalus* that he adulterated the coinage. Some say that having been appointed to superintend the workmen he was persuaded by them, and that he went to Delphi or to the Delian oracle in his own city and inquired of Apollo whether he should do what he was urged to do. When the god gave him permission to alter the political currency, not understanding what this meant, he adulterated the state coinage, and when he was detected, according to some he was banished, while according to others he voluntarily quitted the city for fear of consequences. One version is that his father entrusted him with the money and that he debased it, in consequence of which the father was imprisoned and died, while the son fled, came to Delphi, and inquired, not whether he should falsify the coinage, but what he should do to gain the greatest reputation; and that then it was that he received the oracle.

On reaching Athens he fell in with Antisthenes. Being repulsed by him, because he never welcomed pupils, by sheer persistence Diogenes wore him out. Once when he stretched out his staff against him, the pupil offered his head with the words, "Strike, for you will find no wood hard enough to keep me away from you, so long as I think you've something to say." From that time forward he was his pupil, and, exile as he was, set out upon a simple life.

Through watching a mouse running about, says Theophrastus in the Megarian dialogue, not looking for a place to lie down in, not afraid of the dark, not seeking any of the things which are considered to

Reprinted by permission of the publishers and The Loeb Classical Library from Diogenes Laertius, *Lives of Eminent Philosophers,* Vol. II, translated by R. D. Hicks (Cambridge, Massachusetts: Harvard University Press, 1925).

be dainties, he discovered the means of adapting himself to circumstances. He was the first, say some, to fold his cloak because he was obliged to sleep in it as well, and he carried a wallet to hold his victuals, and he used any place for any purpose, for breakfasting, sleeping, or conversing. And then he would say, pointing to the portico of Zeus and the Hall of Processions, that the Athenians had provided him with places to live in. He did not lean upon a staff until he grew infirm; but afterwards he would carry it everywhere, not indeed in the city, but when walking along the road with it and with his wallet; so say Olympiodorus, once a magistrate at Athens, Polyeuctus the orator, and Lysanias the son of Aeschrio. He had written to some one to try and procure a cottage for him. When this man was a long time about it, he took for his abode the tub in the Metroon, as he himself explains in his letters. And in summer he used to roll in it over hot sand, while in winter he used to embrace statues covered with snow, using every means of inuring himself to hardship.

He was great at pouring scorn on his contemporaries. The school of Euclides he called bilious, and Plato's lectures waste of time, the performances at the Dionysia great peep-shows for fools, and the demagogues the mob's lacqueys. He used also to say that when he saw physicians, philosophers and pilots at their work, he deemed man the most intelligent of all animals; but when again he saw interpreters of dreams and diviners and those who attended to them, or those who were puffed up with conceit of wealth, he thought no animal more silly. He would continually say that for the conduct of life we need right reason or a halter.

Observing Plato one day at a costly banquet taking olives, "How is it," he said, "that you the philosopher who sailed to Sicily for the sake of these dishes, now when they are before you do not enjoy them?" "Nay, by the gods, Diogenes," replied Plato, "there also for the most part I lived upon olives and such like." "Why then," said Diogenes, "did you need to go to Syracuse? Was it that Attica at that time did not grow olives?" But Favorinus in his *Miscellaneous History* attributes this to Aristippus. Again, another time he was eating dried figs when he encountered Plato and offered him a share of them. When Plato took them and ate them, he said, "I said you might share them, not that you might eat them all up."

And one day when Plato had invited to his house friends coming from Dionysius, Diogenes trampled upon his carpets and said, "I trample upon Plato's vainglory." Plato's reply was, "How much pride you expose to view, Diogenes, by seeming not to be proud." Others tell us that what Diogenes said was, "I trample upon the pride of Plato," who retorted, "Yes, Diogenes, with pride of another sort." Sotion, however, in his fourth book makes the Cynic address this remark to Plato himself. Diogenes once asked him for wine, and after that also for some dried figs; and Plato sent him a whole jar full. Then the other said, "If some one asks you how many two and two are, will you answer, Twenty? So, it seems, you neither give as you are asked nor answer as you are questioned." Thus he scoffed at him as one who talked without end.

Being asked where in Greece he saw good men, he replied, "Good men nowhere, but good boys at Lacedaemon." When one day he was gravely discoursing and nobody attended to him, he began whistling, and as people clustered about him, he reproached them with coming in all seriousness to hear nonsense, but slowly and contemptuously when the theme was serious. He would say that men strive in digging and kicking to outdo one another, but no one strives to become a good man and true. And he would wonder that the grammarians should investigate the ills of Odysseus, while they were ignorant of their own. Or that the musicians should tune the strings of the lyre, while leaving the dispositions of their own souls discordant; that the mathematicians should gaze at the sun and the moon, but overlook matters close at hand; that the orators should make a fuss about justice in their speeches, but never practise it; or that the avaricious should cry out against money, while inordinately fond of it. He used also to condemn those who praised honest men for being superior to money, while themselves envying the very rich. He was moved to anger that men should sacrifice to the gods to ensure health and in the midst of the sacrifice should feast to the detriment of health. He was astonished that when slaves saw their masters were gluttons, they did not steal some of the viands. He would praise those who were about to marry and refrained, those who intending to go a voyage never set sail, those who thinking to engage in politics do no such thing, those also who purposing to rear a family do not do so, and those who make ready to live with potentates, yet never come near them after all. He used to say, moreover, that we ought to stretch out our hands to our friends with the fingers open and not closed. Menippus in his *Sale of Diogenes* tells how, when he was captured and put up for sale, he was asked what he could do. He replied, "Govern men." And he told the crier to give notice in case anybody wanted to purchase a master for himself. Having been forbidden to sit down, "It makes no difference," said he, "for in whatever position fishes lie, they still find purchasers." And he said he marvelled that before we buy a jar or dish we try whether it rings true, but if it is a man are content merely to look at him. To Xeniades who purchased him he said, "You must obey me, although I am a slave; for, if a physician or a steersman were in slavery, he would be obeyed." Eubulus in his book entitled *The Sale of Diogenes* tells us that this was how he trained the sons of Xeniades. After their other studies he taught them to ride, to shoot with the bow, to sling stones and to hurl javelins. Later, when they reached the wrestling-school, he would not permit the master to give them full athletic training, but only so much as to heighten their colour and keep them in good condition.

The boys used to get by heart many passages from poets, historians, and the writings of Diogenes himself; and he would practise them in every short cut to a good memory. In the house too he taught them to wait upon themselves, and to be content with plain fare and water to drink. He used to make them crop their hair close and to wear it unadorned, and to go lightly clad, barefoot, silent, and not looking about them in the streets. He would also take them out hunting. They on their part had a great regard for Diogenes and made requests of their parents for him. The same Eubulus relates that he grew old in the house of Xeniades, and when he died was buried by his sons. There Xeniades once asked him how he wished to be buried. To which he replied, "On my face." "Why?" inquired the other. "Because," said he, "after a little time down will be converted into up." This because the Macedonians had now got the supremacy, that is, had risen high from a humble position. Some one took him into a magnificent house and warned him not to expectorate, whereupon having clearing his throat he discharged the phlegm into the man's face, being unable, he said, to find a meaner receptacle. Others father this upon Aristippus. One day he shouted out for men, and when people collected, hit out at them with his stick, saying, "It was men I called for, not scoundrels." This is told by Hecato in the first book of his *Anecdotes*. Alexander is reported to have said, "Had I not been Alexander, I should have liked to be Diogenes."

The word "disabled," Diogenes held, ought to be applied not to the deaf or blind, but to those who have no wallet. One day he made his way with head half shaven into a party of young revellers, as Metrocles relates in his *Anecdotes*, and was roughly handled by them. Afterwards he entered on a tablet the names of those who had struck him and went about with the tablet hung round his neck, till he had covered them with ridicule and brought universal blame and discredit upon them. He described himself as a hound of the sort which all men praise, but no one, he added, of his admirers dared go out hunting along with him. When some one boasted that at the Pythian games he had vanquished men, Diogenes replied, "Nay, I defeat men, you defeat slaves."

To those who said to him, "You are an old man; take a rest," "What?" he replied, "if I were running in the stadium, ought I to slacken my pace when approaching the goal? ought I not rather to put on speed?" Having been invited to a dinner, he declared that he wouldn't go; for, the last time he went, his host had not expressed a proper gratitude. He would walk upon snow barefoot and do the other things mentioned above. Not only so; he even attempted to eat meat raw, but could not manage to digest it. He once found Demosthenes the orator lunching at an inn, and, when he retired within, Diogenes said, "All the more you will be inside the tavern." When some strangers expressed a wish to see Demosthenes, he stretched out his middle finger and said, "There goes the demagogue of Athens." Some one dropped a loaf of bread and was ashamed to pick it up; whereupon Diogenes, wishing to read him a lesson, tied a rope to the neck of a wine-jar and proceeded to drag it across the Ceramicus.

He used to say that he followed the example of the trainers of choruses; for they too set the note a little high, to ensure that the rest should hit the right note. Most people, he would say, are so nearly mad that a finger makes all the difference. For, if you go along with your middle finger stretched out, some one will think you mad, but, if it's the little finger, he will not think so. Very valuable things, said he, were bartered for things of no value, and vice versa. At all events a statue fetches three thousand drachmas, while a quart of barley-flour is sold for two copper coins.

To Xeniades, who purchased him, he said, "Come, see that you obey orders." When he quoted the line,

Backward the streams flow to their founts,

Diogenes asked, "If you had been ill and had purchased a doctor, would you then, instead of obeying him, have said " 'Backward the streams flow to their founts'?"

Some one wanted to study philosophy under him. Diogenes gave him a tunny to carry and told him to follow him. And when for shame the man threw it away and departed, some time after on meeting him he laughed and said, "The friendship between you and me was broken by a tunny." The version given by Diocles, however, is as follows. Some one having said to him, "Lay your commands upon us, Diogenes," he took him away and gave him a cheese to carry, which cost half an obol. The other declined; whereupon he remarked, "The friendship between you and me is broken by a little cheese worth half an obol."

One day, observing a child drinking out of his hands, he cast away the cup from his wallet with the words, "A child has beaten me in plainness of living." He also threw away his bowl when in like manner he saw a child who had broken his plate taking up his lentils with the hollow part of a morsel of bread. He used also to reason thus: "All things belong to the gods. The wise are friends of the gods, and friends hold things in common. Therefore all things belong to the wise." One day he saw a woman kneeling before the gods in an ungraceful attitude, and wishing to free her of superstition, according to Zoilus of Perga, he came forward and said, "Are you not afraid, my good woman, that a god may be standing behind you?—for all things are full of his presence—and you may be put to shame?" He dedicated to Asclepius a bruiser who, whenever people fell on their faces, used to run up to them and bruise them.

All the curses of tragedy, he used to say, had lighted upon him. At all events he was

A homeless exile, to his country dead.
A wanderer who begs his daily bread.

But he claimed that to fortune he could oppose courage, to convention nature, to passion reason. When he was sunning himself in the Craneum, Alexander came and stood over him and said, "Ask of me any boon you like." To which he replied, "stand out of my light." Some one had been reading aloud for a very long time, and when he was near the end of the roll pointed to a space with no writing on it. "Cheer up, my men," cried Diogenes; "there's land in sight." To one who by argument had proved conclusively that he had horns, he said, touching his forehead, "Well, I for my part don't see any." In like manner, when somebody declared that there is no such thing as motion, he got up and walked about. When some one was discoursing on celestial phenomena, "How many days," asked Diogenes, "were you in coming from the sky?" A eunuch of bad character had inscribed on his door the words, "Let nothing evil enter." "How then," he asked, "is the master of the house to get in?" When he had anointed his feet with unguent, he declared that from his head the unguent passed into the air, but from his feet into his nostrils. The Athenians urged him to become initiated, and told him that in the other world those who have been initiated enjoy a special privilege. "It would be ludicrous." quoth he, "if Agesilaus and Epaminondas are to dwell in the mire, while certain folk of no account will live in the Isles of the Blest because they have been initiated."

When mice crept on to the table he addressed them thus, "See now even Diogenes keeps parasites." When Plato styled him a dog, "quite true," he said, "for I come back again to those who have sold me." As he was leaving the public baths, somebody inquired if many men were bathing. He said, No. But to another who asked if there was a great crowd of bathers, he said, Yes. Plato had defined Man as an animal, biped and featherless, and was applauded. Diogenes plucked a fowl and brought it into the lecture-room with the words, "Here is Plato's man." In consequence of which there was added to the definition, "having broad nails." To one who asked what was the proper time for

lunch, he said, "If a rich man, when you will; if a poor man, when you can."

At Megara he saw the sheep protected by leather jackets, while the children went bare. "It's better," said he, "to be a Megarian's ram than his son." To one who had brandished a beam at him and then cried, "Look out," he replied, "What, are you intending to strike me again?" He used to call the demagogues the lackeys of the people and the crowns awarded to them the efflorescence of fame. He lit a lamp in broad daylight and said, as he went about, "I am looking for a man." One day he got a thorough drenching where he stood, and, when the bystanders pitied him, Plato said, if they really pitied him, they should move away, alluding to his vanity. When some one hit him a blow with his fist, "Heracles," said he, "how came I to forget to put on a helmet when I walked out?" Further, when Meidias assaulted him and went on to say, "There are 3000 drachmas to your credit," the next day he took a pair of boxing-gauntlets, gave him a thrashing and said, "There are 3000 blows to *your* credit." When Lysias the druggist asked him if he believed in the gods, "How can I help believing in them," said he, "when I see a god-forsaken wretch like you?" Others give this retort to Theodorus. Seeing some one perform religious purification, he said, "Unhappy man, don't you know that you can no more get rid of errors of conduct by sprinklings than you can of mistakes in grammar?" He would rebuke men in general with regard to their prayers, declaring that they asked for those things which seemed to them to be good, not for such as are truly good. As for those who were excited over their dreams he would say that they cared nothing for what they did in their waking hours, but kept their curiosity for the visions called up in their sleep. At Olympia, when the herald proclaimed Dioxippus to be victor over the men, Diogenes protested, "Nay, he is victorious over slaves, I over men."

Still he was loved by the Athenians. At all events, when a youngster broke up his tub, they gave the boy a flogging and presented Diogenes with another. Dionysius the Stoic says that after Chaeronea he was seized and dragged off to Philip, and being asked who he was, replied, "A spy upon your insatiable greed." For this he was admired and set free.

Alexander having on one occasion sent a letter to Antipater at Athens by a certain Athlios, Diogenes, who was present, said:

Graceless son of graceless sire to graceless
wight by graceless squire.

Perdiccas having threatened to put him to death unless he came to him, "That's nothing wonderful," quoth he, "for a beetle or a tarantula would do the same." Instead of that he would have expected the threat to be that Perdiccas would be quite happy to do without his company. He would often insist loudly that the gods had given to men the means of living easily, but this had been put out of sight, because we required honeyed cakes, unguents and the like. Hence to a man whose shoes were being put on by his servant, he said, "You have not attained to full felicity, unless he wipes your nose as well; and that will come, when you have lost the use of your hands."

Once he saw the officials of a temple leading away some one who had stolen a bowl belonging to the treasurers, and said, "The great thieves are leading away the little thief." Noticing a lad one day throwing stones at a cross (gibbet), "Well done," he said, "you will hit your mark." When some boys clustered round him and said, "Take care he doesn't bite us," he answered, "Never fear, boys, a dog does not eat beetroot." To one who was proud of wearing a lion's skin his words were, "Leave off dishonouring the habiliments of courage." When some one was extolling the good fortune of Callisthenes and saying what splendour he shared in the suite of Alexander, "Not so," said Diogenes, "but rather ill fortune; for he breakfasts and dines when Alexander thinks fit."

Being short of money, he told his friends that he applied to them not for alms, but for repayment of his due. When behaving indecently in the marketplace, he wished it were as easy to relieve hunger by rubbing an empty stomach. Seeing a youth starting off to dine with satraps, he dragged him off, took him to his friends and bade them keep strict watch over him. When a youth effeminately attired put a question to him, he declined to answer unless he pulled up his robe and showed whether he was man or woman. A youth was playing cottabos in the baths. Diogenes said to him, "The better you play, the worse it is for you." At a feast certain people kept throwing all the bones to him as they would have done to a dog. Thereupon he played a dog's trick and drenched them.

Rhetoricians and all who talked for reputation he used to call "thrice human," meaning thereby "thrice wretched." An ignorant rich man he used to call "the sheep with the golden fleece." Seeing a notice on the house of a profligate, "To be sold," he said, "I knew well that after such surfeiting you would throw up the owner." To a young man who complained of the number of people who annoyed him by their attentions he said, "Cease to hang out a sign of invitation." Of a public bath which was dirty he said, "When people have bathed here, where are they to go to get clean?" There was a stout musician whom everybody depreciated and Diogenes alone praised. When asked why, he said, "Because being so big, he yet sings to his lute and does not turn brigand."

The musician who was always deserted by his audience he greeted with a "Hail chanticleer," and when asked why he so addressed him, replied, "Because your song makes every one get up." A young man was delivering a set speech, when Diogenes, having filled the front fold of his dress with lupins, began to eat them, standing right opposite to him. Having thus drawn off the attention of the assemblage, he said he was greatly surprised that they should desert the orator to look at himself. A very superstitious person addressed him thus, "With one blow I will break your head." "And I," said Diogenes, "by a sneeze from the left will make you tremble." Hegesias having asked him to lend him one of his writings, he said, "You are a simpleton, Hegesias; you do not choose painted figs, but real ones; and yet you pass over the true training and would apply yourself to written rules."

When some one reproached him with his exile, his reply was, "Nay, it was through that, you miserable fellow, that I came to be a philosopher." Again, when some one reminded him that the people of Sinope had sentenced him to exile, "And I them," said he, "to home-staying." Once he saw an Olympic victor tending sheep and thus accosted him: "Too quickly, my good friend, have you left Olympia for Nemea." Being asked why athletes are so stupid, his answer was, "Because they are built up of pork and beef." He once begged alms of a statue, and, when asked why he did so, replied, "To get practice in being refused." In asking alms—as he did at first by reason of his poverty—he used this form: "If you have already given to anyone else, give to me also; if not, begin with me."

On being asked by a tyrant what bronze is best for a statue, he replied, "That of which Harmodius and Aristogiton were moulded." Asked how Dionysius treated his friends, "Like purses," he replied; "so long as they are full, he hangs them up, and, when they are empty, he throws them away." Some one lately wed had set up on his door the notice:

The son of Zeus, victorious Heracles
Dwells here; let nothing evil enter in.

To which Diogenes added "After war, alliance." The love of money he declared to be the mother-city of all evils. Seeing a spendthrift eating olives in a tavern, he said, "If you had breakfasted in this fashion, you would not so be dining."

Good men he called images of the gods, and love the business of the idle. To the question what is wretched in life he replied, "An old man destitute." Being asked what creature's bite is the worst, he said, "Of those that are wild a sycophant's; of those that are tame a flatterer's." Upon seeing two centaurs very badly painted, he asked, "Which of these is Chiron?" (worse man). Ingratiating speech he compared to honey used to choke you. The stomach he called livelihood's Charybdis. Hearing a report that Didymon the flute-player had been caught in adultery, his comment was, "His name alone is sufficient to hang him." To the question why gold is pale, his reply was, "Because it has so many thieves plotting against it." On seeing a woman carried in a litter, he remarked that the cage was not in keeping with the quarry.

One day seeing a runaway slave sitting on the brink of a well, he said, "Take care, my lad, you don't fall in." Seeing a boy taking clothes at the baths, he asked, "Is it for a little unguent or is it for a new cloak?" Seeing some women hanged from an olive-tree, he said, "Would that every tree bore similar fruit." On seeing a footpad he accosted him thus:

What mak'st thou here, my gallant?
Com'st thou perchance for plunder of the
*   dead?*

Being asked whether he had any maid or boy to wait on him, he said "No." "If you should die, then, who will carry you out to burial?" "Whoever wants the house," he replied.

Noticing a good-looking youth lying in an exposed position, he nudged him and cried, "Up, man, up, lest some foe thrust a dart into thy back!" To one who was feasting lavishly he said:

Short-liv'd thou'lt be, my son, by what thou
*   —buy'st.*

As Plato was conversing about Ideas and using the nouns "tablehood" and "cuphood," he said, "Table and cup I see; but your tablehood and cuphood, Plato, I can nowise see." "That's readily accounted for," said Plato, "for you have the eyes to see the visible table and cup; but not the understanding by which ideal tablehood and cuphood are discerned."

On being asked by somebody, "What sort of a man do you consider Diogenes to be?" "A Socrates gone mad," said he. Being asked what was the right time to marry, Diogenes replied, "For a young man not yet: for an old man never at all." Being asked what he would take to be soundly cuffed, he replied, "A helmet." Seeing a youth dressing with elaborate care, he said, "If it's for men, you're a fool; if for women, a knave." One day he detected a youth blushing. "Courage," quoth he, "that is the hue of virtue." One day after listening to a couple of lawyers disputing, he condemned them both, saying that the one had no doubt stolen, but the other had not lost anything. To the question what wine he found pleasant to drink, he replied, "That for which other people pay." When he was told that many people laughed at him, he made answer, "But I am not laughed down."

When some one declared that life is an evil, he corrected him: "Not life itself, but living ill." When he was advised to go in pursuit of his runaway slave, he replied, "It would be absurd, if Manes can live without Diogenes, but Diogenes cannot get on without Manes." When breakfasting on olives amongst which a cake had been inserted, he flung it away and addressed it thus:

Stranger, betake thee from the princes' path.

And on another occasion thus:

He lashed an olive.

Being asked what kind of hound he was, he replied, "When hungry, a Maltese; when full, a Molossian—two breeds which most people praise, though for fear of fatigue they do not venture out hunting with them. So neither can you live with me, because you are afraid of the discomforts."

Being asked if the wise eat cakes, "Yes," he said, "cakes of all kinds, just like other men." Being asked why people give to beggars but not to philosophers, he said, "Because they think they may one day be lame or blind, but never expect that they will turn to philosophy." He was begging of a miserly man who was slow to respond; so he said, "My friend, it's for food that I'm asking, not for funeral expenses." Being reproached one day for having falsified the currency, he said, "That was the time when I was such as you are now; but such as I am now, you will never be." To another who reproached him for the same offence he made a more scurrilous repartee.

On coming to Myndus and finding the gates large, though the city itself was very small, he cried, "Man of Myndus, bar your gates, lest the city should run away." Seeing a man who had been caught stealing purple, he said:

Fast gripped by purple death and forceful fate.

When Craterus wanted him to come and visit him, "No," he replied, "I would rather live on a few grains of salt at Athens than enjoy sumptuous fare at Craterus's table." He went up to Anaximenes the rhetorician, who was fat, and said, "Let us beggars have something of your paunch; it will be a relief to you, and we shall get advantage." And when the same man was discoursing, Diogenes distracted his audience by producing some salt fish. This annoyed the lecturer, and Diogenes said, "An obol's worth of salt fish has broken up Anaximenes' lecture-class."

Being reproached for eating in the market-place, "Well, it was in the market-place," he said, "that I felt hungry." Some authors affirm that the following also belongs to him: that Plato saw him washing lettuces, came to him and quietly said to him, "Had you paid court to Dionysius, you wouldn't now be washing lettuces," and that he with equal calmness made answer, "If you had washed lettuces, you wouldn't have paid court to Dionysius." When some one said, "Most people laugh at you," his reply was, "And so very likely do the asses at them; but as they don't care for the asses, so neither do I care for them." One day observing a youth studying philosophy, he said, "Well done, Philosophy, that thou divertest admirers of bodily charms to the real beauty of the soul."

When some one expressed astonishment at the votive offerings in Samothrace, his comment was, "There would have been far more, if those who were not saved had set up offerings." But others attribute this remark to Diagoras of Melos. To a handsome youth, who was going out to dinner, he said, "You will come back a worse man." When he came back and said next day, "I went and am none the worse for it," Diogenes said, "Not worse-man (Chiron), but Lax-man (Eurytion)." He was asking alms of a bad-tempered man, who said, "Yes, if you can persuade me." "If I could have persuaded you," said Diogenes, "I would have persuaded you to hang yourself." He was returning from Lacedaemon to Athens; and on some one asking, "Whither and whence?" he replied, "From the men's apartments to the women's."

He was returning from Olympia, and when somebody inquired whether there was a great crowd, "Yes," he said, "a great crowd, but few who could be called men." Libertines he compared to fig-trees growing upon a cliff: whose fruit is not enjoyed by any man, but is eaten by ravens and vultures. When Phryne set up a golden statue of Aphrodite in Delphi, Diogenes is said to have written upon it: "From the licentiousness of Greece." Alexander once came and stood opposite him and said, "I am Alexander the great king." "And I," said he, "am Diogenes the Cynic." Being asked what he had done to be called a hound, he said, "I fawn on those who give me anything, I yelp at those who refuse, and I set my teeth in rascals."

He was gathering figs, and was told by the keeper that not long before a man had hanged himself on that very fig-tree. "Then," said he, "I will now purge it." Seeing an Olympian victor casting repeated glances at a courtesan, "See," he said, "yonder ram frenzied for battle, how he is held fast by the neck fascinated by a common minx." Handsome courtesans he would compare to a deadly honeyed potion. He was breakfasting in the marketplace, and the bystanders gathered round him with cries of "dog." "It is you who are dogs," cried he, "when you stand round and watch me at my breakfast." When two cowards hid away from him, he called out, "Don't be afraid, a hound is not fond of beetroot." After seeing a stupid wrestler practising as a doctor he inquired of him, "What does this mean? Is it that you may now have your revenge on the rivals who formerly beat you?" Seeing the child of a courtesan throw stones at a crowd, he cried out, "Take care you don't hit your father."

A boy having shown him a dagger that he had received from an admirer, Diogenes remarked, "A pretty blade with an ugly handle." When some people commended a person who had given him a gratuity, he broke in with "You have no praise for me who was worthy to receive it." When some one asked that he might have back his cloak, "If it was a gift," replied Diogenes, "I possess it; while, if it was a loan, I am using it." A suppositious son having told him that he had gold in the pocket of his dress, "True," said he, "and therefore you sleep with it under your pillow." On being asked what he had gained from philosophy, he replied, "This at least, if nothing else—to be prepared for every fortune." Asked where he came from, he said, "I am a citizen of the world." Certain parents were sacrificing to the gods, that a son might be born to them. "But," said he, "do you not sacrifice to ensure what manner of man he shall turn out to be?" When asked for a subscription towards a club, he said to the president:

Despoil the rest; off Hector keep thy hands.

The mistresses of kings he designated queens; for, said he, they make the kings do their bidding. When the Athenians gave Alexander the title of Dionysus, he said, "Me too you might make Sarapis." Some one having reproached him for going into dirty places, his reply was that the sun too visits cesspools without being defiled.

When he was dining in a temple, and in the course of the meal loaves not free from dirt were put on the table, he took them up and threw them away, declaring that nothing unclean ought to enter a temple. To the man who said to him, "You don't know anything, although you are a philosopher," he replied, "Even if I am but a pretender to wisdom, that in itself is philosophy." When some one brought a child to him and declared him to be highly gifted and of excellent character, "What need then," said he, "has he of me?" Those who say admirable things, but fail to do them, he compared to a harp; for the harp, like them, he said, has neither hearing nor perception.

He was going into a theatre, meeting face to face those who were coming out, and being asked why, "This," he said, "is what I practise doing all my life."

Seeing a young man behaving effeminately, "Are you not ashamed," he said, "that your own intention about yourself should be worse than nature's: for nature made you a man but you are forcing yourself to play the woman." Observing a fool tuning a psaltery, "Are you not ashamed," said he, "to give this wood concordant sounds, while you fail to harmonize your soul with life?" To one who protested that he was ill adapted for the study of philosophy, he said "Why then do you live, if you do not care to live well?" To one who despised his father, "Are you not ashamed," he said, "to despise him to whom you owe it that you can so pride yourself?" Noticing a handsome youth chattering in unseemly fashion, "Are you not ashamed," he said, "to draw a dagger of lead for an ivory scabbard?"

Being reproached with drinking in a tavern, "Well," said he, "I also get my hair cut in a barber's shop." Being reproached with accepting a cloak from Antipater, he replied:

The gods' choice gifts are nowise to be spurned.

When some one first shook a beam at him and then shouted "Look out," Dioge-nes struck the man with his staff and added "Look out." To a man who was urgently pressing his suit to a courtesan he said, "Why, hapless man, are you at such pains to gain your suit, when it would be better for you to lose it?" To one with perfumed hair he said, "Beware lest the sweet scent on your head cause an ill odour in your life." He said that bad men obey their lusts as servants obey their masters.

The question being asked why footmen are so called, he replied, "Because they have the feet of men, but souls such as you, my questioner, have." He asked a spendthrift for a mina. The man inquired why it was that he asked others for an obol but him for a mina. "Because," said Diogenes, "I expect to receive from others again, but whether I shall ever get anything from you again lies on the knees of the gods." Being reproached with begging when Plato did not beg, "Oh yes," says he, "he does, but when he does so—

He holds his head down close, that none may hear."

Seeing a bad archer, he sat down beside the target with the words, "in order not to get hit." Lovers, he declared, derive their pleasures from their misfortune.

Being asked whether death was an evil thing, he replied, "How can it be evil, when in its presence we are not aware of it?" When Alexander stood opposite him and asked, "Are you not afraid of me?" "Why, what are you?" said he, "a good thing or a bad?" Upon Alexander replying "A good thing," "Who then," said Diogenes, "is afraid of the good?" Education, according to him, is a controlling grace to the young, consolation to the old, wealth to the poor, and ornament to the rich. When Didymon, who was a rake, was once treating a girl's eye, "Beware," says Diogenes, "lest the oculist instead of curing the eye should ruin the pupil." On somebody declaring that his own friends were plotting against him, Diogenes exclaimed, "What is to be done then, if you have to treat friends and enemies alike?"

Being asked what was the most beautiful thing in the world, he replied, "Freedom of speech." On entering a boys' school, he found there many statues of the Muses, but few pupils. "By the help of the gods," said he, "schoolmaster, you have plenty of pupils." It was his habit to do everything in public, the works of Demeter and of Aphrodite alike. He used to draw out the following arguments, "If to breakfast be not absurd, neither is it absurd in the market-place; but to breakfast is not absurd, therefore it is not absurd to breakfast in the market-place." Behaving indecently in public, he wished "it were as easy to banish hunger by rubbing the belly." Many other sayings are attributed to him, which it would take long to enumerate.

He used to affirm that training was of two kinds, mental and bodily: the latter being that whereby, with constant exercise, perceptions are formed such as secure freedom of movement for virtuous deeds; and the one half of this training is incomplete without the other, good health and strength being just as much included among the essential things, whether for body or soul. And he would adduce indisputable evidence to show how easily from gymnastic training we arrive at virtue. For in the manual crafts and other arts it can be seen that the craftsmen develop extraordinary manual skill through practice. Again, take the case of flute-players and of athletes: what surpassing skill they acquire by their own incessant toil; and, if they had transferred their efforts to the training of the mind, how certainly their labours would not have been unprofitable or ineffective.

Nothing in life, however, he maintained, has any chance of succeeding without strenuous practice; and this is capable of overcoming anything. Accordingly, instead of useless toils men should choose such as nature recommends, whereby they might have lived happily. Yet such is their madness that they choose to be miserable. For even the despising of pleasure is itself most pleasurable, when we are habituated to it; and just as those accustomed to a life of

pleasure feel disgust when they pass over to the opposite experience, so those whose training has been of the opposite kind derive more pleasure from despising pleasure than from the pleasures themselves. This was the gist of his conversation; and it was plain that he acted accordingly, adulterating currency in very truth, allowing convention no such authority as he allowed to natural right, and asserting that the manner of life he lived was the same as that of Heracles when he preferred liberty to everything.

He maintained that all things are the property of the wise, and employed such arguments as those cited above. All things belong to the gods. The gods are friends to the wise, and friends share all property in common; therefore all things are the property of the wise. Again as to law: that it is impossible for society to exist without law; for without a city no benefit can be derived from that which is civilized. But the city is civilized, and there is no advantage in law without a city; therefore law is something civilized. He would ridicule good birth and fame and all such distinctions, calling them showy ornaments of vice. The only true commonwealth was, he said, that which is as wide as the universe. He advocated community of wives, recognizing no other marriage than a union of the man who persuades with the woman who consents. And for this reason he thought sons too should be held in common.

And he saw no impropriety either in stealing anything from a temple or in eating the flesh of any animal; nor even anything impious in touching human flesh, this, he said, being clear from the custom of some foreign nations. Moreover, according to right reason, as he put it, all elements are contained in all things and pervade everything: since not only is meat a constituent of bread, but bread of vegetables; and all other bodies also, by means of certain invisible passages and particles, find their way in and unite with all substances in the form of vapour. This he makes plain in the *Thyestes*, if the tragedies are really his and not the work of his friend Philiscus of Aegina or of Pasiphon, the son of Lucian, who according to Favorinus in his *Miscellaneous History* wrote them after the death of Diogenes. He held that we should neglect music, geometry, astronomy, and the like studies, as useless and unnecessary.

He became very ready also at repartee in verbal debates, as is evident from what has been said above.

Further, when he was sold as a slave, he endured it most nobly. For on a voyage to Aegina he was captured by pirates under the command of Scirpalus, conveyed to Crete and exposed for sale. When the auctioneer asked in what he was proficient, he replied, "In ruling men." Thereupon he pointed to a certain Corinthian with a fine purple border to his robe, the man named Xeniades above-mentioned, and said, "Sell me to this man; he needs a master." Thus Xeniades came to buy him, and took him to Corinth and set him over his own children and entrusted his whole household to him. And he administered it in all respects in such a manner that Xeniades used to go about saying, "A good genius has entered my house."

Cleomenes in his work entitled *Concerning Pedagogues* says that the friends of Diogenes wanted to ransom him, whereupon he called them simpletons; for, said he, lions are not the slaves of those who feed them, but rather those who feed them are at the mercy of the lions: for fear is the mark of the slave, whereas wild beasts make men afraid of them. The man had in fact a wonderful gift of persuasion, so that he could easily vanquish anyone he liked in argument. At all events a certain Onesicritus of Aegina is said to have sent to Athens the one of his two sons named Androsthenes, and he having become a pupil of Diogenes stayed there; the father then sent the other also, the aforesaid Philiscus, who was the elder, in search of him; but Philiscus also was detained in the same way. When, thirdly, the father himself arrived, he was just as much attracted to the pursuit of philosophy as his sons and joined the circle—

so magical was the spell which the discourses of Diogenes exerted. Amongst his hearers was Phocion surnamed the Honest, and Stilpo the Megarian, and many other men prominent in political life.

Diogenes is said to have been nearly ninety years old when he died. Regarding his death there are several different accounts. One is that he was seized with colic after eating an octopus raw and so met his end. Another is that he died voluntarily by holding his breath. This account was followed by Cercidas of Megalopolis (or of Crete) who in his meliambics writes thus:

> Not so he who aforetime was a citizen of
>   Sinope,
> That famous one who carried a staff, dou-
>   bled his cloak, and lived in the open air.
> But he soared aloft with his lip tightly
>   pressed against his teeth
> And holding his breath withal. For in truth
>   he was rightly named
> Diogenes, a true-born son of Zeus, a hound
>   of heaven.

Another version is that, while trying to divide an octopus amongst the dogs, he was so severely bitten on the sinew of the foot that it caused his death. His friends, however, according to Antisthenes in his *Succession of Philosophers,* conjectured that it was due to the retention of his breath. For he happened to be living in the Craneum, the gymnasium in front of Corinth. When his friends came according to custom and found him wrapped up in his cloak, they thought that he must be asleep, although he was by no means of a drowsy or somnolent habit. They therefore drew aside his cloak and found that he was dead. This they supposed to have been his deliberate act in order to escape thenceforward from life.

Hence, it is said, arose a quarrel among his disciples as to who should bury him: nay, they even came to blows; but, when their fathers and men of influence arrived, under their direction he was buried beside the gate leading to the Isthmus. Over his grave they set up a pillar and a dog in Parian marble upon it. Subsequently his fellow-citizens honoured him with bronze statues, on which these verses were inscribed:

> *Time makes even bronze grow old: but thy glory, Diogenes, all eternity will never destroy. Since thou alone didst point out to mortals the lesson of self-sufficingness and the easiest path of life.*

We too have written on him in the proceleusmatic metre:

> *Diogenes, come tell me what fate took you to*
> *   the world below?*
> *A dog's savage tooth.*

But some say that when dying he left instructions that they should throw him out unburied, that every wild beast might feed on him, or thrust him into a ditch and sprinkle a little dust over him. But according to others his instructions were that they should throw him into the Ilissus, in order that he might be useful to his brethren.

Questions

1. What lesson do you suppose Diogenes thought there was to be learned from Antisthenes that was worth being struck? How is this lesson taught? How is it learned?

2. When Diogenes was sold as a slave and became a tutor, he would have the boys ". . . get by heart many passages from poets, historians, and the writings of Diogenes himself." Why did he teach this way? What is the point of learning, say a poem, "by heart?"

3. Consider the wit and sarcasm of Diogenes. Is there a point to it? (Of course, the point may well be quite different in various episodes, so we must give careful attention to the episodes. Since they represent his *life,* they are our only basis for understanding his character.) If you are inclined to say that Diogenes' sarcasm is all rather pointless, could that be what Diogenes means when he calls himself a "Socrates gone mad?" Is he saying that the intelligence of Socrates is present without the purpose to give it direction and substance? What is present in Socrates' life that is absent from Diogenes'?

6

Is Any Theft Simple?

Confessions

IV.   9.   Theft is punished by Thy law, O Lord, and the law written in the hearts of men, which iniquity itself effaces not. For what thief will abide a thief? not even a rich thief, one stealing through want. Yet I lusted to thieve, and did it, compelled by no hunger, nor poverty, but through a cloyedness of well-doing, and pamperedness of iniquity. For I stole that of which I had enough, and much better. Nor cared I to enjoy what I stole, but joyed in the theft and sin itself. A pear tree there was near our vineyard, laden with fruit, tempting neither for colour nor taste. To shake and rob this, some lewd young fellows of us went, late one night (having according to our pestilent custom prolonged our sports in the streets till then), and took huge loads, not for our eating, but to fling to the very hogs, having only tasted them. And this, but to do what we liked only because it was misliked.

Reprinted by permission of the publishers from *Great Books of the Western World*, Vol. 18, "The Confessions," Saint Augustine, translated by Edward Bouverie Puser (Chicago: Encyclopaedia Britannica, Inc., 1952).

Behold my heart, O God, behold my heart, which Thou hadst pity upon in the bottom of the bottomless pit. Now, behold, let my heart tell Thee what it sought there, that I should be gratuitously evil, having no temptation to ill but the ill itself. It was foul, and I loved it; I loved to perish, I loved mine own fault, not that for which I was faulty, but my fault itself. Foul soul, falling from Thy firmament to utter destruction; not seeking aught through the shame, but the shame itself!

V.   10.   For there is an attractiveness in beautiful bodies, in gold and silver, and all things; and in bodily touch, sympathy hath much influence, and each other sense hath his proper object answerably tempered. Worldly honour hath also its grace, and the power of overcoming, and of mastery; whence springs also the thirst of revenge. But yet, to obtain all these, we may not depart from Thee, O Lord, nor decline from Thy law. The life also which here we live hath its own enchantment, through a certain proportion of its own, and a correspondence with all things beautiful here below. Human friendship also is endeared with a sweet tie, by reason of the unity formed of many souls. Upon occasion of all these, and the like, is sin committed, while through an immoderate inclination towards these goods of the lowest order, the better and higher are forsaken—Thou, our Lord God, Thy truth, and Thy law. For these lower things have their delights, but not like my God, Who made all things: for in Him doth the righteous delight, and He is the joy of the upright in heart. (Ps. 64.10)

11.   When, then, we ask why a crime was done, we believe it not, unless it appear that there might have been some desire of obtaining some of those which we called lower goods, or a fear of losing them. For they are beautiful and comely; although, compared with those higher and beatific goods, they be abject and low. A man hath murdered another; why? he loved his wife or his estate; or would rob for his own livelihood; or feared to lose some such thing by him; or, wronged, was on fire to be revenged. Would any commit murder upon no cause, delighted simply in murdering? Who would believe it? For as for that furious and savage man, of whom it is said that he was gratuitously evil and cruel, yet is the cause assigned; "lest," saith he, "through idleness hand or heart should grow inactive." And to what end? That, through that practice of guilt, he might, having taken the city, attain to honours, empire, riches, and be freed from fear of the laws, and his embarrassments from domestic needs, and consciousness of villainies. So then, not even Catiline himself loved his own villainies, but something else, for whose sake he did them.

VI.   12.   What then did wretched I so love in thee, thou theft of mine, thou deed of darkness, in that sixteenth year of my age? Lovely thou wert not, because thou wert theft. But art thou anything, that thus I speak to thee? Fair were the pears we stole, because they were Thy creation, Thou fairest of all, Creator of all, Thou good God; God, the sovereign good and my true good. Fair were those pears, but

not them did my wretched soul desire; for I had store of better, and those I gathered only that I might steal. For, when gathered, I flung them away, my only feast therein being my own sin, which I was pleased to enjoy. For if aught of those pears came within my mouth, what sweetened it was the sin. And now, O Lord my God, I enquire what in that theft delighted me; and behold it hath no loveliness; I mean not such loveliness as in justice and wisdom; nor such as is in the mind and memory, and senses, and animal life of man; nor yet as the stars are glorious and beautiful in their orbs; or the earth, or sea, full of embryolife, replacing by its birth that which decayeth; nay, nor even that false and shadowy beauty which belongeth to deceiving vices.

13.   For so doth pride imitate exaltedness; whereas Thou Alone art God exalted over all. Ambition, what seeks it but honours and glory? whereas Thou Alone art to be honoured above all, and glorious for evermore. The cruelty of the great would fain be feared, but who is to be feared but God alone, out of whose power what can be wrested or withdrawn? when, or where, or whither, or by whom? The tendernesses of the wanton would fain be counted love: yet is nothing more tender than Thy charity; nor is aught loved more healthfully than Thy truth, bright and beautiful above all. Curiosity makes semblance of a desire of knowledge; whereas Thou supremely knowest all. Yea, ignorance and foolishness itself is cloked under the name of simplicity and uninjuriousness; because nothing is found more single than Thee: and what less injurious, since they are his own works, which injure the sinner? Yea, sloth would fain be at rest; but what stable rest besides the Lord? Luxury affects to be called plenty and abundance; but Thou art the fulness and neverfailing plenteousness of incorruptible pleasures. Prodigality presents a shadow of liberality: but Thou art the most overflowing Giver of all good. Covetousness would possess many things: and Thou possessest all things. Envy disputes for ex-

cellency: what more excellent than Thou? Anger seeks revenge: who revenges more justly than Thou? Fear startles at things unwonted and sudden, which endanger things beloved, and takes forethought for their safety: but to Thee what unwonted or sudden, or who separateth from Thee what Thou lovest? Or where but with Thee is unshaken safety? Grief pines away for things lost, the delight of its desires; because it would have nothing taken from it, as nothing can from Thee.

14. Thus doth the soul commit fornication when she turns from Thee, seeking, without Thee, what she findeth not pure and untainted till she returns to Thee. Thus all pervertedly imitate Thee, who remove far from Thee, and lift themselves up against Thee. But even by thus imitating Thee, they imply Thee to be the Creator of all nature; whence there is no place whither altogether to retire from Thee. What then did I love in that theft? and wherein did I even corruptly and pervertedly imitate my Lord? Did I wish even by stealth to do contrary to Thy law, because by power I could not, so that being a prisoner, I might mimic a maimed liberty by doing with impunity things unpermitted me, a darkened likeness of Thy Omnipotency? Behold Thy servant fleeing from his Lord, and obtaining a shadow. O rottenness, O monstrousness of life, and depth of death! could I like what I might not, only because I might not?

VII. 15. "What shall I render unto the Lord," (Ps. 16.12) that, whilst my memory recalls these things, my soul is not affrighted at them? I will love Thee, O Lord, and thank Thee, and confess unto Thy name; (Rev. 3.5.) because Thou hast forgiven me these so great and heinous deeds of mine. To Thy grace I ascribe it, and to Thy mercy, that Thou hast melted away my sins as it were ice. To Thy grace I ascribe also whatsoever I have not done of evil; for what might I not have done, who even loved a sin for its own sake? Yea, all I confess to have been forgiven me; both what evils I committed by my own wilfulness, and what by Thy guidance I committed not.

What man is he who, weighing his own infirmity, dares to ascribe his purity and innocency to his own strength; that so he should love Thee the less, as if he had less needed Thy mercy, whereby Thou remittest sins to those that turn to Thee? For whosoever, called by Thee, followed Thy voice and avoided those things which he reads me recalling and confessing of myself, let him not scorn me, who being sick, was cured by that Physician, through Whose aid it was that he was not, or rather was less, sick: and for this let him love Thee as much, yea and more; since by Whom he sees me to have been recovered from such deep consumption of sin, by Him he sees himself to have been from the like consumption of sin preserved.

VIII. 16. "What fruit had I then" (wretched man!) in those things, of the remembrance whereof I am now ashamed: (Rom. 6.21) Especially in that theft which I loved for the theft's sake; and it too was nothing, and therefore the more miserable I, who loved it. Yet alone I had not done it: such was I then, I remember, alone I had never done it. I loved then in it also the company of the accomplices, with whom I did it? I did not then love nothing else but the theft, yea rather I did love nothing else; for that circumstance of the company was also nothing. What is, in truth? who can teach me, save He that enlighteneth my heart and discovereth its dark corners? What is it which hath come into my mind to enquire, and discuss, and consider? For had I then loved the pears I stole, and wished to enjoy them, I might have done it alone, and the bare commission of the theft sufficed to attain my pleasure; nor needed I have inflamed the itching of my desires by the excitement of accomplices. But since my pleasure was not in those pears, it was in the offence itself, which the company of fellow-sinners occasioned.

IX. 17. What then was this feeling? For of a truth it was too foul: and woe was me, who had it. But yet what was it? "Who can understand his errors?" (Ps. 19.12) It was the sport, which, as it were, tickled our hearts, that we beguiled, those who little thought what we were doing, and much misliked it. Why then was my delight of such sort, that I did it not alone? Because none doth ordinarily laugh alone? ordinarily no one; yet laughter sometimes masters men alone and singly when no one whatever is with them, if anything very ludicrous presents itself to their senses or mind. Yet I had not done this alone; alone I had never never done it. Behold my God, before Thee, the vivid remembrance of my soul; alone, I had never committed that theft, wherein what I stole pleased me not, but that I stole; nor had it alone like me to do it, nor had I done it. O friendship too unfriendly! thou incomprehensible inveigler of the soul, thou greediness to do mischief out of mirth and wantonness, thou thirst of others' loss, without lust of my own gain or revenge: but when it is said, "Let's go, let's do it," we are ashamed not to be shameless.

X. 18. Who can disentangle that twisted and intricate knottiness? Foul is it: I hate to think on it, to look on it. But Thee I long for, O Righteousness and Innocency, beautiful and comely to all pure eyes, and of a satisfaction unsating. With Thee is rest entire, and life imperturbable. Whoso enters into Thee enters into the joy of his Lord: (Matt. 25.21) and shall not fear, and shall do excellently in the All-Excellent. I sank away from Thee, and I wandered, O my God, too much astray from Thee my stay, in these days of my youth, and I became to myself a barren land.

Questions

1. What does it mean ". . . to do what we liked only because it was misliked"?

2. What does it mean to be "gratuitously evil"? Why does Augustine regard this episode as displaying gratuitous evil?

3. "When, then, we ask why a crime was done," what are we asking for? What *kind* of answer do we seek? What kind of answer *should* we seek? (Consider a committee appointed by the government to research "the causes of crime." *How* is this usually done? Does this have anything to do with understanding morality?)

4. Augustine, now in his later years, is attempting to understand something he did when he was sixteen. What kind of character is shown by this endeavor? In attempting to describe this character, consider what Augustine's concerns were at sixteen, what they are now, and the nature of the change that has taken place.

5. What does Augustine mean by the words, ". . . when it is said, 'Let's go, let's do it,' we are ashamed not to be shameless"? *How* do the opinions of our peers affect our thoughts and actions? *Should* they have any influence? How can one escape this influence? (You should be developing the ability to supply additional contexts related to the discussion.)

6. If you are working with a text of ethical theories, describe this episode in terms of the theories you have studied. It might be particularly helpful to evaluate it from the perspectives of Plato, Kant, and Nietzsche.

7

Ending an Affair

Boswell's London Journal 1762-1763

[Our lives, even as our thoughts, are episodic; thus, the great difficulty in understanding a life or in thinking a thought whole. Boswell, in his personal journals and in his magnificent biography of Johnson, comes as near as is possible to presenting a *complete* person. In this, he, no less than Augustine or Rousseau or Kierkegaard, is the standard. (The *kind* of person each presents, of course, is quite different.) Philosophical issues, are always concerned with what a human being is essentially. *Is* there anything essential that undergirds all the episodes of each human life? In order to address this question we have taken passages from the journal (covering roughly nine weeks) in which Boswell confronts his own sexuality. It should be well noted, though, that the journal in its entirety displays a *whole* person attempting to think his way through his life. Anger, piety, ambition, humility, arrogance, pride, fear, generosity, compassion—

Boswell reflects upon them all. He seeks to understand himself. He does this by keeping a journal. His writing is his thought. His thought encompasses more than sex.

editor]

Thursday 25 November. I went to Love's and drank tea. I had now been some time in town without female sport. I determined to have nothing to do with whores, as my health was of great consequence to me. I went to a girl with whom I had an intrigue at Edinburgh, but my affection cooling, I had left her. I knew she was come up. I waited on her and tried to obtain my former favours, but in vain. She would by no means listen.[1] I was really unhappy for

From *Boswell's London Journal 1762–1763*, edited by Frederick A. Pottle. Copyright 1950 by Yale University. Reprinted by the very kind permission of Professor Pottle, McGraw-Hill Book Company, and Yale University.

[1]She was probably a servant; the juxtaposition of references to her and to Love here and in the memoranda hints that she was a servant in Love's family. (Mrs. Love had just "come up" from Edinburgh.) In the memoranda and in earlier notes, where she is several times mentioned, she receives no other designation than the Greek character ϕ. Perhaps Phemie or Effie?

want of women. I thought it hard to be in such a place without them. I picked up a girl in the Strand; went into a court with intention to enjoy her in armour.[2] But she had none. I toyed with her. She wondered at my size, and said if I ever took a girl's maidenhead, I would make her squeak. I gave her a shilling, and had command enough of myself to go without touching her. I afterwards trembled at the danger I had escaped. I resolved to wait cheerfully till I got some safe girl or was liked by some woman of fashion.

Sunday 28 November. I breakfasted with Mr. Douglas. I went to St. James's Church and heard service and a good sermon on "By what means shall a young man learn to order his ways," in which the advantages of early piety were well displayed. What a curious, inconsistent thing is the mind of man! In the midst of a divine service I was laying plans for having women, and yet I had the most sincere feelings of religion. I imagine that my want of belief is the occasion of this, so that I can have all the feelings. I would try to make out a little consistency this way. I have a warm heart and a vivacious fancy. I am therefore given to love, and also to piety or gratitude to God, and to the most brilliant and showy method of public worship.

Saturday 4 December. I breakfasted with Dempster. He accompanied me into the City. He parted from me at St. Paul's, and I went to Child's, where there was not much said. I dined and drank tea with Lady Betty Macfarlane. We were but cold and dull. The Laird was low and disagreeable. I resolved to dine there no more; at least very, very seldom. At night Erskine and I strolled through the streets and St. James's Park. We were accosted there by several ladies of the town. Erskine was very humorous and said some very wild things to them. There

---

[2]That is, making use of a prophylactic sheath.

was one in a red cloak of a good buxom person and comely face whom I marked as a future piece, in case of exigency.

Tuesday 14 December. It is very curious to think that I have now been in London several weeks without ever enjoying the delightful sex, although I am surrounded with numbers of freehearted ladies of all kinds: from the splendid Madam at fifty guineas a night, down to the civil nymph with white-thread stockings who tramps along the Strand and will resign her engaging person to your honour for a pint of wine and a shilling. Manifold are the reasons for this my present wonderful continence. I am upon a plan of economy, and therefore cannot be at the expense of first-rate dames. I have suffered severely from the loathsome distemper, and therefore shudder at the thoughts of running any risk of having it again. Besides, the surgeons' fees in this city come very high. But the greatest reason of all is that fortune, or rather benignant Venus, has smiled upon me and favoured me so far that I have had the most delicious intrigues with women of beauty, sentiment, and spirit, perfectly suited to my romantic genius.

Indeed, in my mind, there cannot be higher felicity on earth enjoyed by man than the participation of genuine reciprocal amorous affection with an amiable woman. There he has a full indulgence of all the delicate feelings and pleasures both of body and mind, while at the same time in this enchanting union he exults with a consciousness that he is the superior person. The dignity of his sex is kept up. These paradisial scenes of gallantry have exalted my ideas and refined my taste, so that I really cannot think of stooping so far as to make a most intimate companion of a groveling-minded, ill-bred, worthless creature, nor can my delicacy be pleased with the gross voluptuousness of the stews. I am therefore walking about with a healthful stout body and a cheerful mind, in search of a woman worthy of my love, and who thinks me worthy of hers, without any interested views, which is the only sure way to find out if a woman really loves a man. If I should be a single man for the whole winter, I will be satisfied. I have had as much elegant pleasure as I could have expected would come to my share in many years.

However, I hope to be more successful. In this view, I had now called several times for a handsome actress of Covent Garden Theatre, whom I was a little acquainted with, and whom I shall distinguish in this my journal by the name of Louisa.[3] This lady had been indisposed and saw no company, but today I was admitted. She was in a pleasing undress and looked very pretty. She received me with great politeness. We chatted on the common topics. We were not easy—there was a constraint upon us— we did not sit right on our chairs, and we were unwilling to look at one another. I talked to her on the advantage of having an agreeable acquaintance, and hoped I might see her now and then. She desired me to call in whenever I came that way, without ceremony. "And pray," said she, "when shall I have the pleasure of your company at tea?" I fixed Thursday, and left her, very well satisfied with my first visit.

Thursday 16 December. In the afternoon I went to Louisa's. A little black young fellow, her brother, came in. I could have wished him at the Bay of Honduras. However, I found him a good quiet obliging being who gave us no disturbance. She talked on a man's liking a woman's company, and of the injustice people treated them with in suspecting anything bad. This was a fine artful pretty speech. We talked of French manners, and how they studied to make one another happy. "The English," said I, "accuse them of being false, because they misunderstand them. When a French-

man makes warm professions of regard, he does it only to please you for the time. It is words of course. There is no more of it. But the English, who are cold and phlegmatic in their address, take all these fine speeches in earnest, and are confounded to find them otherwise, and exclaim against the perfidious Gaul most unjustly. For when Frenchmen put a thing home seriously and vow fidelity, they have the strictest honour. O they are the people who enjoy time; so lively, pleasant, and gay. You never hear of madness or self-murder among them. Heat of fancy evaporates in fine brisk clear vapour with them, but amongst the English often falls heavy upon the brain."

We chatted pretty easily. We talked of love as a thing that could not be controlled by reason, as a fine passion. I could not clearly discern how she meant to behave to me. She told me that a gentleman had come to her and offered her £50, but that her brother knocked at the door and the man run out of the house without saying a word. I said I wished he had left his money. We joked much about the £50. I said I expected some night to be surprised with such an offer from some decent elderly gentlewoman. I made just a comic parody to her story. I sat till past eight. She said she hoped it would not be long before she had the pleasure of seeing me again.

This night I made no visible progress in my amour, but I in reality was doing a great deal. I was getting well acquainted with her. I was appearing an agreeable companion to her; I was informing her by my looks of my passion for her.

Friday 17 December. I engaged in this amour just with a view of convenient pleasure but the god of pleasing anguish now seriously seized my breast. I felt the fine delirium of love. I waited on Louisa at one, found her alone, told her that her goodness in hoping to see me *soon* had brought me back: that it appeared long to me since I saw her. I was a little bashful. However, I took a good heart and talked with ease and dignity. "I hope, Madam, you are at present

---

[3]The memoranda identify Louisa as one Mrs. Lewis, about whom, except for what we learn from Boswell himself, next to nothing is known. She played the Queen in *Hamlet* at Covent Garden on 27 September 1762, her first appearance there. On 20 October she played Mrs. Ford in the *Merry Wives.* Genest does not mention her again for the season.

a single woman." "Yes, sir." "And your affections are not engaged?" "They are not, Sir." "But this is leading me into a strange confession. I assure you, Madam, my affections are engaged." "Are they, Sir?" "Yes, Madam, they are engaged to you." (She looked soft and beautiful.) "I hope we shall be better acquainted and like one another better." "Come, Sir, let us talk no more of that now." "No, Madam, I will not. It is like giving the book in the preface." "Just so, Sir, telling in the preface what should be in the middle of the book." (I think such conversations are best written in the dialogue way.) "Madam, I was very happy to find you. From the first time that I saw you, I admired you." "O, Sir." "I did, indeed. What I like beyond everything is an agreeable female companion, where I can be at home and have tea and genteel conversation. I was quite happy to be here." "Sir, you are welcome here as often as you please. Every evening, if you please." "Madam I am infinitely obliged to you." This is just what I wanted. I left her, in good spirits, and dined at Sheridan's.

Monday 20 December. I went to Louisa's after breakfast. "Indeed," said I, "it was hard upon me to leave you so soon yesterday. I am quite happy in your company." "Sir," said she, "You are very obliging. But," said she, "I am in bad humour this morning. There was a person who professed the greatest friendship for me; I now applied for their assistance, but was shifted. It was such a trifle that I am sure they could have granted it. So I have been railing against my fellow-creatures." "Nay, dear Madam, don't abuse them all on account of an individual. But pray what was this favour? Might I know?" (She blushed.) "Why, Sir, there is a person has sent to me for a trifling debt. I sent back word that it was not convenient for me to let them have it just now, but in six weeks I should pay it."

I was a little confounded and embarrassed here. I dreaded bringing myself into a scrape. I did not know what she might call a trifling sum. I half-resolved to say no

more. However, I thought that she might now be trying my generosity and regard for her, and truly this was the real test. I thought I would see if it was in my power to assist her.

"Pray, Madam, what was the sum?" "Only two guineas, Sir." Amazed and pleased, I pulled out my purse. "Madam," said I, "if I can do you any service, you may command me. Two guineas is at present all that I have, but a trifle more. There they are for you. I told you that I had very little, but yet I hope to live. Let us just be honest with one another. Tell me when you are in any little distress, and I will tell you what I can do." She took the guineas. "Sir, I am infinitely obliged to you. As soon as it is in my power, I shall return them. Indeed I could not have expected this from you." Her gratitude warmed my heart. "Madam! though I have little, yet as far as ten guineas, you may apply to me. I would live upon nothing to serve one that I regarded."

I did not well know what to think of this scene. Sometimes I thought it artifice, and that I was taken in. And then again, I viewed it just as a circumstance that might very easily happen. Her mentioning returning the money looked well. My naming the sum of ten guineas was rash; however, I considered that it cost me as much to be cured of what I contracted from a whore, and that ten guineas was but a moderate expense for women during the winter.

I had all along treated her with a distant politeness. On Saturday I just kissed her hand. She now sung to me. I got up in raptures and kissed her with great warmth. She received this very genteelly. I had a delicacy in presuming too far, lest it should look like demanding goods for my money. I resumed the subject of love and gallantry. She said, "I pay no regard to the opinion in the world so far as contradicts my own sentiments." "No, Madam, we are not to mind the arbitrary rules imposed by the multitude." "Yet, Sir, there is a decency to be kept with the public. And I must do so, whose bread depends upon them." "Certainly, Madam. But when may I wait upon you? Tomorrow evening?" "Sir, I am obliged to be all day with a lady who is not well." "Then next day, Madam." "What? to drink a dish of tea, Sir?" "No, no, not to drink a dish of tea." (Here I looked sheepish.) "What time may I wait upon you?" "Whenever you please, Sir." I kissed her again, and went away highly pleased with the thoughts of the affair being settled.

Wednesday 22 December. I stood and chatted a while with the sentries before Buckingham House. One of them, an old fellow, said he was in all the last war. "At the battle of Dettingen," said he, "I saw our cannon make a lane through the French army as broad as that" (pointing to the Mall), "which was filled up in as short time as I'm telling you it." They asked me for a pint of beer, which I gave them. I talked on the sad mischief of war and on the frequency of poverty. "Why, Sir," said he, "God made all right at first when he made mankind. ("I believe," said the other, "he made but few of them.") But, Sir, if God was to make the world today, it would be crooked again tomorrow. But the time will come when we shall all be rich enough. To be sure, salvation is promised to those that die in the field." I have great pleasure in conversing with the lower part of mankind, who have very curious ideas.

This forenoon I went to Louisa's in full expectation of consummate bliss. I was in a strange flutter of feeling. I was ravished at the prospect of joy, and yet I had such an anxiety upon me that I was afraid that my powers would be enervated. I almost wished to be free of this assignation. I entered her apartment in a sort of confusion. She was elegantly dressed in the morning fashion, and looked delightfully well. I felt the tormenting anxiety of serious love. I sat down and I talked with the distance of a new acquaintance and not with the ease and ardour of a lover, or rather a gallant. I talked of her lodgings being neat, opened the door of her bedchamber, looked into it. Then sat down by her in a most melancholy

plight. I would have given a good deal to be out of the room.

We talked of religion. Said she, "People who deny that, show a want of sense." "For my own part, Madam, I look upon the adoration of the Supreme Being as one of the greatest enjoyments we have. I would not choose to get rid of my religious notions. I have read books that staggered me. But I was glad to find myself regain my former opinions." "Nay, Sir, what do you think of the Scriptures having stood the test of ages?" "Are you a Roman Catholic, Madam?" "No, Sir. Though I like some parts of their religion, in particular, confession; not that I think the priest can remit sins, but because the notion that we are to confess to a decent clergyman may make us cautious what we do." "Madam," said I, "I would ask you to do nothing that you should be sorry to confess. Indeed I have a great deal of principle in matters of gallantry, and never yet led any woman to do what might afterwards make her uneasy. If she thinks it wrong, I never insist." She asked me some questions about my intrigues, which I nicely eluded.

I then sat near her and began to talk softly, but finding myself quite dejected with love, I really cried out and told her that I was miserable; and as I was stupid, would go away. But saluting her with warmth, my powers were excited, I felt myself vigorous. I sat down again. I beseeched her, "You know, Madam, you said you was not a Platonist. I beg it of you to be so kind. You said you are above the finesse of your sex." (Be sure always to make a woman better than her sex.) "I adore you." "Nay, dear Sir" (I pressing her to me and kissing her now and then), "pray be quiet. Such a thing requires time to consider of." "Madam, I own this would be necessary for any man but me. But you must take my character from myself. I am very good-tempered, very honest, and have little money. I should have some reward for my particular honesty." "But, Sir, give me time to recollect myself." "Well then, Madam, when shall I see you?"

"On Friday, Sir." "A thousand thanks." I left her and came home and took my bread and cheese with great contentment, and then went and chatted a while with Webster.

Friday 24 December. I waited on Louisa. Says she, "I have been very unhappy since you was here. I have been thinking of what I said to you. I find that such a connection would make me miserable." "I hope, Madam, I am not disagreeable to you." "No, Sir, you are not. If it was the first duke in England I spoke to, I should just say the same thing." "But pray, Madam, what is your objection?" "Really, Sir, I have many disagreeable apprehensions. It may be known. Circumstances might be very troublesome. I beg it of you, Sir, consider of it. You own good sense will agree with me. Instead of visiting me as you do now, you would find a discontented, unhappy creature." I was quite confused. I did not know what to say. At last I agreed to think of it and see her on Sunday. I came home and dined in dejection. Yet I mustered up vivacity, and away I went in full dress to Northumberland House. There was spirit, to lay out a couple of shillings and be a man of fashion in my situation. There was true economy.

Sunday 26 December. I went to Whitehall Chapel and heard service. I took a whim to go through all the churches and chapels in London, taking one each Sunday. At one I went to Louisa's. I told her my passion in the warmest terms. I told her that my happiness absolutely depended upon her. She said it was running the greatest risk. "Then," said I, "Madam, you will show the greatest generosity to a most sincere lover." She said that we should take time to consider of it, and that then we could better determine how to act. We agreed that the time should be a week, and that if I remained of the same opinion, she would then make me blessed. There is no telling how easy it made my mind to be convinced that she did not despise me, but on the

contrary had a tender heart and wished to make me easy and happy.

Friday 31 December. I waited on Louisa. The conversation turned upon love, whether we would or not. She mentioned one consequence that in an affair of gallantry might be troublesome. "I suppose, Madam," said I, "you mean if a third person should be interested in the affair. Why, to be sure, if such a person should appear, he must be taken care of. For my own part, I have the strongest principles of that kind." "Well, Sir," said she, with a sweet complacency. "But we won't talk any more on the subject."

Sunday 2 January. I had George Home at breakfast with me. He is a good honest fellow and applies well to his business as a merchant. He had seen me all giddiness at his father's, and was astonished to find me settled on so prudent a plan. As I have made it a rule to dine every Sunday at home, and have got my landlady to give us regularly on that day a piece of good roast beef with a warm apple-pie, I was a little difficulted today, as our time of dining is three o'clock, just my hour of assignation. However, I got dinner to be at two and at three I hastened to my charmer.

Here a little speculation on the human mind may well come in. For here was I, a young man full of vigour and vivacity, the favourite lover of a handsome actress and going to enjoy the full possession of my warmest wishes. And yet melancholy threw a cloud over my mind. I could relish nothing. I felt dispirited and languid. I approached Louisa with a kind of an uneasy tremor. I sat down. I toyed with her. Yet I was not inspired by Venus. I felt rather a delicate sensation of love than a violent amorous inclination for her. I was very miserable. I thought myself feeble as a gallant, although I had experienced the reverse many a time. Louisa knew not my powers. She might imagine me impotent. I sweated almost with anxiety, which made me worse.

She behaved extremely well; did not seem to remember the occasion of our meeting at all. I told her I was very dull. She said, "People cannot always command their spirits." The time of church was almost elapsed when I began to feel that I was still a man. I fanned the flame by pressing her alabaster breasts and kissing her delicious lips. I then barred the door of her dining-room, led her all fluttering into her bedchamber, and was just making a triumphal entry when we heard her landlady coming up. "O Fortune why did it happen thus?" would have been the exclamation of a Roman bard. We were stopped most suddenly and cruelly from the fruition of each other. She ran out and stopped the landlady from coming up. Then returned to me in the dining-room. We fell into each other's arms, sighing and panting, "O dear, how hard this is." "O Madam, see what you can contrive for me." "Lord, Sir, I am so frightened."

Her brother then came in. I recollected that I had been at no place of worship today. I begged pardon for a little and went to Covent Garden Church, where there is evening service between five and six. I heard a few prayers and then returned and drank tea. She entertained us with her adventures when travelling through the country. Some of them were excellent. I told her she might make a novel. She said if I would put them together that she would give me material. I went home at seven. I was unhappy at being prevented from the completion of my wishes, and yet I thought that I had saved my credit for prowess, that I might through anxiety have not acted a vigorous part; and that we might contrive a meeting where I could love with ease and freedom.

Monday 3 January. I begged Louisa to invent some method by which we might meet in security. I insisted that she should go and pass the night with me somewhere. She begged time to think of it.

Tuesday 4 January. Louisa told me that she would go with me to pass the night when she was sure that she would not be wanted at the playhouse next day; and she mentioned Saturday as most convenient, being followed by Sunday, on which nothing is done. "But, Sir," said she, "may not this be attended with expense? I hope you'll excuse me." There was something so kind and so delicate in this hint that it charmed me. "No, Madam, it cannot be a great expense, and I can save on other articles to have money for this."

Tuesday 11 January. This day I had some agreeable conversation with my dear Louisa. All was now agreed upon. I had been at Hayward's on Saturday morning and told that we could not be there that night, as my wife was not come to town. But that we would be there next week and take our chance for a bed. And here a hint or two of Louisa's history may well come in. She was born of very creditable parents in London. But being too strictly confined, she ran off and married heedlessly. She was obliged for subsistence to go upon the stage, and travelled in different companies. Her husband proved a harsh, disagreeable creature, with whom she led a terrible life; at last, as it was discovered that they were illegally married, they parted by consent, and she got into Covent Garden Theatre.

Wednesday 12 January. Louisa and I agreed that at eight at night she would meet me in the Piazzas of Covent Garden. I was quite elevated, and felt myself able and undaunted to engage in the wars of the Paphian Queen.

At the appointed hour of eight I went to the Piazzas, where I sauntered up and down for a while in a sort of trembling suspense, I knew not why. At last my charming companion appeared, and I immediately conducted her to a hackney-coach which I had ready waiting, pulled up the blinds, and away we drove to the destined scene of delight. We contrived to seem as if we had come off a journey, and carried in a bundle our night-clothes, handkerchiefs, and other little things. We also had with us some almond biscuits, or as they call them in London, macaroons, which looked like provision on the road. On our arrival at Hayward's we were shown into the parlour, in the same manner that any decent couple would be. I here thought proper to conceal my own name (which the people of the house had never heard), and assumed the name of Mr. Digges. We were shown up to the very room where he slept. I said my cousin, as I called him, was very well. That Ceres and Bacchus might in moderation lend their assistance to Venus, I ordered a genteel supper and some wine.

Louisa told me she had two aunts who carried her over to France when she was a girl, and that she could once speak French as fluently as English. We talked a little in it, and agreed that we would improve ourselves to reading and speaking it every day. I asked her if we did not just look like man and wife. "No," said she, "we are too fond for married people." No wonder that she may have a bad idea of that union, considering how bad it was for her. She has contrived a pretty device for a seal. A heart is gently warmed by Cupid's flame, and Hymen comes with his rude torch and extinguishes it. She said she found herself quite in a flutter. "Why, really," said I, "reason sometimes has no power. We have no occasion to be frightened, and yet we are both a little so. Indeed, I preserve a tolerable presence of mind." I rose and kissed her, and conscious that I had no occasion to doubt my qualifications as a gallant, I joked about it: "How curious would it be if I should be so frightened that we should rise as we lay down." She reproved my wanton language by a look of modesty. The bells of St. Bride's church rung their merry chimes hard by. I said that the bells in Cupid's court would be this night set a-ringing for joy at our union.

We supped cheerfully and agreeably and drank a few glasses, and then the maid came and put the sheets, well aired, upon the bed. I now contemplated my fair prize. Louisa is just twenty-four, of a tall rather than short figure, finely made in person, with a handsome face an an enchanting languish in her eyes. She dresses with taste. She has sense, good humour, and vivacity, and looks quite a woman in genteel life. As I mused on this elevating subject, I could not help being somehow pleasingly confounded to think that so fine a woman was at this moment in my possession, that without any motives of interest she had come with me to an inn, agreed to be my intimate companion, as to be my bedfellow all night, and to permit me the full enjoyment of her person.

When the servant left the room, I embraced her warmly and begged that she would not now delay my felicity. She declined to undress before me, and begged I would retire and send her one of the maids. I did so, gravely desiring the girl to go up to Mrs. Digges. I then took a candle in my hand and walked out to the yard. The night was very dark and very cold. I experienced for some minutes the rigours of the season, and called into my mind many terrible ideas of hardships, that I might make a transition from such dreary thoughts to the most gay and delicious feelings. I then caused make a bowl of negus, very rich of the fruit, which I caused to be set in the room as a reviving cordial.

I came softly into the room, and in a sweet delirium slipped into bed and was immediately clasped in her snowy arms and pressed in her milk-white bosom. Good heavens, what a loose did we give to amorous dalliance! The friendly curtain of darkness concealed our blushes. In a moment I felt myself animated with the strongest powers of love, and, from my dearest creature's kindness, had a most luscious feast. Proud of my godlike vigour, I soon resumed the noble game. I was in full glow of health.

Sobriety had preserved me from effeminacy and weakness, and my bounding blood beat quick and high alarms. A more voluptuous night I never enjoyed. Five times was I fairly lost in supreme rapture. Louisa was madly fond of me; she declared I was a prodigy, and asked me if this was not extraordinary for human nature. I said twice as much might be, but this was not, although in my own mind I was somewhat proud of my performance. She said it was what there was no just reason to be proud of. But I told her I could not help it.

She said it was what we had in common with the beasts. I said no. For we had it highly improved by the pleasures of sentiment. I asked her what she thought enough. She gently chid me for asking such questions, but said two times. I mentioned the Sunday's assignation, when I was in such bad spirits, told her in what agony of mind I was, and asked her if she would not have despised me for my imbecility. She declared she would not, as it was what people had not in their own power.

She often insisted that we should compose ourselves to sleep before I would consent to it. At last I sunk to rest in her arms and she in mine. I found the negus, which had a fine flavour, very refreshing to me. Louisa had an exquisite mixture of delicacy and wantonness that made me enjoy her with more relish. Indeed I could not help roving in fancy to the embraces of some other ladies which my lively imagination strongly pictures. I don't know if that was altogether fair. However, Louisa had all the advantage. She said she was quite fatigued and could neither stir leg nor arm. She begged I would not despise her, and hoped my love would not be altogether transient. I have painted this night as well as I could. The description is faint; but I surely may be styled a Man of Pleasure.

Sunday 16 January. I heard service and sermon in the New Church in the Strand which insensibly relieved me from my cloudy spirits. I had not been at Lady Betty's since Thursday sennight, as I wanted to having nothing but English ideas, and to be as manly as I possibly could. However, I thought they might take amiss my being absent for so long a time without being able to assign them any rational reason for it. I therefore went there after church and found them at breakfast. They were glad to

see me, and very kind. I hoped they were not angry at me for running through London whimsically so long without ever calling on them. They said, by no means. For they had now got a method to account for all my actions, which was just to say, "It is part of his plan"; and that they would always be glad to see me. I said I valued them much more after being some time absent from them. I really liked them this day better than ever.

I then went to Louisa and was permitted the rites of love with great complacency; yet I felt my passion for Louisa much gone. I felt a degree of coldness for her and I observed an affectation about her which disgusted me. I had a strong proof of my own inconstancy of disposition, and I considered that any woman who married me must be miserable. Here I argued wrong. For as a licentious love is merely the child of passion, it has no sure ground to hope for a long continuance, as passion may be extinguished with the most sudden and trifling breath of wind; but rational esteem founded on just motives must in all probability endure, especially when the opinion of the world and many other considerations contribute to strengthen and preserve it. Louisa and I began this day to read French. Our book was a little light piece of French gallantry entitled *Journal Amoureux.* She pronounced best and I translated best. Between us we did very well.

Monday 17 January. Louisa and I continued our study of French, which was useful as it gave us some employment and prevented us from tiring on account of conversation becoming insipid from a sameness that must necessarily happen when only two people are much together. I this day again had full fruition of her charms. I still, though, found that the warm enthusiasm of love was over. Yet I continued to mention my fears of her having some other favourite. I first said that I would watch her carefully, and would come at different times and by surprise if possible, that I might find out the truth. But I recovered myself and said I was sure I had no reason, so would not anxiously inquire. "Indeed, Sir," said she, "it is better not. For it is a maxim with me, where there is no confidence, there is no breach of trust."

Tuesday 18 January. I this day began to feel an unaccountable alarm of unexpected evil: a little heat in the members of my body sacred to Cupid, very like a symptom of that distemper with which Venus, when cross, takes it into her head to plague her votaries. But then I had run no risks. I had been with no woman but Louisa; and sure she could not have such a thing. Away then with such idle fears, such groundless, uneasy apprehensions! When I came to Louisa's, I felt myself stout and well, and most courageously did I plunge into the fount of love, and had vast pleasure as I enjoyed her as an actress who had played many a fine lady's part. She was remarkably fond of me today, and sighing said, "What will become of me if I lose you now?"

Wednesday 19 January. This was a day eagerly expected by Dempster, Erskine, and I, as it was fixed as the period of our gratifying a whim proposed by me: which was that on the first day of the new tragedy called *Elvira's* being acted, we three should walk from the one end of London to the other, dine at Dolly's, and be in the theatre at night; and as the play would probably be bad, and as Mr. David Malloch, the author, who has changed his name to David Mallet, Esq., was an arrant puppy, we determined to exert ourselves in damning it. I this morning felt stronger symptoms of the sad distemper, yet I was unwilling to imagine such a thing. However, the severe exercise of today, joined with hearty eating and drinking, I was sure would confirm or remove my suspicions.

We walked up to Hyde Park Corner, from whence we set out at ten. Our spirits were high with the notion of the adventure, and the variety that we met with as we went along is amazing. As the Spectator observes, one end of London is like a different country from the other in look and in manners. We eat an excellent breakfast at the Somerset Coffee-house. We turned down Gracechurch Street and went upon the top of London Bridge, from whence we viewed with a pleasing horror the rude and terrible appearance of the river, partly froze up, partly covered with enormous shoals of floating ice which often crashed against each other. Dempster said of this excursion from the road that our Epic Poem would be somewhat dull if it were not enlivened by such episodes. As we went along, I felt the symptoms increase, which was very confounding and very distressing to me. I thought the best thing I could do was not to keep it secret, which would be difficult and troublesome, but fairly to own it to Dempster and Erskine and ask their advice and sympathy. They really sympathized, and yet they could not help smiling a little at my catching a tartar so very unexpectedly, when I imagined myself quite safe, and had been vaunting most heroically of my felicity in having the possession of a fine woman, to whom I ascribed so many endearing qualities that they really doubted of her existence, and used to call her my ideal lady.

Thursday 20 January. I rose very disconsolate, having rested very ill by the poisonous infection raging in my veins and anxiety and vexation boiling in my breast. I could scarcely credit my own senses. What! thought I, can this beautiful, this sensible, and this agreeable woman be so sadly defiled? Can corruption lodge beneath so fair a form? Can she who professed delicacy of sentiment and sincere regard for me, use me so very basely and so very cruelly? No, it is impossible. I have just got a gleet by irritating the parts too much with excessive venery. And yet these damned twinges, that scalding heat, and that deep-tinged loathsome matter are the strongest proofs of an infection. But she certainly must think that I would soon discover her falsehood. But perhaps she was ignorant of her being ill. A pretty conjecture indeed! No, she could not be ignorant. Yes, yes, she intended to make the most of me. And now I recollect that the day we went to Hayward's, she showed me a bill of thirty shillings about which she was in some uneasiness and no doubt expected that I would pay it. But I was too cautious, and she had not effrontery enough to try my generosity in direct terms so soon after my letting her have two guineas. And am I then taken in? Am I, who have had safe and elegant intrigues with fine women, become the dupe of a strumpet? Am I now to be laid up for many weeks to suffer extreme pain and full confinement, and to be debarred all the comforts and pleasures of life? And then must I have my poor pocket drained by the unavoidable expense of it? And shall I no more (for a long time at least) take my walk, healthful and spirited, round the Park before breakfast, view the brilliant Guards on the Parade, and enjoy all my pleasing amusements? And then am I prevented from making love to Lady Mirabel, or any other woman of fashion? O dear, O dear! What a cursed thing this is! What a miserable creature am I!

In this woeful manner did I melancholy ruminate. I thought of applying to a quack who would cure me quickly and cheaply. But then the horrors of being imperfectly cured and having the distemper thrown into my blood terrified me exceedingly. I therefore pursued my resolution of last night to go to my friend Douglas, whom I knew to be skillful and careful; and although it should cost me more, yet to get sound health was a matter of great importance, and I might save upon other articles. I accordingly went and breakfasted with him.

Mrs. Douglas, who has a prodigious memory and knows a thousand anecdotes, expecially of scandal, told me that Congreve the poet lived in the family of old Lord Godolphin, who is yet alive, and that Lady Godolphin was notoriously fond of him. In so much that her lord having gone abroad upon an embassy for two years, on his return she presented him with a fine girl by the author of *Love For Love,* which he was so indulgent as to accept of; nay, after Congreve's death, he joined with her in grief, and allowed her to have an image of him in wax daily set at table and nightly in her bedchamber, to which she spoke, believing it through heat of fancy, or believing it in appearance, to be Congreve himself. The young lady was most tenderly educated, and it is a certain fact that she was never suffered to see the moon for fear she should cry for it. She is now Duchess of Leeds, and has turned out extremely well.

After breakfast Mrs. Douglas withdrew, and I opened my sad case to Douglas, who upon examining the parts, declared I had got an evident infection and that the woman who gave it me could not but know of it. I joked with my friend about the expense, asked him if he would take a draught on my arrears, and bid him visit me seldom that I might have the less to pay. To these jokes he seemed to give little heed, but talked seriously in the way of his business. And here let me make a just and true observation, which is that the same man as a friend and as a surgeon exhibits two very opposite characters. Douglas as a friend is most kind, most anxious for my interest, made me live ten days in his house, and suggested every plan of economy. But Douglas as a surgeon will be as ready to keep me long under his hands, and as desirous to lay hold of my money, as any man. In short, his views alter quite. I have to do not with him but his profession.

I then went to Louisa. With excellent address did I carry on this interview, as the following scene, I trust, will make appear.

LOUISA: My dear Sir! I hope you are well today.

BOSWELL: Excessively well, I thank you. I hope I find you so.

LOUISA: No, really, Sir. I am distressed with a thousand things. (Cunning jade, her circumstances!) I really don't know what to do.

BOSWELL: Do you know that I have been very unhappy since I saw you?

LOUISA: How so, Sir?

BOSWELL: Why, I am afraid that you don't love me so well, nor have not such a regard for me, as I thought you had.

LOUISA: Nay, dear Sir! (Seeming unconcerned.)

BOSWELL: Pray, Madam, have I no reason?

LOUISA: No, indeed, Sir, you have not.

BOSWELL: Have I no reason, Madam? Pray think.

LOUISA: Sir!

BOSWELL: Pray, Madam, in what state of health have you been in for some time?

LOUISA: Sir, you amaze me.

BOSWELL: I have but too strong, too plain reason to doubt of your regard. I have for some days observed the symptoms of disease, but was unwilling to believe you so very ungenerous. But now, Madam, I am thoroughly convinced.

LOUISA: Sir, you have terrified me. I protest I know nothing of the matter.

BOSWELL: Madam, I have had no connection with any woman but you these two months. I was with my surgeon this morning, who declared I had got a strong infection, and that she from whom I had it could not be ignorant of it. Madam, such a thing in this case is worse than from a woman of the town, as from her you may expect it. You have used me very ill. I did not deserve it. You know you said where there was no confidence, there was no breach of trust. But surely I placed some confidence in you. I am sorry that I was mistaken.

LOUISA: Sir, I will confess to you that about three years ago I was very bad. But for these fifteen months I have been quite well. I appeal to God Almighty that I am speaking true; and for these six months I have had to do with no man but yourself.

BOSWELL: But by G-d, Madam, I have been with none but you, and here am I very bad.

LOUISA: Well, Sir, by the same solemn oath I protest that I was ignorant of it.

BOSWELL: Madam, I wish much to believe you. But I own I cannot upon this occasion believe a miracle.

LOUISA: Sir, I cannot say more to you. But you leave me in the greatest misery. I shall lose your esteem. I shall be hurt in the opinion of everybody, and in my circumstances.

BOSWELL (to himself): What the devil does the confounded jilt mean by being hurt in her circumstances? This is the grossest cunning. But I won't take notice of that at all. —Madam, as to the opinion of everybody, you need not be afraid. I was going to joke and say that I never boast of a lady's *favours*. But I give you my word of honour that you shall not be discovered.

LOUISA: Sir, this is being more generous than I could expect.

BOSWELL: I hope, Madam, you will own that since I have been with you I have always behaved like a man of honour.

LOUISA: You have indeed, Sir.

BOSWELL (rising): Madam, your most obedient servant.

During all this conversation I really behaved with a manly composure and polite dignity that could not fail to inspire an awe, and she was pale as ashes and trembled and faltered. Thrice did she insist on my staying a little longer, as it was probably the last time that I should be with her. She could say nothing to the purpose. And I sat silent. As I was going, said she, "I hope, Sir, you will give me leave to inquire after your health." "Madam," said I, archly, "I fancy it will be needless for some weeks." She again renewed her request. But unwilling to be plagued any more with her, I put her off by saying I might perhaps go to the country, and left her. I was really confounded at her behaviour. There is scarcely a possibility that she could be innocent of the crime of horrid imposition. And yet her positive asseverations really stunned me. She is in all probability a most consummate dissembling whore.

Thus ended my intrigue with the fair Louisa, which I flattered myself so much with, and from which I expected at least a winter's safe copulation. It is indeed very hard. I cannot say, like young fellows who get themselves clapped in a bawdy-house, that I will take better care again. For I really did take care. However, since I am fairly trapped, let me make the best of it. I have not got it from imprudence. It is merely the chance of war.

Thursday 3 February. I was not so well yesterday. I was somewhat morose. I thought the treacherous Louisa deserved to suffer for her depravity. I therefore wrote her the following letter:

MADAM:—My surgeon will soon have a demand upon me of five guineas for curing the disease which you have given me. I must therefore remind you of the little sum which you had of me some time ago. You cannot have forgot upon what footing I let you have it. I neither *paid* it for prostitution nor *gave* it in charity. It was fairly borrowed, and you promised to return it. I give you notice that I expect to have it before Saturday sennight.

I have been very bad, but I scorn to upbraid you. I think it below me. If you are not rendered callous by a long course of disguised wickedness, I should think the consideration of your deceit and baseness, your corruption both of body and mind, would be a very severe punishment. Call not that a misfortune which is the consequence of your own unworthiness. I desire no mean evasions. I want no letters. Send the money sealed up. I have nothing more to say to you.

James Boswell.

This, I thought, might be a pretty bitter potion to her. Yet I thought to mention the money was not so genteel. However, if I get it (which is not probable), it will be of real

service to me; and to such a creature as her a pecuniary punishment will give most pain. Am not I too vindictive? It appears so; but upon better consideration I am only sacrificing at the shrine of Justice; and sure I have chosen a victim that deserves it.

Questions

1. What *kind* of reason is Boswell giving when he says, "I determined to have nothing to do with whores, as my health was of great consequence to me"?

2. What is it to be "unhappy for want of women"? What is it for a woman to be "unhappy for want of men"? Contrast this with being "unhappy for want of" *one you love.* What is the difference between the former two cases and the latter case?

3. "What a curious, inconsistent thing is the mind of man," says Boswell. What does it take to notice this? Can anything be done about the inconsistency? If so, what?

4. Boswell regards the "enchanting union" of sexual congress as showing the male to be "the superior person." And yet he is ". . . in search of a woman worthy of (his) love, . . . who thinks (him) worthy of hers, without any interested views, which is the only sure way to find out if a woman really loves a man." Is there any inconsistency here? If so, of what sort? In any event, describe the character that is shown by this view.

5. Consider the entire episode of "winning" Louisa and then ending the affair. Does Boswell's action (or possibly reaction) seem rather too harsh? If so, why? Does one first need to know whether it is possible to have gonorrhea and be unaware of it before the (moral) right and wrong can be assayed? (Boswell, remember, apparently asked his physician this. Why?)

6. If you are working with a text of ethical theories, describe this episode in terms of the theories you have studied. It might be particularly helpful to evaluate it from the perspectives of Kant, Mill, Nietzsche, and Moore.

8

Ending a Feud

Selection from
"The Life of Samuel Johnson"

[The narrator is Boswell. The year is 1776, roughly fourteen years after the episode from his journals.

editor]

My desire of being acquainted with celebrated men of every description, had made me, much about the same time, obtain an introduction to Dr. Samuel Johnson and to John Wilkes, Esq. Two men more different could perhaps not be selected out of all mankind. They had even attacked one another with some asperity in their writings; yet I lived in habits of friendship with both.

But I conceived an irresistable wish, if possible, to bring Dr. Johnson and Mr. Wilkes together. How to manage it, was a nice and difficult matter.

My worthy booksellers and friends, Messieurs Dilly in the Poultry, at whose hospi-

Reprinted by permission of the publishers from *Great Books of the Western World*, Vol. 44, "The Life of Samuel Johnson," James Boswell (Chicago: Encyclopaedia Britannica, Inc., 1952).

table and well-covered table I have seen a greater number of literary men, than at any other, except that of Sir Joshua Reynolds, had invited me to meet Mr. Wilkes and some more gentlemen, on Wednesday, May 15. "Pray, (said I,) let us have Dr. Johnson."—"What, with Mr. Wilkes? not for the world, (said Mr. Edward Dilly;) Dr. Johnson would never forgive me."—"Come, (said I,) if you'll let me negociate for you, I will be answerable that all shall go well." DILLY: "Nay, if you will take it upon you, I am sure I shall be very happy to see them both here."

Notwithstanding the high veneration which I entertained for Dr. Johnson, I was sensible that he was sometimes a little actuated by the spirit of contradiction, and by means of that I hoped I should gain my point. I was persuaded that if I had come upon him with a direct proposal, "Sir, will you dine in company with Jack Wilkes?" he would have flown into a passion, and would probably have answered, "Dine with Jack Wilkes, Sir! I'd as soon dine with Jack Ketch." I therefore, while we were sitting quietly by ourselves at his house in an evening, took occasion to open my plan thus: —"Mr. Dilly, Sir, sends his respectful compliments to you, and would be happy if you would do him the honour to dine with him on Wednesday next along with me, as I must soon go to Scotland." JOHNSON: "Sir, I am obliged to Mr. Dilly. I will wait upon him—" BOSWELL: "Provided, Sir, I suppose, that the company which he is to have, is agreeable to you." JOHNSON: "What do you mean, Sir? What do you take me for? Do you think I am so ignorant of the world, as to imagine that I am to prescribe to a gentleman what company he is to have at his table?" BOSWELL: "I beg your pardon, Sir, for wishing to prevent you from meeting people whom you might not like. Perhaps he may have some of what he calls his patriotick friends with him." JOHNSON: "Well, Sir, and what then? What care *I* for his *patriotick friends*? Poh!" BOSWELL: "I should not be surprised to find Jack Wilkes there." JOHNSON: "And if Jack Wilkes *should* be there, what is that to *me*, Sir? My dear friend, let us have no more of this. I am sorry to be angry with you; but really it is treating me strangely to talk to me as if I could not meet any company whatever, occasionally." BOSWELL: "Pray, forgive me, Sir; I meant well. But you shall meet whoever comes, for me." Thus I secured him, and told Dilly that he would find him very well pleased to be one of his guests on the day appointed.

Upon the much expected Wednesday, I called on him about half an hour before dinner, as I often did when we were to dine out together, to see that he was ready in time, and to accompany him. I found him buffeting his books, as upon a former occasion, covered with dust, and making no preparation for going abroad. "How is this, Sir? (said I). Don't you recollect that you are to dine at Mr. Dilly's?" JOHNSON: "Sir, I did not think of going to Dilly's: it went out of my head. I have ordered dinner at home with Mrs. Williams." BOSWELL: "But my dear Sir, you know you were engaged to Mr. Dilly, and I told him so. He will expect you, and will be much disappointed if you don't come." JOHNSON: "You must talk to Mrs. Williams about this."

Here was a sad dilemma. I feared that what I was so confident I had secured, would yet be frustrated. He had accustomed himself to shew Mrs. Williams such a degree of humane attention, as frequently imposed some restraint upon him; and I knew that if she should be obstinate, he would not stir. I hastened down stairs to the blind lady's room, and told her I was in great uneasiness, for Dr. Johnson had engaged to me to dine that day at Mr. Dilly's, but that he had told me he had forgotten his engagement, and had ordered dinner at home. "Yes, Sir, (said she, pretty peevishly,) Dr. Johnson is to dine at home."— "Madam, (said I,) his respect for you is such, that I know he will not leave you, unless you absolutely desire it. But as you have so much of his company, I hope you will be good enough to forgo it for a day: as Mr. Dilly is a very worthy man, has frequently had agreeable parties at his house for Dr. Johnson, and will be vexed if the Doctor neglects him to-day. And then, Madam, be pleased to consider my situation; I carried the message, and I assured Mr. Dilly that Dr. Johnson was to come; and no doubt he has made a dinner, and invited a company, and boasted of the honour he expected to have. I shall be quite disgraced if the Doctor is not there." She gradually softened to my solicitations, which were certainly as earnest as most entreaties to ladies upon any occasion, and was graciously pleased to empower me to tell Dr. Johnson, "That all things considered, she thought he should certainly go." I flew back to him, still in dust, and careless of what should be the event, "indifferent in his choice to go or stay"; but as soon as I had announced to him Mrs. William's consent, he roared, "Frank, a clean shirt," and was very soon drest. When I had him fairly seated in a hackney-coach with me, I exulted as much as a fortune-hunter who has got an heiress into a post-chaise with him to set out for Gretna-Green.

When we entered Mr. Dilly's drawing-room, he found himself in the midst of a company he did not know. I kept myself snug and silent, watching how he would conduct himself. I observed him whispering to Mr. Dilly, "Who is that gentleman, Sir?"—"Mr. Arthur Lee."—JOHNSON: "Too, too, too," (under his breath,) which was one of his habitual mutterings. Mr. Arthur Lee could not but be very obnoxious to Johnson, for he was not only a *patriot,* but an *American.* He was afterwards minister from the United States at the Court of Madrid. "And who is the gentleman in lace?"—"Mr. Wilkes, Sir." This information confounded him still more; he had some difficulty to restrain himself, and taking up a book, sat down upon a window-seat and read, or at least kept his eye upon it intently for some time, till he composed himself. His feelings, I dare say, were aukward enough. But he no doubt recollected his having rated me for supposing that he could be at all disconcerted by any company, and he, therefore, resolutely set himself to behave quite as an easy man of the world, who could adapt himself at once to the disposition and manners of those whom he might chance to meet.

The cheering sound of "Dinner is upon the table," dissolved his reverie, and we *all* sat down without any symptom of ill humour. There were present, beside Mr. Wilkes, and Mr. Arthur Lee, who was an old companion of mine when he studied physick at Edinburgh, Mr. (now Sir John) Miller, Dr. Lettsom, and Mr. Slater, the druggist. Mr. Wilkes placed himself next to Dr. Johnson, and behaved to him with so much attention and politeness, that he gained upon him insensibly. No man ate more heartily than Johnson, or loved better what was nice and delicate. Mr. Wilkes was very assiduous in helping him to some fine veal. "Pray give me leave, Sir;—It is better here—A little of the brown—Some fat, Sir —A little of the stuffing—Some gravy—Let me have the pleasure of giving you some butter—Allow me to recommend a squeeze of this orange;—or the lemon, perhaps, may have more zest."—"Sir, Sir, I am obliged to you, Sir," cried Johnson, bowing, and turning his head to him with a look for some time of "surly virtue," but, in a short while, of complacency.

Foote being mentioned, Johnson said, "He is not a good mimick." One of the company added, "A merry Andrew, a buffoon." JOHNSON: "But he has wit too, and is not deficient in ideas, or in fertility and variety of imagery, and not empty of reading; he has knowledge enough to fill up his part. One species of wit he has in an eminent degree, that of escape. You drive him into a corner with both hands; but he's gone, Sir, when you think you have got him —like an animal that jumps over your head. Then he has a great range for wit; he never lets truth stand between him and a jest, and he is sometimes mighty coarse. Garrick is under many restraints from which Foote is free." WILKES: "Garrick's wit is more like Lord Chesterfield's." JOHNSON: "The first time I was in company with Foote was at Fitzherbert's. Having no good opinion of the fellow, I was resolved not to be pleased; and it is very difficult to please a man against his will. I went on eating my dinner pretty sullenly, affecting not to mind him. But the dog was so very comical, that I was obliged to lay down my knife and fork, throw myself back upon my chair, and fairly laugh it out. No, Sir, he was irresistible. He upon one occasion experienced, in an extraordinary degree, the efficacy of his powers of entertaining. Amongst the many and various modes which he tried of getting money, he became a partner with a small-beer brewer, and he was to have a share of the profits for procuring customers amongst his numerous acquaintance. Fitzherbert was one who took his small-beer; but it was so bad that the servants resolved not to drink it. They were at some loss how to notify their resolution, being afraid of offending their master, who they knew liked Foote much as a companion. At last they fixed upon a little black boy, who was rather a favourite, to be their deputy, and deliver their remonstrance; and having invested him with the whole authority of the kitchen, he was to inform Mr. Fitzherbert, in all their names, upon a certain day, that they would drink Foote's small-beer no longer. On that day Foote happened to dine at Fitzherbert, and this boy served at table; he was so delighted with Foote's stories, and merriment, and grimace, that when he went down stairs, he told them, 'This is the finest man I have ever seen. I will not deliver your message. I will drink his small-beer.' "

Somebody observed that Garrick could not have done this. WILKES: "Garrick would have made the small-beer still smaller. He is now leaving the stage; but he will play *Scrub* all his life." I knew that Johnson would let nobody attack Garrick but himself, as Garrick said to me, and I had heard him praise his liberality; so to bring out his commendation of his celebrated pupil, I said, loudly, "I have heard Garrick is liberal." JOHNSON: "Yes, Sir, I know that Garrick has given away more money than any man in England that I am acquainted with, and that not from ostentatious views. Garrick was very poor when he began life; so when he came to have money, he probably was very unskilful in giving away, and saved when he should not. But Garrick began to be liberal as soon as he could; and I am of opinion, the reputation of avarice which he has had, has been very lucky for him, and prevented his having many enemies. You despise a man for avarice, but do not hate him. Garrick might have been much better attacked for living with more splendour than is suitable to a player: if they had had the wit to have assaulted him in that quarter, they might have galled him more. But they have kept clamouring about his avarice, which has rescued him from much obloquy and envy."

Mr. Wilkes remarked, that "among all the bold flights of Shakespeare's imagination, the boldest was making Birnamwood march to Dunsinane; creating a wood where there never was a shrub; a wood in Scotland! ha! ha! ha!" And he also observed, that "the clannish slavery of the

Highlands of Scotland was the single exception to Milton's remark of 'The Mountain Nymph, sweet Liberty,' being worshipped in all hilly countries."—"When I was at Inverary (said he,) on a visit to my old friend, Archibald, Duke of Argyle, his dependents congratulated me on being such a favourite of his Grace. I said, 'It is then, gentlemen, truly lucky for me; for if I had displeased the Duke, and he had wished it, there is not a Campbell among you but would have been ready to bring John Wilkes's head to him in a charger. It would have been only

"Off with his head! so much for Aylesbury."

I was then member for Aylesbury."

WILKES: "We have no City-Poet now: that is an office which has gone into disuse. The last was Elkanah Settle. There is something in *names* which one cannot help feeling. Now *Elkanah Settle* sounds so *queer,* who can expect much from that name? We should have no hesitation to give it for John Dryden, in preference to Elkanah Settle, from the names only, without knowing their different merits." JOHNSON: "I suppose Sir, Settle did as well for Aldermen in his time, as John Home could do now. Where did Beckford, and Trecothick learn English?"

Mr. Arthur Lee mentioned some Scotch who had taken possession of a barren part of America, and wondered why they should choose it. JOHNSON: "Why, Sir, all barrenness is comparative. The *Scotch* would not know it to be barren." BOSWELL: "Come, come, he is flattering the English. You have now been in Scotland, Sir, and say if you did not see meat and drink enough there." JOHNSON: "Why yes, Sir; meat and drink enough to give the inhabitants sufficient strength to run away from home." All these quick and lively sallies were said sportively, quite in jest, and with a smile, which showed that he meant only wit. Upon this topick he and Mr. Wilkes could perfectly assimilate; here was a bond of union between them, and I was conscious that as both of them had visited Caledonia, both were fully satisfied of the strange narrow ignorance of those who imagine that it is a land of famine. But they amused themselves with persevering in the old jokes. When I claimed a superiority for Scotland over England in one respect, that no man can be arrested there for a debt merely because another swears it against him; but there must first be the judgement of a court of law ascertaining its justice; and that a seizure of the person, before judgement is obtained, can take place only, if his creditor should swear that he is about to fly from the country, or, as it is technically expressed, is *in meditatione fugae*: WILKES: "That, I should think may be safely sworn of all the Scotch nation." JOHNSON: (To Mr. Wilkes) "You must know, Sir, I lately took my friend Boswell, and shewed him genuine civilized life in an English provincial town. I turned him loose at Lichfield, my native city, that he might see for once real civility: for you know he lives among savages in Scotland, and among rakes in London." WILKES: "Except when he is with grave, sober, decent people, like you and me." JOHNSON: (smiling) "And we ashamed of him."

They were quite frank and easy. Johnson told the story of his asking Mrs. Macaulay to allow her footman to sit down with them, to prove the ridiculousness of the arguments for the equality of mankind: and he said to me afterwards, with a nod of satisfaction, "You saw Mr. Wilkes acquiesced." Wilkes talked with all imaginable freedom of the ludicrous title given to the Attorney-General, *Diabolus Regis*; adding, "I have reason to know something about that officer; for I was prosecuted for a libel." Johnson, who many people would have supposed must have been furiously angry at hearing this talked of so lightly, said not a word. He was now, *indeed*, "a good-humoured fellow."

After dinner we had an accession of Mrs. Knowles, the Quaker lady, well known for her various talents, and of Mr. Alderman Lee. Amidst some patriotick groans, somebody (I think the Alderman) said, "Poor old England is lost." JOHNSON: "Sir, it is not so much to be lamented that old England is lost, as that the Scotch have found it."

WILKES: "Had Lord Bute governed Scotland only, I should not have taken the trouble to write his eulogy, and dedicate 'MORTIMER' to him."

Mr. Wilkes held a candle to shew a fine print of a beautiful female figure which hung in the room, and pointed out the elegant contour of the bosom with the finger of an arch connoisseur. He afterwards in a conversation with me waggishly insisted, that all the time Johnson shewed visible signs of a fervent admiration of the corresponding charms of the fair Quaker.

I attended Dr. Johnson home, and had the satisfaction to hear him tell Mrs. Williams how much he had been pleased with Mr. Wilkes's company, and what an agreeable day he had passed.

I talked a good deal to him of the celebrated Margaret Caroline Rudd, whom I had visited, induced by the fame of her talents, address, and irresistible power of fascination. To a lady who disapproved of my visiting her, he said on a former occasion, "Nay, Madam, Boswell is in the right; I should have visited her myself, were it not that they have now a trick of putting every thing into the newspapers." This evening he exclaimed, "I envy him his acquaintance with Mrs. Rudd."

On the evening of the next day I took leave of him, being to set out for Scotland. I thanked him with great warmth for all his kindness. "Sir, (said he,) you are very welcome. Nobody repays it with more."

Questions

1. Why, do you think, does Boswell want "to bring Dr. Johnson and Mr. Wilkes together"? Do his motives have anything to do with the morality of his actions?

2. This episode takes place some fourteen years after Boswell's affair with Louisa. Notice this offhand remark concerning his persuasion of Mrs. Williams: "She gradually softened to my solicitations, which were certainly as earnest as most en-

treaties to ladies upon any occasion. . . ." What does this mean? Given this remark and the journal episode, can we construct Boswell's view of women? If so, what is that view? What kind of character does this display?

3. Is Boswell quite honest with Johnson? Is he justified in what he does? Explain.

4. Suppose that Dr. Johnson and Wilkes had ended up getting in a fistfight. Would this change the way in which question three should be answered? Explain.

5. How does Boswell regard other people? Explain why this is moral, amoral, or immoral.

6. If you are working with a text of ethical theories, describe this episode in terms of the theories you have studied. It might be particularly helpful to evaluate it from the perspectives of Aristotle, Epicurus, Kant, Nietzsche, and Prichard.

9

On Not Taking an Oath

Selection from
Concluding Unscientific Postscript

[At an earlier point in the book, Johannes Climacus, the "author" of *Concluding Unscientific Postscript,* recounted how "four years ago" he decided to become an author. This decision presented a problem: insofar as "spiritual existence" had been made "easier and easier" by other authors, what was there for him to do? He finally said to himself, "You must do something, but inasmuch as with your limited capacities it will be impossible to make anything easier than it has become, you must, with the same humanitarian enthusiasm as the others, undertake to make something harder." This episode exhibits some of the "difficulties" in "spiritual existence."

editor]

The story is quite a simple one. It was about five years ago, on a Sunday—aye,

Selection from Søren Kierkegaard, *Concluding Unscientific Postscript,* translated by David Swenson and Walter Lowrie (copyright 1941 © 1969 by Princeton University Press; Princeton Paperback, 1968) pp. 210–216. Reprinted by permission of Princeton University Press and the American Scandinavian Foundation.

now perhaps the reader will be disposed not to believe me, because it was again on a Sunday, but it is none the less quite certain that it was a Sunday, about two months after the one previously mentioned. It was late in the day, evening was approaching. And the evening's farewell to the day, and to him who has lived the day, is a speech of mysterious meanings. Its reminder is like the watchful mother's admonition to her child, to come home betimes; but its invitation, even if the farewell is without guilt in being so misunderstood, is an inexplicable beckoning, as if rest could be found only by remaining for the tryst of the night, not with a woman, but femininely with the infinite; persuaded by the night wind, when it monotonously repeats itself, when it breathes through forest and dale, sighing as if it sought for something; persuaded by the distant echo in one's own soul of the night's stillness, as if it had a premonition of something to come; persuaded by the lofty calm of the heavens above, as if this something had been found; persuaded by the audible soundlessness of the dew, as if this were the explanation and the refreshment of the infinite, like the half-understood fruitfulness of the quiet night, like the semi-transparency of the night mist.

Contrary to my usual custom I had come into the garden which is called the garden of the dead, where again the visitor's farewell is rendered doubly difficult, since it is meaningless to say: yet once more, when the last time is already past, and since there is no reason for ceasing to say farewell, when the beginning is made after the last time is past. Most of the visitors had already gone home, only an individual here and there vanished among the trees; not glad to meet anyone, he avoided the contact, seeking the dead and not the living. And always in this garden there prevails a beautiful understanding among the visitors, that one does not come here to see and to be seen, but each visitor avoids the other. Nor does one need company, least of all a gossipy friend, here where all is eloquence, where the dead man calls out the brief word engraved upon his tombstone. He does not expound and expand like a clergyman, but is like a silent man who says only this one word, but says it with a passion as if to burst the tomb—or is it not strange to have inscribed upon his tombstone: "We shall meet again"; and then to remain in the grave? And yet what inwardness is the word precisely because of the contradiction; for if one who may come again tomorrow says, "We shall meet again," this is not particularly moving. To have everything against you, not to have a single direct expression for your inwardness, and yet to stand by your words: that is true inwardness. For inwardness is false precisely in the degree that the outward expression in mien and visage, in words and assurances, is at once ready to hand; not precisely because the expression itself is untrue, but the falsity consists in the fact that the inwardness is merely a phase. The dead man is silent while time goes by; on the renowned warrior's grave they have laid his sword, and insolence has torn the paling about it to pieces, but the warrior does not rise to seize

his sword to defend himself and his resting-place; he does not gesticulate, he gives no assurances, he does not flare up in momentary inwardness; but silent as the tomb, and still as death, he stands by his word. All honor to the living who outwardly conduct themselves as a dead man in relation to his inwardness, and precisely thereby preserve it. Such inwardness is not as a moment's excitement, or as a woman's beguilement, but as the eternal which has been won through death. Such an one is a man; for that a woman bubbles over in momentary inwardness is not unbeautiful, nor is it unbeautiful that she soon forgets it again; the one corresponds to the other, and both to the feminine and to that which in daily life is usually understood by inwardness.

Weary from walking I sat down on a bench, a wondering witness to how that proud ruler, the sun, now for thousands of years the hero of the day, and destined to remain such until the final day, how the sun in its flaming departure cast a glorifying radiance over the entire landscape; over the top of the wall which surrounds the yard, my eyes looked into that eternal symbol of eternity: the infinite horizon. What sleep is for the body, such rest is for the soul, an opportunity to breathe in peace. Suddenly I discovered to my astonishment that the trees which concealed me from the eyes of others, had concealed others from mine; for I heard a voice almost at my side. It has always wounded my sensibilities to witness another person's expression of feeling, as he gives himself up to it only when he believes himself unobserved; for there is an emotional inwardness which is properly hidden, and revealed only to God, just as a woman's beauty desires to be concealed from all, and revealed only to the beloved: hence I resolved to remove myself. But the first words I heard gripped me strongly; and since I feared that the noise of my departure might be more embarrassing than if I remained sitting, I chose the latter course, and thus remained a witness to a situation which however solemn, suffered no violation by my presence.

Through the leaves I saw that there were two: an elderly man with snow-white hair, and a child, a boy of about ten. They were both dressed in mourning, and sat before a freshly dug grave, from which it was natural to conclude that it was a recent loss in which they were engrossed. The aged man's venerable figure was clothed in increased solemnity by the glory of the setting sun; and his voice, calm and yet thrilled with feeling, enunciated each word clearly, reflecting the inwardness that possessed the speaker, who now and then ceased speaking when his voice choked with tears, or his mood ended in a sigh. For feeling is like the river Niger in Africa: its source is not known, nor its outlet, but only its course. From the conversation I learned that the little boy was the old man's grandson, and he whose grave was being visited, the boy's father. In all probability the rest of the family must already have been removed by death, since no other name was mentioned, a circumstance which I also verified upon a later visit, when I read upon the tablet the name, and the names of the many dead.

The old man talked with the child about his no longer having a father, of his having no one to cling to except an old man who was too old for him, and who himself longed to leave the world; but that there was a God in heaven, from whom all fatherhood in heaven and on the earth is named, and that there was one name in which alone there was salvation, the name of the Lord Jesus Christ. He ceased speaking for a moment, and then said half aloud to himself: "That this solace should have become my fear, that he, my son, now buried there in the grave, should have relinquished it. To what end then all my hope, my care, to what end his wisdom, when as now his death in the midst of his error must make a believer's soul uncertain of his salvation, must bring my gray hairs in sorrow to the grave, must cause a believer to leave the world in anxiety, an old man to hasten like a doubter after a certainty, and to look despondently about him upon those he leaves behind!"

Then he again addressed himself to the boy. He told him that there was a wisdom which tried to fly beyond faith, that on the other side of faith there was a wide stretch of country like the blue mountains, an illusory land, which to a mortal eye might appear to yield a certainty higher than that of faith; but the believer feared this mirage, as the sailor fears a similar appearance on the sea; that it was an illusion of eternity in which a mortal cannot live, but only lose his faith when he permits his gaze to be fascinated by the sight. He fell silent, and then once more spoke half aloud to himself: "Alas, that my unhappy son should have permitted himself to be deceived! To what end all his learning, which made it impossible for him to explain himself to me, so that I could not even speak to him about his error, because it was too high for me!" Then he arose and brought the child over to the grave, and said with a voice whose impressiveness I shall never forget: "Poor boy, you are only a child, and yet you will soon be alone in the world! Do you promise me by the memory of your dead father, who, if he could speak to you now, would speak thus, and speaks to you with my voice; do you promise me by the sight of my old age and my gray hairs; do you promise me by the solemnity of this sacred ground, by the God whose name you have learned to call upon, by the name of Jesus Christ, in whom alone there is salvation; do you promise me that you will hold fast to this faith in life and in death, that you will not permit yourself to be deceived by an illusion, however the face of the world changes —do you promise this?" Overwhelmed by the impression, the little one threw himself down upon his knees, but the old man lifted him up and pressed him to his heart.

I must in deference to the truth admit that this was the most moving scene I had ever witnessed. What may perhaps for a moment dispose one or another reader to assume that the whole story is fictitious, namely, that an old man should talk thus to a child, was precisely what moved me most of all: the unhappy old man who had been left alone in the world with a child; who had no one to talk with about his anxiety except the child; who had but one to save, the child, not able to presuppose sufficient maturity on the child's part to understand him, and yet not daring to wait for the coming of maturity because he himself is an old man. It is beautiful to be old, beautiful to see the new generation grow up about one, a happy reckoning, to add the sum each time the number is increased; but if it comes to reckon in reverse, to subtract instead of to add, each time death takes its toll—until the end is come, and only an old man is left to strike the balance: what then is so heavy as to be old! Just as need can force a man to extreme measures, so it seemed to me that the old man's sufferings found their strongest expression in what poetically must be called an improbability: that an old man has in a child his only confidant, and that a sacred promise, an oath, is demanded of a child.

Although merely a spectator and witness, I was myself deeply moved. At one moment it seemed to me that I was myself the young man whom his father had buried in so great fear; the next, it seemed to me that I was the child, bound by the sacred promise. However, I felt no impulse to rush forward, to express to the old man my sympathy, assuring him with tears and trembling voice that I should never forget the scene, or even begging him to pledge me in an oath. For only over-precipitate people, clouds without water and storm-driven mists, are quick to take an oath; because the fact is that they are unable to keep it, and therefore must perpetually be taking it. I, for my part, am of the opinion that "never to forget this impression," is something quite different from saying once in a solemn moment: "I will never forget it." The first is inwardness, the second is perhaps only a momentary inwardness. And if one never does forget it, it does not seem that the solemnity with which it was said is so particularly important, since the continuing solemnity with which one, day by day, prevents the forgetfulness, is the truer solemnity. The womanish is always dangerous. A tender pressure of the hand, a passionate embrace, a tear in the eye: these things are not quite the same as the silent consecration of a resolve. The inwardness of the spirit is, after all, always a stranger and a foreigner in the body: why, then, gesticulations? Shakespeare makes Brutus say so truly, when the conspirators bind themselves by an oath to their enterprise:

"No, not an oath: . . .
Swear priests, and cowards, and men caute-
lous,
Old feeble carrions, and such suffering souls
That welcome wrongs; . . . but do not stain
The even virtue of our enterprise,
Nor the insuppressive mettle of our spirits,
To think that, or our cause, or our perfor-
mance
Did need an oath. "[1]

The momentary outpouring of inwardness most often leaves behind a lassitude which is dangerous. And besides, a very simple observation has in still another way taught me caution in connection with the making of oaths or promises, so that the true inwardness is even compelled to express itself contrariwise. Flighty and easily excitable souls are more prone to nothing than to the taking of a sacred promise, because the inner weakness needs the strong stimulus of the moment. To administer a sacred pledge to such a person is a very dubious thing, and it is far better to prevent the solemn episode from taking place, while still binding oneself by a little *reservatio mentalis*, providing the giving of the pledge seems at all or moderately justified. This is to the other's advantage, prevents a profanation of the holy, and frees him from being bound by an oath that he would eventually break. Thus if Brutus, in view of the fact that the conspirators, with a possible exception or two, were flighty fellows, and

---

[1] *Julius Caesar* by William Shakespeare.

hence precipitate to take oaths and to give and require sacred pledges, had thrust them away from him, had for this reason prohibited the taking of a pledge; while in view of the fact that he considered the cause just, and also thought it just that they should turn to him for assistance, if he had in all quietness dedicated himself—in that case it seems to me that his inwardness would have been greater. Now he is somewhat declamatory, and though there is truth in what he says, there is a strain of falsity in his saying it to the conspirators, without being quite clear in his own mind to what sort of men he is speaking.

And so I, too, went home. Fundamentally I had understood the old gentleman at once, for my studies had in many ways led me to take note of a dubious relationship between a modern Christian speculation and Christianity, but the matter had not in any decisive manner enlisted my interest. Now it was invested with its own proper significance. The venerable old man with his faith seemed to be an individual with an absolutely justified grievance, a man whom existence had mistreated, because a modern speculation, like a change in the currency, had made property values in the realm of faith insecure. His sorrow over the loss of his son, not only by death, but as he understood it, still more terribly through speculative philosophy, moved me profoundly; while the contradiction in his position, that he could not even explain how the enemy had conducted the campaign, became for me a decisive challenge to trace out a definite clue. The entire matter appealed to me as a very complicated criminal case, where the crisscrossing of many trails made it difficult to find the truth. This was something for me. And I thought to myself: "You are now tired of life's diversions, you are tired of the maidens, whom you love only in passing; you must have something fully to occupy your time. Here it is: to discover where the misunderstanding lies between speculative philosophy and Christianity." This therefore became my

resolve. I have certainly never spoken to any human being about my plan, and I am sure my landlady has not seen any change in me, either the same evening or the day after.

"But," said I to myself, "since you are not a genius, and have by no means a call to bestow a beatific happiness upon all mankind, and since you have not promised anyone anything, you can address yourself to your enterprise *con amore,* and methodically, as if a poet and a dialectician watched over your every step, now that you have reached a more specific understanding of your own notion that you must try to make something difficult." My studies, which had already in a manner brought me to my goal, were now systematically organized; but whenever I was tempted to transform my investigations into an erudite learning, there always came before my mind the venerable figure of the old man. But chiefly I sought by reflection to trace the misunderstanding to its roots. My many failures I need not here recite, but finally it became clear to me that the misdirection of speculative philosophy, and its consequent assumed justification for reducing faith to the status of a relative moment, could not be anything accidental, but must be rooted deeply in the entire tendency of the age. It must, in short, doubtless be rooted in the fact that on account of our vastly increased knowledge, men had forgotten what it means to EXIST, and what INWARDNESS signifies.

Questions

1. Is there any significance to Johannes Climacus' poetic description of "evening"? Is this simply a delightful literary flourish? Compare this with his characterization of "the sun" and "the infinite horizon."

2. Discuss the concept of "the feminine" present in this episode, contrasting it with Boswell's view of "women."

3. What is meant by "All honor to the living who outwardly conduct themselves as a dead man in relation to his inwardness, and precisely thereby preserve it"? If someone is really sincere about something, shouldn't he talk about it?

4. What is the "illusory land" of which the old man speaks? How does one avoid it?

5. If Johannes is so moved by this "scene," why doesn't he "rush forward"?

6. What is the difference between, " 'never to forget this impression' " and "saying once in a solemn moment: 'I will never forget it.' "?

7. How does one *remember* "what it means to EXIST, and what INWARDNESS signifies"?

8. If you are working with a text of ethical theories, describe this episode in terms of the theories you have studied. It might be particularly helpful to evaluate it from the perspectives of Kant, Nietzsche, and Prichard.

10

Education

Hard Times

Chapter 1: The One Thing Needful.

"Now, what I want is, Facts. Teach these boys and girls nothing but Facts. Facts alone are wanted in life. Plant nothing else, and root out everything else. You can only form the minds of reasoning animals upon facts; nothing else will ever be of any service to them. This is the principle on which I bring up my own children, and this is the principle on which I bring up these children. Stick to Facts, sir!"

The scene was a plain, bare, monotonous vault of a school-room, and the speaker's square forefinger emphasised his observations by underscoring every sentence with a line on the schoolmaster's sleeve. The emphasis was helped by the speaker's square wall of a forehead, which had his eyebrows for its base, while his eyes found commodious cellarage in two dark caves, overshadowed by the wall. The emphasis was helped by the speaker's mouth, which was wide, thin, and hard set. The emphasis was helped by the speaker's voice, which was inflexible, dry, and dictatorial. The emphasis was helped by the speaker's hair, which bristled on the skirts of his bald head, a plantation of firs to keep the wind from its shining surface, all covered with knobs, like the crust of a plum pie, as if the head had scarcely warehouse-room for the hard facts stowed inside. The speaker's obstinate carriage, square coat, square legs, square shoulders,—nay, his very neckcloth, trained to take him by the throat with an unaccommodating grasp, like a stubborn fact, as it was,—all helped the emphasis.

"In this life, we want nothing but Facts, sir; nothing but Facts!"

The speaker, and the schoolmaster, and the third grown person present, all backed a little, and swept with their eyes the inclined plane of little vessels then and there arranged in order, ready to have imperial gallons of facts poured into them until they were full to the brim.

Reprinted from *The Works of Charles Dickens*, vol. IV, P. F. Collier, Publisher, 1870, by permission of Macmillan and Co. and Fawcett Publications, Inc.

Chapter 2: Murdering the Innocents.

Thomas Gradgrind, sir. A man of realities. A man of facts and calculations. A man who proceeds upon the principle that two and two are four, and nothing over, and who is not to be talked into allowing for anything over. Thomas Gradgrind, sir—peremptorily Thomas—Thomas Gradgrind. With a rule and a pair of scales, and the multiplication table always in his pocket, sir, ready to weigh and measure any parcel of human nature, and tell you exactly what it comes to. It is a mere question of figures, a case of simple arithmetic. You might hope to get some other nonsensical belief into the head of George Gradgrind, or Augustus Gradgrind, or John Gradgrind, or Joseph Gradgrind (all suppositious, non-existent persons), but into the head of Thomas Gradgrind—no, sir!

In such terms Mr. Gradgrind always mentally introduced himself, whether to his private circle of acquaintance, or to the public in general. In such terms, no doubt, substituting the words "boys and girls," for "sir," Thomas Gradgrind now presented Thomas Gradgrind to the little pitchers before him, who were to be filled so full of facts.

Indeed, as he eagerly sparkled at them from the cellarage before mentioned, he seemed a kind of cannon loaded to the muzzle with facts, and prepared to blow them clean out of the regions of childhood at one discharge. He seemed a galvanising apparatus, too, charged with a grim mechanical substitute for the tender young imaginations that were to be stormed away.

"Girl number twenty," said Mr. Gradgrind, squarely pointing with his square forefinger, "I don't know that girl. Who is that girl?"

"Sissy Jupe, sir," explained number twenty, blushing, standing up, and curtseying.

"Sissy is not a name," said Mr. Gradgrind. "Don't call yourself Sissy. Call yourself Cecilia."

"It's father as calls me Sissy, sir," returned the young girl in a trembling voice, and with another curtsey.

"Then he has no business to do it," said Mr. Gradgrind. "Tell him he mustn't. Cecilia Jupe. Let me see. What is your father?"

"He belongs to the horse-riding, if you please, sir."

Mr. Gradgrind frowned, and waved off the objectionable calling with his hand.

"We don't want to know anything about that, here. You mustn't tell us about that, here. Your father breaks horses, don't he?"

"If you please, sir, when they can get any to break, they do break horses in the ring, sir."

"You mustn't tell us about the ring here. Very well, then. Describe your father as a horsebreaker. He doctors sick horses, I dare say?"

"Oh yes, sir."

"Very well, then. He is a veterinary surgeon, a farrier, and horsebreaker. Give me your definition of a horse."

(Sissy Jupe thrown into the greatest alarm by this demand.)

"Girl number twenty unable to define a horse!" said Mr. Gradgrind, for the general behoof of all the little pitchers. "Girl number twenty possessed of no facts, in reference to one of the commonest of animals! Some boy's definition of a horse. Bitzer, yours."

The square finger, moving here and there, lighted suddenly on Bitzer, perhaps because he chanced to sit in the same ray of sunlight which, darting in at one of the bare windows of the intensely whitewashed room, irradiated Sissy. For, the boys and girls sat on the face of the inclined plane in two compact bodies, divided up the centre by a narrow interval; and Sissy, being at the corner of a row on the sunny side, came in for the beginning of a sunbeam, of which Bitzer, being in the corner of a row on the other side, a few rows in advance, caught the end. But, whereas the girl was so dark-eyed and dark-haired, that she seemed to receive a deeper and more lustrous colour from the sun, when it shone upon her, the boy was so light-eyed and light-haired that the self-same rays appeared to draw out of him what little colour he ever possessed. His cold eyes would hardly have been eyes, but for the short ends of lashes which, by bringing them into immediate contrast with something paler than themselves, expressed their form. His short-cropped hair might have been a mere continuation of the sandy freckles on his forehead and face. His skin was so unwholesomely deficient in the natural tinge, that he looked as though, if he were cut, he would bleed white.

"Bitzer," said Thomas Gradgrind. "Your definition of a horse."

"Quadruped. Graminivorous. Forty teeth, namely twenty four grinders, four eye-teeth, and twelve incisive. Sheds coat in the spring; in marshy countries, sheds hoofs, too. Hoofs hard, but requiring to be shod with iron. Age known by marks in mouth." Thus (and much more) Bitzer.

"Now girl number twenty," said Mr. Gradgrind. "You know what a horse is."

She curtseyed again, and would have blushed deeper, if she could have blushed deeper than she had blushed all the time. Bitzer, after rapidly blinking at Thomas Gradgrind with both eyes at once, and so catching the light upon his quivering ends of lashes that they looked like the antennæ of busy insects, put his knuckles to his freckled forehead, and sat down again.

The third gentleman now stepped forth. A mighty man at cutting and drying, he was; a government officer; in his way (and in most other people's too), a professed pugilist; always in training, always with a system to force down the general throat like a bolus, always to be heard at the bar of his little Public-office, ready to fight all England. To continue in fistic phraseology, he had a genius for coming up to the scratch, wherever and whatever it was, and proving himself an ugly customer. He would go in and damage any subject whatever with his right, follow up with his left, stop, exchange, counter, bore his opponent (he always fought All England) to the ropes, and fall upon him neatly. He was certain to knock the wind out of common sense, and render that unlucky adversary deaf to the call of time. And he had it in charge from high authority to bring about the great public-office Millennium, when Commissioners should reign upon earth.

"Very well," said this gentleman, briskly smiling, and folding his arms. "That's a horse. Now, let me ask you girls and boys, Would you paper a room with representations of horses?"

After a pause, one half the children cried in chorus, "Yes sir!" Upon which the other half, seeing in the gentleman's face that Yes was wrong, cried out in chorus, "No sir!"— as the custom is, in these examinations.

"Of course, No. Why wouldn't you?"

A pause. One corpulent slow boy, with a wheezy manner of breathing, ventured the answer, Because he wouldn't paper a room at all, but would paint it.

"You *must* paper it," said the gentleman, rather warmly.

"You must paper it," said Thomas Gradgrind, "whether you like it or not. Don't tell *us* you wouldn't paper it. What do you mean boy?"

"I'll explain to you, then," said the gentleman, after another and dismal pause, "why you wouldn't paper a room with representations of horses. Do you ever see horses walking up and down the sides of rooms in reality—in fact? Do you?"

"Yes sir!" from one half. "No, sir!" from the other.

"Of course no," said the gentleman with an indignant look at the wrong half. "Why, then, you are not to see anywhere, what you don't see in fact; you are not to have anywhere, what you don't have in fact. What is called Taste, is only another name for Fact."

Thomas Gradgrind nodded his approbation.

"This is a new principal, a discovery, a great discovery," said the gentleman.

"Now I'll try you again. Suppose you were going to carpet a room. Would you use a carpet having a representation of flowers upon it?"

There being a general conviction by this time that "No sir!" was always the right answer to this gentleman, the chorus of No was very strong. Only a few feeble stragglers said Yes; among them Sissy Jupe.

"Girl number twenty," said the gentleman, smiling in calm strength of knowledge.

Sissy blushed, and stood up.

"So you would carpet your room—or your husband's room, if you were a grown woman, and had a husband—with representations of flowers, would you," said the gentleman. "Why would you?"

"If you please, sir, I am very fond of flowers," returned the girl.

"And is that why you would put tables and chairs upon them, and have people walking over them with heavy boots?"

"It wouldn't hurt them, sir. They wouldn't crush and wither if you please, sir. They would be the pictures of what was very pretty and pleasant, and I would fancy—"

"Ay, ay, ay! But you mustn't fancy," cried the gentleman, quite elated by coming so happily to his point. "That's it! You are never to fancy."

"You are not, Cecelia Jupe," Thomas Gradgrind solemnly repeated, "to do anything of that kind."

"Fact, fact, fact!" said the gentleman. And "Fact, fact, fact!" repeated Thomas Gradgrind.

"You are to be in all things regulated and governed," said the gentleman, "by fact. We hope to have before long, a board of fact, composed of commissioners of fact, who will force the people to be a people of fact, and of nothing but fact. You must discard the word fancy altogether. You have nothing to do with it. You are not to have, in any object of use or ornament, what would be a contradiction in fact. You don't walk upon flowers in fact; you cannot be allowed to walk upon flowers in carpets.

You don't find that foreign birds and butterflies come and perch upon your crockery; you can not be permitted to paint foreign birds and butterflies upon your crockery. You never meet with quadrupeds going up and down walls; you must have not have quadrupeds represented upon walls. You must use," said the gentleman, "for all these purposes, combinations and modifications (in primary colours) of mathematical figures which are susceptible of proof and demonstration. This is the new discovery. This is fact. This is taste."

The girl curtseyed and sat down. She was very young, and she looked as if she were frightened by the matter of fact prospect the world afforded.

"Now, if Mr. M'Choakumchild," said the gentleman, "will proceed to give his first lesson here, Mr. Gradgrind, I shall be happy, at your request, to observe his mode of procedure."

Mr. Gradgrind was much obliged. "Mr. M'Choakumchild, we only wait for you."

So, Mr. M'Choakumchild began in his best manner. He and some one hundred and forty other schoolmasters, had been lately turned at the same time, in the same factory, on the same principles, like so many pianoforte legs. He had been put through an immense variety of paces, and had answered volumes of head-breaking questions. Orthography, etymology, syntax, and prosody, biography, astronomy, geography, and general cosmography, the sciences of compound proportion, algebra, land-surveying and levelling, vocal music and drawing from models, were all the ends of his ten chilled fingers. He had worked his stony way into Her Majesty's most Honourable Privy Council's Schedule B, and had taken the bloom off the higher branches of mathematics and physical science, French, German, Latin, and Greek. He knew all about all the Water Sheds of all the world (whatever they are), and all the histories of all the peoples, and all the names of all the rivers and mountains, and all the productions, manners, and customs of all the countries, and all their boundaries and bearings on the two and thirty points of the compass. Ah, rather overdone, M'Choakumchild. If he had only learned a little less, how infinitely better he might have been taught much more!

He went to work in this preparatory lesson, not unlike Morgiana in the Forty Thieves: looking into all the vessels ranged before him, one after another, to see what they contained. Say, good M'Chaokumchild. When from thy boiling store, thou shalt fill each jar brim full by and by, dost thou think that thou wilt always kill outright the robber Fancy lurking within—or sometimes only maim him and distort him!

Questions

1. What is the view of education which underlies Mr. Gradgrind's school? Your analysis should include particular attention to his emphasis on "Facts" and the manner in which children are viewed (e.g., the narrator characterizing the students as "vessels," Gradgrind referring to them by number, and so on).

2. If Euthyphro had attended Mr. Gradgrind's school, would he have been able to answer Socrates' questions? Explain.

3. What is an education *for*? Some people have contended that all education is, or should be, career education. If that is so, is Gradgrind's method correct? If that view is mistaken, or confused, how would you convince Mr.Gradgrind that it is?

4. What should be the role of government in education?

5. What is "Fancy"? For what might it be used?

6. What happens when "Fancy" is "maimed and distorted"?

11

Keeping an Oath

The Controversy

[Grigory—a loyal serf of the Karamazov estate. He, more than their father, had raised the brothers.

Fyodor (Pavlovitch) Karamazov—the patriarch (as it were) of the estate. (Most of the property had been acquired with his wives' money.)

Smerdyakov—presumably Fyodor's bastard son by "stinking Lizaveta." (She was a mentally retarded girl whom, rumor had it, Fyodor had raped. She died giving birth to Smerdyakov in the Karamazov garden house.) Grigory had raised Smerdyakov as a serf on the estate.

Ivan Karamazov—Fyodor's first son by his second wife. He is an intellectual who lives in Moscow but is home to discuss property matters with his father.

Alyosha Karamazov—Fyodor's second son by his second wife. He still lives at home but is considering entering a monastery.
                                                         editor]

Reprinted with permission of Macmillan Publishing Co., Inc., from *The Brothers Karamazov*, by Fyodor Dostoevsky, translated by Constance Garnett. Published in the United States by Macmillan Publishing Co., Inc.

But Balaam's ass had suddenly spoken. The subject was a strange one. Grigory had gone in the morning to make purchases, and had heard from the shopkeeper Lukyanov the story of a Russian soldier which had appeared in the newspaper of that day. This soldier had been taken prisoner in some remote part of Asia, and was threatened with an immediate agonizing death if he did not renounce Christianity and follow Islam. He refused to deny his faith, and was tortured, flayed alive, and died, praising and glorifying Christ. Grigory had related the story at table. Fyodor Pavlovitch always liked, over the dessert after dinner, to laugh and talk, if only with Grigory. This afternoon he was in a particularly good-humored and expansive mood. Sipping his brandy and listening to the story, he observed that they ought to make a saint of a soldier like that, and to take his skin to some monastery. "That would make the people flock, and bring the money in."

Grigory frowned, seeing that Fyodor Pavlovitch was by no means touched, but, as usual, was beginning to scoff. At that moment Smerdyakov, who was standing by the door, smiled. Smerdyakov often waited at table towards the end of dinner, and since Ivan's arrival in our town he had done so every day.

"What are you grinning at?" asked Fyodor Pavlovitch, catching the smile instantly, and knowing that it referred to Grigory.

"Well, my opinion is," Smerdyakov began suddenly and unexpectedly in a loud voice, "that if that laudable soldier's exploit was so very great there would have been, to my thinking, no sin in it if he had on such an emergency renounced, so to speak, the name of Christ and his own christening, to save by that same his life, for good deeds, by which, in the course of years to expiate his cowardice."

"How could it not be a sin? You're talking nonsense. For that you'll go straight to hell and be roasted there like mutton," put in Fyodor Pavlovitch.

It was at this point that Alyosha came in, and Fyodor Pavlovitch, as we have seen, was highly delighted at his appearance.

"We're on your subject, your subject," he chuckled gleefully, making Alyosha sit down to listen.

"As for mutton, that's not so, and there'll be nothing there for this, and there shouldn't be either, if it's according to justice," Smerdyakov maintained stoutly.

"How do you mean 'according to justice'?" Fyodor Pavlovitch cried still more gayly, nudging Alyosha with his knee.

"He's a rascal, that's what he is!" burst from Grigory. He looked Smerdyakov wrathfully in the face.

"As for being a rascal, wait a little, Grigory Vassilyevitch," answered Smerdyakov with perfect composure. "You'd better consider yourself that, once I am taken prisoner by the enemies of the Christian race, and they demand from me to curse the name of God and to renounce my holy christening, I am fully entitled to act by my own reason, since there would be no sin in it."

"But you've said that before. Don't waste words. Prove it," cried Fyodor Pavlovitch.

"Soup-maker!" muttered Grigory contemptuously.

"As for being a soup-maker, wait a bit, too, and consider for yourself, Grigory Vassilyevitch, without abusing me. For as soon as I say to those enemies, 'No, I'm not a Christian, and I curse my true God,' then at once, by God's high judgment, I become immediately and specially anathema accursed, and am cut off from the Holy Church, exactly as though I were a heathen, so that at that very instant, not only when I say it aloud, but when I think of saying it, before a quarter of a second has passed, I am cut off. Is that so or not, Grigory Vassilyevitch?"

He addressed Grigory with obvious satisfaction, though he was really answering Fyodor Pavlovitch's questions, and was well aware of it, and intentionally pretending that Grigory had asked the questions.

"Ivan," cried Fyodor Pavlovitch suddenly, "stoop down for me to whisper. He's got this all up for your benefit. He wants you to praise him. Praise him."

Ivan listened with perfect seriousness to his father's excited whisper.

"Stay, Smerdyakov, be quiet a minute," cried Fyodor Pavlovitch once more. "Ivan, your ear again."

Ivan bent down again with a perfectly grave face.

"I love you as I do Alyosha. Don't think I don't love you. Some brandy?"

"Yes.—But you're rather drunk yourself," thought Ivan, looking steadily at his father.

He was watching Smerdyakov with great curiosity.

"You're anathema accursed, as it is," Grigory suddenly burst out, "and how dare you argue, you rascal, after that, if—"

"Don't scold him, Grigory, don't scold him," Fyodor Pavlovitch cut him short.

"You should wait, Grigory Vassilyevitch, if only a short time, and listen, for I haven't finished all I had to say. For at the very moment I become accursed, at that same highest moment, I become exactly like a heathen, and my christening is taken off me and becomes of no avail. Isn't that so?"

"Make haste and finish, my boy," Fyodor Pavlovitch urged him, sipping from his wine-glass with relish.

"And if I've ceased to be a Christian, then I told no lie to the enemy when they asked whether I was a Christian or not a Christian, seeing I had already been relieved by God Himself of my Christianity by reason of the thought alone, before I had time to utter a word to the enemy. And if I have already been discharged, in what manner and with what sort of justice can I be held responsible as a Christian in the other world for having denied Christ, when, through the very thought alone, before denying Him I had been relieved from my christening? If I'm no longer a Christian, then I can't renounce Christ, for I've nothing then to renounce. Who will hold an unclean Tatar responsible, Grigory Vassilyevitch, even in heaven, for not having been born a Christian? And who would punish him for that, considering that you can't take two skins off one ox? For God Almighty Himself, even if He did make the Tatar responsible, when he dies would give him the smallest possible punishment, I imagine (since he must be punished), judging that he is not to blame if he has come into the world an unclean heathen, from heathen parents. The Lord God can't surely take a Tatar and say he was a Christian? That would mean that the Almighty would tell a real untruth. And can the Lord of Heaven and earth tell a lie, even in one word?"

Grigory was thunderstruck and looked at the orator, his eyes nearly starting out of his head. Though he did not clearly understand what was said, he had caught something in this rigmarole, and stood, looking like a man who has just hit his head against a wall. Fyodor Pavlovitch emptied his glass and went off into his shrill laugh.

"Alyosha! Alyosha! What do you say to that! Ah, you casuist! He must have been with the Jesuits, somewhere, Ivan. Oh, you stinking Jesuit, who taught you? But you're talking nonsense, you casuist, nonsense, nonsense, nonsense. Don't cry, Grigory, we'll reduce him to smoke and ashes in a moment. Tell me this, O ass; you may be right before your enemies, but you have renounced your faith all the same in your own heart, and you say yourself that in that very hour you became anathema accursed. And if once you're anathema they won't pat you on the head for it in hell. What do you say to that, my fine Jesuit?"

"There is no doubt that I have renounced it in my own heart, but there was no special sin in that. Or if there was sin, it was the most ordinary."

"How's that the most ordinary?"

"You lie, accursed one!" hissed Grigory.

"Consider yourself, Grigory Vassilyevitch," Smerdyakov went on, staid and unruffled, conscious of his triumph, but, as it were, generous to the vanquished foe. "Consider yourself, Grigory Vassilyevitch; it is said in the Scripture that if you have faith, even as a mustard seed, and bid a mountain move into the sea, it will move without the least delay at your bidding. Well, Grigory Vassilyevitch, if I'm without faith and you have so great a faith that you are continually swearing at me, you try yourself telling this mountain, not to move into the sea for that's a long way off, but even to our stinking little river which runs at the bottom of the garden. You'll see for yourself that it won't budge, but will remain just where it is however much you shout at it, and that shows, Grigory Vassilyevitch, that you haven't faith in the proper manner, and only abuse others about it. Again, taking into consideration that no one in our day, not only you, but actually no one, from the highest person to the lowest peasant, can shove mountains into the sea—except perhaps some one man in the world, or, at most, two, and they most likely are saving their souls in secret somewhere in the Egyptian desert, so you wouldn't find them —if so it be, if all the rest have no faith, will God curse all the rest? that is, the population of the whole earth, except about two hermits in the desert, and in His well-known mercy will He not forgive one of them? And so I'm persuaded that though I may once have doubted I shall be forgiven if I shed tears of repentance."

"Stay!" cried Fyodor Pavlovitch, in a transport of delight. "So you do suppose there are two who can move mountains? Ivan, make a note of it, write it down. There you have the Russian all over!"

"You're quite right in saying it's characteristic of the people's faith," Ivan assented, with an approving smile.

"You agree. Then it must be so, if you agree. It's true, isn't it, Alyosha? That's the Russian faith all over, isn't it?"

"No, Smerdyakov has not the Russian faith at all," said Alyosha firmly and gravely.

"I'm not talking about his faith. I mean those two in the desert, only that idea. Surely that's Russian, isn't it?"

"Yes, that's purely Russian," said Alyosha smiling.

"Your words are worth a gold piece, O ass, and I'll give it to you to-day. But as to the rest you talk nonsense, nonsense, nonsense. Let me tell you, stupid, that we here are all of little faith, only from carelessness, because we haven't time; things are too much for us, and, in the second place, the Lord God has given us so little time, only twenty-four hours in the day, so that one hasn't even time to get sleep enough, much less to repent of one's sins. While you have denied your faith to your enemies when you'd nothing else to think about but to show your faith! So I consider, brother, that it constitutes a sin."

"Constitute a sin it may, but consider yourself, Grigory Vassilyevitch, that it only extenuates it, if it does constitute. If I had believed then in very truth, as I ought to have believed, then it really would have been sinful if I had not faced tortures for my faith, and had gone over to the pagan Mohammedan faith. But, of course, it wouldn't have come to torture then, because I should only have had to say at that

instant to the mountain, 'Move and crush the tormentor,' and it would have moved and at the very instant have crushed him like a black-beetle, and I should have walked away as though nothing had happened, praising and glorifying God. But, suppose at that very moment I had tried all that, and cried to that mountain, 'Crush these tormentors,' and it hadn't crushed them, how could I have helped doubting, pray, at such a time, and at such a dread hour of mortal terror? And apart from that, I should know already that I could not attain to the fullness of the Kingdom of Heaven (for since the mountain had not moved at my word, they could not think very much of my faith up aloft, and there could be no very great reward awaiting me in the world to come). So why should I let them flay the skin off me as well, and to no good purpose? For, even though they had flayed my skin half off my back, even then the mountain would not have moved at my word or at my cry. And at such a moment not only doubt might come over one but one might lose one's reason from fear, so that one would not be able to think at all. And, therefore, how should I be particularly to blame if not seeing my advantage or reward there or here, I should, at least, save my skin. And so trusting fully in the grace of the Lord I should cherish the hope that I might be altogether forgiven."

Questions

1. There is a good deal of what is called *ad hominem* argument here. Is this form of argument sometimes appropriate? Consider what it is *to argue* about a generality and to *argue to the person* concerning a specific incident. Explain.

2. Consider the content of Smerdyakov's argument. Has he discovered a loophole in the "logic of God"? Does this mean that any "soup-maker" can confound God? What conception of Deity is involved in the argument?

3. Why *didn't* the soldier act as Smerdyakov would have had him act? Was the soldier not quick-witted or intelligent enough?

4. What was the nature of the Russian soldier's obligation?

5. How many mountain-movers would it take to show that there is genuine faith (or "faith in the proper manner")?

6. What does it mean to be "of little faith . . . only from carelessness"? What contrast is Fyodor suggesting?

7. If you are working with a text of ethical theories, describe this episode in terms of the theories you have studied. It might be particularly helpful to evaluate it from the perspectives of Thomas Aquinas, Kant, Moore, and Prichard.

12

Christian Ethics?

God Sees the Truth, but Waits

In the town of Vladímir lived a young merchant named Iván Dmítrich Aksënov. He had two shops and a house of his own.

Aksënov was a handsome, fair-haired, curly-headed fellow, full of fun and very fond of singing. When quite a young man he had been given to drink and was riotous when he had had too much; but after he married he gave up drinking except now and then.

One summer Aksënov was going to the Nizhny Fair, and as he bade good-bye to his family his wife said to him, "Iván Dmítrich, do not start to-day; I have had a bad dream about you."

Aksënov laughed, and said, "You are afraid that when I get to the fair I shall go on the spree."

His wife replied: "I do not know what I am afraid of; all I know is that I had a bad dream. I dreamt you returned from the

Reprinted from *Twenty-Three Tales,* by Leo Tolstoy, translated by Louise and Aylmer Maude (London: Oxford University Press, 1965).

town, and when you took off your cap I saw that your hair was quite grey."

Aksënov laughed. "That's a lucky sign," said he. "See if I don't sell out all my goods and bring you some presents from the fair."

So he said good-bye to his family and drove away.

When he had travelled half-way, he met a merchant whom he knew, and they put up at the same inn for the night. They had some tea together, and then went to bed in adjoining rooms.

It was not Aksënov's habit to sleep late, and, wishing to travel while it was still cool, he aroused his driver before dawn and told him to put in the horses.

Then he made his way across to the landlord of the inn (who lived in a cottage at the back), paid his bill, and continued his journey.

When he had gone about twenty-five miles he stopped for the horses to be fed. Askënov rested awhile in the passage of the inn, then he stepped out into the porch and, ordering a *samovár*[1] to be heated, got out his guitar and began to play.

Suddenly a *tróyka*[2] drove up with tinkling bells, and an official alighted, followed by two soldiers. He came to Aksënov and began to question him, asking him who he was and whence he came. Aksënov answered him fully, and said, "Won't you have some tea with me?" But the official went on cross-questioning him and asking him, "Where did you spend last night? Were you alone, or with a fellow-merchant? Did you see the other merchant this morning? Why did you leave the inn before dawn?"

Aksënov wondered why he was asked all these questions, but he described all that had happened, and then added, "Why do you cross-question me as if I were a thief or a robber? I am travelling on business of my own, and there is no need to question me."

Then the official, calling the soldiers, said, "I am the police-officer of this district, and I question you because the merchant with whom you spent last night has been found with his throat cut. We must search your things."

They entered the house. The soldiers and the police-officer unstrapped Aksënov's luggage and searched it. Suddenly the officer drew a knife out of a bag, crying, "Whose knife is this?"

Aksënov looked, and seeing a blood-stained knife taken from his bag, he was frightened.

"How is it there is blood on this knife?"

Aksënov tried to answer, but could hardly utter a word, and only stammered: "I—don't know—not mine."

Then the police-officer said, "This morning the merchant was found in bed with his throat cut. You are the only person who could have done it. The house was locked from inside, and no one else was there. Here is this blood-stained knife in your bag, and your face and manner betray you! Tell me how you killed him and how much money you stole?"

Aksënov swore he had not done it; that he had not seen the merchant after they had had tea together; that he had no money except eight thousand rúbles of his own, and that the knife was not his. But his voice was broken, his face pale, and he trembled with fear as though he were guilty.

The police-officer ordered the soldiers to bind Aksënov and to put him in the cart. As they tied his feet together and flung him into the cart, Aksënov crossed himself and wept. His money and goods were taken from him, and he was sent to the nearest town and imprisoned there. Enquiries as to his character were made in Vladímir. The merchants and other inhabitants of that town said that in former days he used to drink and waste his time, but that he was a good man. Then the trial came on: he was charged with murdering a merchant from Ryazán and robbing him of twenty thousand rúbles.

His wife was in despair, and did not know what to believe. Her children were all quite small; one was a baby at the breast. Taking them all with her, she went to the town where her husband was in gaol. At first she was not allowed to see him; but, after much begging, she obtained permission from the officials and was taken to him. When she saw her husband in prison-dress and in chains, shut up with thieves and criminals, she fell down and did not come to her senses for a long time. Then she drew her children to her, and sat down near him. She told him of things at home, and asked about what had happened to him. He told her all, and she asked, "What can we do now?"

"We must petition the Tsar not to let an innocent man perish."

His wife told him that she had sent a petition to the Tsar, but that it had not been accepted.

Aksënov did not reply, but only looked downcast.

Then his wife said, "It was not for nothing I dreamt your hair had turned grey. You remember? You should not have started that day." And passing her fingers through

---

[1]The *samovár* ("self-boiler") is an urn in which water can be heated and kept on the boil.

[2]A three-horse conveyance.

his hair she said: "Ványa dearest, tell your wife the truth; was it not you who did it?"

"So you, too, suspect me!" said Aksënov, and, hiding his face in his hands, he began to weep. Then a soldier came to say that the wife and children must go away, and Aksënov said good-bye to his family for the last time.

When they were gone, Aksënov recalled what had been said, and when he remembered that his wife also had suspected him, he said to himself, "It seems that only God can know the truth; it is to Him alone we must appeal and from Him alone expect mercy."

And Aksënov wrote no more petitions, gave up all hope, and only prayed to God.

Aksënov was condemned to be flogged and sent to the mines. So he was flogged with a knout, and when the wounds caused by the knout were healed, he was driven to Siberia with other convicts.

For twenty-six years Aksënov lived as a convict in Siberia. His hair turned white as snow, and his beard grew long, thin, and grey. All his mirth went; he stooped; he walked slowly, spoke little, and never laughed, but he often prayed.

In prison Aksënov learnt to make boots, and earned a little money, with which he bought *The Lives of the Saints.* He read this book when it was light enough in the prison; and on Sundays in the prison-church he read the epistle and sang in the choir, for his voice was still good.

The prison authorities liked Aksënov for his meekness, and his fellow-prisoners respected him; they called him "Grandfather," and "The Saint." When they wanted to petition the prison authorities about anything, they always made Aksënov their spokesman, and when there were quarrels among the prisoners they came to him to put things right, and to judge the matter.

No news reached Aksënov from his home, and he did not even know if his wife and children were still alive.

One day a fresh gang of convicts came to the prison. In the evening the old prisoners collected round the new ones and asked them what towns or villages they came from, and what they were sentenced for. Among the rest Aksënov sat down near the new-comers, and listened with downcast air to what was said.

One of the new convicts, a tall, strong man of sixty, with a closely-cropped grey beard, was telling the others what he had been arrested for.

"Well, friends," he said, "I only took a horse that was tied to a sledge, and I was arrested and accused of stealing. I said I had only taken it to get home quicker, and had then let it go; besides, the driver was a personal friend of mine. So I said, 'It's all right.' 'No,' said they, 'you stole it.' But how or where I stole it they could not say. I once really did something wrong, and ought by rights to have come here long ago, but that time I was not found out. Now I have been sent here for nothing at all . . . Eh, but it's lies I'm telling you; I've been to Siberia before, but I did not stay long."

"Where are you from?" asked some one.

"From Vladímir. My family are of that town. My name is Makár, and they also call me Semënich."

Aksënov raised his head and said: "Tell me, Semënich, do you know anything of the merchants Aksënov, of Vladímir? Are they still alive?"

"Know them? Of course I do. The Aksënovs are rich, though their father is in Siberia: a sinner like ourselves, it seems! As for you, Gran'dad, how did you come here?"

Aksënov did not like to speak of his misfortune. He only sighed, and said, "For my sins I have been in prison these twenty-six years."

"What sins?" asked Makár Semënich.

But Aksënov only said, "Well, well—I must have deserved it!" He would have said no more, but his companions told the new-comer how Aksënov came to be in Siberia: how some one had killed a merchant and had put a knife among Aksënov's things, and he had been unjustly condemned.

When Makár Semënich heard this he looked at Aksënov, slapped his own knee, and exclaimed, "Well, this is wonderful! Really wonderful! But how old you've grown, Gran'dad!"

The others asked him why he was so surprised, and where he had seen Aksënov before; but Makár Semënich did not reply. He only said: "It's wonderful that we should meet here, lads!"

These words made Aksënov wonder whether this man knew who had killed the merchant; so he said, "Perhaps, Semënich, you have heard of that affair, or maybe you've seen me before?"

"How could I help hearing? The world's full of rumours. But it's long ago, and I've forgotten what I heard."

"Perhaps you heard who killed the merchant?" asked Aksënov.

Makár Semënich laughed, and replied, "It must have been him in whose bag the knife was found! If some one else hid the knife there—'He's not a thief till he's caught,' as the saying is. How could any one put a knife into your bag while it was under your head? It would surely have woke you up?"

When Aksënov heard these words he felt sure this was the man who had killed the merchant. He rose and went away. All that night Aksënov lay awake. He felt terribly unhappy, and all sorts of images rose in his mind. There was the image of his wife as she was when he parted from her to go to the fair. He saw her as if she were present; her face and her eyes rose before him, he heard her speak and laugh. Then he saw his children, quite little, as they were at that time: one with a little cloak on, another at his mother's breast. And then he remembered himself as he used to be—young and merry. He remembered how he sat playing the guitar in the porch of the inn where he was arrested, and how free from care he had been. He saw in his mind the place where he was flogged, the executioner, and the people standing around; the chains, the convicts, all the twenty-six years of his prison life, and his premature old age. The

thought of it all made him so wretched that he was ready to kill himself.

"And it's all that villain's doing!" thought Aksënov. And his anger was so great against Makár Semënich that he longed for vengeance, even if he himself should perish for it. He kept saying prayers all night, but could get no peace. During the day he did not go near Makár Semënich, nor even look at him.

A fortnight passed in this way. Aksënov could not sleep at nights and was so miserable that he did not know what to do.

One night as he was walking about the prison he noticed some earth that came rolling out from under one of the shelves on which the prisoners slept. He stopped to see what it was. Suddenly Makár Semënich crept out from under the shelf, and looked up at Aksënov with frightened face. Aksënov tried to pass without looking at him, but Makár seized his hand and told him that he had dug a hole under the wall, getting rid of the earth by putting it into his high boots and emptying it out every day on the road when the prisoners were driven to their work.

"Just you keep quiet, old man, and you shall get out too. If you blab they'll flog the life out of me, but I will kill you first."

Aksënov trembled with anger as he looked at his enemy. He drew his hand away, saying, "I have no wish to escape, and you have no need to kill me; you killed me long ago! As to telling of you—I may do so or not, as God shall direct."

Next day, when the convicts were led out to work, the convoy soldiers noticed that one or the other of the prisoners emptied some earth out of his boots. The prison was searched and the tunnel found. The Governor came and questioned all the prisoners to find out who had dug the hole. They all denied any knowledge of it. Those who knew would not betray Makár Semënich, knowing he would be flogged almost to death. At last the Governor turned to Aksënov, whom he knew to be a just man, and said:

"You are a truthful old man; tell me, before God, who dug the hole?"

Makár Semënich stood as if he were quite unconcerned, looking at the Governor and not so much as glancing at Aksënov. Aksënov's lips and hands trembled, and for a long time he could not utter a word. He thought, "Why should I screen him who ruined my life? Let him pay for what I have suffered. But if I tell, they will probably flog the life out of him, and maybe I suspect him wrongly. And, after all, what good would it be to me?"

"Well, old man," repeated the Governor, "tell us the truth: who has been digging under the wall?"

Aksënov glanced at Makár Semënich and said, "I cannot say, your honour. It is not God's will that I should tell! Do what you like with me; I am in your hands."

However much the Governor tried, Aksënov would say no more, and so the matter had to be left.

That night, when Aksënov was lying on his bed and just beginning to doze, some one came quietly and sat down on his bed. He peered through the darkness and recognized Makár.

"What more do you want of me?" asked Aksënov. "Why have you come here?"

Makár Semënich was silent. So Aksënov sat up and said, "What do you want? Go away or I will call the guard!"

Makár Semënich bent close over Aksënov, and whispered, "Iván Dmítrich, forgive me!"

"What for?" asked Aksënov.

"It was I who killed the merchant and hid the knife among your things. I meant to kill you too, but I heard a noise outside; so I hid the knife in your bag and escaped through the window."

Aksënov was silent and did not know what to say. Makár Semënich slid off the bed-shelf and knelt upon the ground. "Iván Dmítrich," said he, "forgive me! For the love of God, forgive me! I will confess that it was I who killed the merchant, and you will be released and can go to your home."

"It is easy for you to talk," said Aksënov, "but I have suffered for you these twenty-six years. Where could I go to now? . . . My wife is dead, and my children have forgotten me. I have nowhere to go. . . ."

Makár Semënich did not rise, but beat his head on the floor. "Iván Dmítrich, forgive me!" he cried. "When they flogged me with the knout it was not so hard to bear as it is to see you now . . . yet you had pity on me and did not tell. For Christ's sake forgive me, wretch that I am!" And he began to sob.

When Aksënov heard him sobbing he, too, began to weep.

"God will forgive you!" said he. "Maybe I am a hundred times worse than you." And at these words his heart grew light and the longing for home left him. He no longer had any desire to leave the prison, but only hoped for his last hour to come.

In spite of what Aksënov had said, Makár Semënich confessed his guilt. But when the order for his release came, Aksënov was already dead.

(Written in 1872.)

Where Love Is, God Is

In a certain town there lived a cobbler, Martin Avdéich by name. He had a tiny room in a basement, the one window of which looked out on to the street. Through it one could only see the feet of those who passed by, but Martin recognized the people by their boots. He had lived long in the place and had many acquaintances. There was hardly a pair of boots in the neighbourhood that had not been once or twice through his hands, so he often saw his own handiwork through the window. Some he had resoled, some patched, some stitched up, and to some he had even put fresh uppers. He had plenty to do, for he worked well, used good material, did not charge too much, and could be relied on. If he could do a job by the day required, he undertook it; if not, he told the truth and gave no false promises; so he was well known and never short of work.

Martin had always been a good man, but in his old age he began to think more about his soul and to draw nearer to God. While he still worked for a master, before he set up on his own account, his wife had died, leaving him with a three-year-old son. None of his elder children had lived, they had all died in infancy. At first Martin thought of sending his little son to his sister's in the country, but then he felt sorry to part with the boy, thinking: "It would be hard for my little Kapitón to have to grow up in a strange family, I will keep him with me."

Martin left his master and went into lodgings with his little son. But he had no luck with his children. No sooner had the boy reached an age when he could help his father and be a support as well as a joy to him, than he fell ill and, after being laid up for a week with a burning fever, died. Martin buried his son, and gave way to despair so great and overwhelming that he murmured against God. In his sorrow he prayed again and again that he too might die, reproaching God for having taken the son he loved, his only son, while he, old as he was, remained alive. After that Martin left off going to church.

One day an old man from Martin's native village, who had been a pilgrim for the last eight years, called in on his way from the Tróitsa Monastery. Martin opened his heart to him and told him of his sorrow.

"I no longer even wish to live, holy man," he said. "All I ask of God is that I soon may die. I am now quite without hope in the world."

The old man replied: "You have no right to say such things, Martin. We cannot judge God's ways. Not our reasoning, but God's will, decides. If God willed that your son should die and you should live, it must be best so. As to your despair—that comes because you wish to live for your own happiness."

"What else should one live for?" asked Martin.

"For God, Martin," said the old man. "He gives you life, and you must live for Him. When you have learnt to live for Him, you will grieve no more, and all will seem easy to you."

Martin was silent awhile, and then asked: "But how is one to live for God?"

The old man answered: "How one may live for God has been shown us by Christ. Can you read? Then buy the Gospels and read them: there you will see how God would have you live. You have it all there."

These words sank deep into Martin's heart, and that same day he went and bought himself a Testament in large print, and began to read.

At first he meant only to read on holidays, but having once begun he found it made his heart so light that he read every day. Sometimes he was so absorbed in his reading that the oil in his lamp burnt out before he could tear himself away from the book. He continued to read every night, and the more he read the more clearly he understood what God required of him, and how he might live for God. And his heart grew lighter and lighter. Before, when he went to bed he used to lie with a heavy heart, moaning as he thought of his little Kapitón; but now he only repeated again and again: "Glory to Thee, glory to Thee, O Lord! Thy will be done!"

From that time Martin's whole life changed. Formerly, on holidays he used to go and have tea at the public-house and did not even refuse a glass or two of vódka. Sometimes, after having had a drop with a friend, he left the public-house not drunk, but rather merry, and would say foolish things: shout at a man, or abuse him. Now all that sort of thing passed away from him. His life became peaceful and joyful. He sat down to his work in the morning, and when he had finished his day's work he took the lamp down from the wall, stood it on the table, fetched his book from the shelf, opened it, and sat down to read. The more he read the better he understood and the clearer and happier he felt in his mind.

It happened once that Martin sat up late, absorbed in his book. He was reading Luke's Gospel; and in the sixth chapter he came upon the verses:

"To him that smiteth thee on the one cheek offer also the other; and from him that taketh away thy cloke withhold not thy coat also. Give to every man that asketh thee; and of him that taketh away thy goods ask them not again. And as ye would that men should do to you, do ye also to them likewise."

He also read the verses where our Lord says:

"And why call ye me, Lord, Lord, and do not the things which I say? Whosoever cometh to me, and heareth my sayings, and doeth them, I will shew you to whom he is like: He is like a man which built an house, and digged deep, and laid the foundation on a rock: and when the flood arose, the stream beat vehemently upon that house, and could not shake it: for it was founded upon a rock. But he that heareth, and doeth not, is like a man that without a foundation built an house upon the earth, against which the stream did beat vehemently, and immediately it fell; and the ruin of that house was great."

When Martin read these words his soul was glad within him. He took off his spectacles and laid them on the book, and leaning his elbows on the table pondered over what he had read. He tried his own life by the standard of those words, asking himself:

"Is my house built on the rock, or on sand? If it stands on the rock, it is well. It seems easy enough while one sits here alone, and one thinks one has done all that God commands; but as soon as I cease to be on my guard, I sin again. Still I will persevere. It brings such joy. Help me, O Lord!"

He thought all this, and was about to go to bed, but was loth to leave his book. So he went on reading the seventh chapter—about the centurion, the widow's son, and the answer to John's disciples—and he came to the part where a rich Pharisee invited the Lord to his house; and he read how the woman who was a sinner, anointed his feet and washed them with her tears, and how he justified her. Coming to the forty-fourth verse, he read:

"And turning to the woman, he said unto Simon, Seest thou this woman? I entered into thine house, thou gavest me no water for my feet: but she hath wetted my feet with her tears, and wiped them with her hair. Thou gavest me no kiss; but she, since the time I came in, hath not ceased to kiss my feet. My head with oil thou didst not anoint: but she hath anointed my feet with ointment."

He read these verses and thought: "He gave no water for his feet, gave no kiss, his head with oil he did not anoint. . . ." And Martin took off his spectacles once more, laid them on his book, and pondered.

"He must have been like me, that Pharisee. He too thought only of himself—how to get a cup of tea, how to keep warm and comfortable; never a thought of his guest. He took care of himself, but for his guest he cared nothing at all. Yet who was the guest? The Lord himself! If he came to me, should I behave like that?"

Then Martin laid his head upon both his arms and, before he was aware of it, he fell asleep.

"Martin!" he suddenly heard a voice, as if some one had breathed the word above his ear.

He started from his sleep. "Who's there?" he asked.

He turned round and looked at the door; no one was there. He called again. Then he heard quite distinctly: "Martin, Martin! Look out into the street to-morrow, for I shall come."

Martin roused himself, rose from his chair and rubbed his eyes, but did not know whether he had heard these words in a dream or awake. He put out the lamp and lay down to sleep.

Next morning he rose before daylight and after saying his prayers he lit the fire and prepared his cabbage soup and buckwheat porridge. Then he lit the samovár, put on his apron, and sat down by the window to his work. As he sat working Martin thought over what had happened the night before. At times it seemed to him like a dream, and at times he thought that he had really heard the voice. "Such things have happened before now," thought he.

So he sat by the window, looking out into the street more than he worked, and whenever any one passed in unfamiliar boots he would stoop and look up, so as to see not the feet only but the face of the passer-by as well. A house-porter passed in new felt boots; then a water-carrier. Presently an old soldier of Nicholas' reign came near the window spade in hand. Martin knew him by his boots, which were shabby old felt ones, goloshed with leather. The old man was called Stepánich: a neighbouring tradesman kept him in his house for charity, and his duty was to help the house-porter. He began to clear away the snow before Martin's window. Martin glanced at him and then went on with his work.

"I must be growing crazy with age," said Martin, laughing at his fancy. "Stepánich comes to clear away the snow, and I must needs imagine it's Christ coming to visit me. Old dotard that I am!"

Yet after he had made a dozen stitches he felt drawn to look out of the window again. He saw that Stepánich had leaned his spade against the wall and was either resting himself or trying to get warm. The man was old and broken down, and had evidently not enough strength even to clear away the snow.

"What if I called him in and gave him some tea?" thought Martin. "The samovár is just on the boil."

He stuck his awl in its place, and rose; and putting the samovár on the table, made tea. Then he tapped the window with his fingers. Stepánich turned and came to the window. Martin beckoned to him to come in and went himself to open the door.

"Come in," he said, "and warm yourself a bit. I'm sure you must be cold."

"May God bless you!" Stepánich answered. "My bones do ache to be sure." He came in, first shaking off the snow, and lest he should leave marks on the floor he began wiping his feet, but as he did so he tottered and nearly fell.

"Don't trouble to wipe your feet," said Martin; "I'll wipe up the floor—it's all in the day's work. Come, friend, sit down and have some tea."

Filling two tumblers, he passed one to his visitor, and pouring his own out into the saucer, began to blow on it.

Stepánich emptied his glass, and, turning it upside down,[3] put the remains of his piece of sugar on the top. He began to express his thanks, but it was plain that he would be glad of some more.

"Have another glass," said Martin, refilling the visitor's tumbler and his own. But while he drank his tea Martin kept looking out into the street.

"Are you expecting any one?" asked the visitor.

"Am I expecting any one? Well now, I'm ashamed to tell you. It isn't that I really expect any one; but I heard something last night which I can't get out of my mind. Whether it was a vision, or only a fancy, I can't tell. You see, friend, last night I was reading the Gospel, about Christ the Lord, how he suffered and how he walked on earth. You have heard tell of it, I dare say."

"I have heard tell of it," answered Stepánich; "but I'm an ignorant man and not able to read."

"Well, you see, I was reading of how he walked on earth. I came to that part, you

---

[3]Turning the glass upside down was the customary way of intimating that one had had enough.

know, where he went to a Pharisee who did not receive him well. Well, friend, as I read about it, I thought how that man did not receive Christ the Lord with proper honour. Suppose such a thing could happen to such a man as myself, I thought, what would I not do to receive him! But that man gave him no reception at all. Well, friend, as I was thinking of this I began to doze, and as I dozed I heard some one call me by name. I got up, and thought I heard some one whispering, "Expect me; I will come to-morrow." This happened twice over. And to tell you the truth, it sank so into my mind that, though I am ashamed of it myself, I keep on expecting him, the dear Lord!"

Stepánich shook his head in silence, finished his tumbler and laid it on its side; but Martin stood it up again and refilled it for him.

"Here, drink another glass, bless you! And I was thinking, too, how he walked on earth and despised no one, but went mostly among common folk. He went with plain people, and chose his disciples from among the likes of us, from workmen like us, sinners that we are. 'He who raises himself,' he said, 'shall be humbled; and he who humbles himself shall be raised.' 'You call me Lord,' he said, 'and I will wash your feet.' 'He who would be first,' he said, 'let him be the servant of all; because', he said, 'blessed are the poor, the humble, the meek, and the merciful.' "

Stepánich forgot his tea. He was an old man, easily moved to tears, and as he sat and listened the tears ran down his cheeks.

"Come, drink some more," said Martin. But Stepánich crossed himself, thanked him, moved away his tumbler, and rose.

"Thank you, Martin Avdéich," he said, "you have given me food and comfort both for soul and body."

"You're very welcome. Come again another time. I am glad to have a guest," said Martin.

Stepánich went away; and Martin poured out the last of the tea and drank it up. Then he put away the tea things and sat down to his work, stitching the back seam of a boot. And as he stitched he kept looking out of the window, waiting for Christ and thinking about him and his doings. And his head was full of Christ's sayings.

Two soldiers went by: one in Government boots, the other in boots of his own; then the master of a neighbouring house, in shining goloshes; then a baker carrying a basket. All these passed on. Then a woman came up in worsted stockings and peasant-made shoes. She passed the window, but stopped by the wall. Martin glanced up at her through the window and saw that she was a stranger, poorly dressed and with a baby in her arms. She stopped by the wall with her back to the wind, trying to wrap the baby up though she had hardly anything to wrap it in. The woman had only summer clothes on, and even they were shabby and worn. Through the window Martin heard the baby crying, and the woman trying to soothe it but unable to do so. Martin rose, and going out of the door and up the steps he called to her.

"My dear, I say, my dear!"

The woman heard and turned round.

"Why do you stand out there with the baby in the cold? Come inside. You can wrap him up better in a warm place. Come this way!"

The woman was surprised to see an old man in an apron, with spectacles on his nose, calling to her, but she followed him in.

They went down the steps, entered the little room, and the old man led her to the bed.

"There, sit down, my dear, near the stove. Warm yourself and feed the baby."

"Haven't any milk. I have eaten nothing myself since early morning," said the woman, but still she took the baby to her breast.

Martin shook his head. He brought out a basin and some bread. Then he opened the oven door and poured some cabbage soup into the basin. He took out the porridge pot also, but the porridge was not yet ready, so he spread a cloth on the table and served only the soup and bread.

"Sit down and eat, my dear, and I'll mind the baby. Why, bless me, I've had children of my own; I know how to manage them."

The woman crossed herself, and sitting down at the table began to eat, while Martin put the baby on the bed and sat down by it. He chucked and chucked, but having no teeth he could not do it well and the baby continued to cry. Then Martin tried poking at him with his finger; he drove his finger straight at the baby's mouth and then quickly drew it back, and did this again and again. He did not let the baby take his finger in its mouth, because it was all black with cobbler's wax. But the baby first grew quiet watching the finger, and then began to laugh. And Martin felt quite pleased.

The woman sat eating and talking, and told him who she was, and where she had been.

"I'm a soldier's wife," said she. "They sent my husband somewhere, far away, eight months ago, and I have heard nothing of him since. I had a place as cook till my baby was born, but then they would not keep me with a child. For three months now I have been struggling, unable to find a place, and I've had to sell all I had for food. I tried to go as a wet-nurse, but no one would have me; they said I was too starved-looking and thin. Now I have just been to see a tradesman's wife (a woman from our village is in service with her) and she has promised to take me. I thought it was all settled at last, but she tells me not to come till next week. It is far to her place, and I am fagged out, and baby is quite starved, poor mite. Fortunately our landlady has pity on us, and lets us lodge free, else I don't know what we should do."

Martin sighed. "Haven't you any warmer clothing?" he asked.

"How could I get warm clothing?" said she. "Why, I pawned my last shawl for six-pence yesterday."

Then the woman came and took the child, and Martin got up. He went and looked among some things that were hanging on the wall, and brought back an old cloak.

"Here," he said, "though it's a worn-out old thing, it will do to wrap him up in."

The woman looked at the cloak, then at the old man, and taking it, burst into tears. Martin turned away, and groping under the bed brought out a small trunk. He fumbled about in it, and again sat down opposite the woman. And the woman said:

"The Lord bless you, friend. Surely Christ must have sent me to your window, else the child would have frozen. It was mild when I started, but now see how cold it has turned. Surely it must have been Christ who made you look out of your window and take pity on me, poor wretch!"

Martin smiled and said, "It is quite true; it was He made me do it. It was no mere chance made me look out."

And he told the woman his dream, and how he had heard the Lord's voice promising to visit him that day.

"Who knows? All things are possible," said the woman. And she got up and threw the cloak over her shoulders, wrapping it round herself and round the baby. Then she bowed, and thanked Martin once more.

"Take this for Christ's sake," said Martin, and gave her sixpence to get her shawl out of pawn. The woman crossed herself, and Martin did the same, and then he saw her out.

After the woman had gone, Martin ate some cabbage soup, cleared the things away, and sat down to work again. He sat and worked, but did not forget the window, and every time a shadow fell on it he looked up at once to see who was passing. People he knew and strangers passed by, but no one remarkable.

After a while Martin saw an apple-woman stop just in front of his window. She had a large basket, but there did not seem to be many apples left in it; she had evidently sold most of her stock. On her back she had a sack full of chips, which she was taking home. No doubt she had gathered them at some place where building was going on.

The sack evidently hurt her and she wanted to shift it from one shoulder to the other, so she put it down on the footpath and, placing her basket on a post, began to shake down the chips in the sack. While she was doing this a boy in a tattered cap ran up, snatched an apple out of the basket and tried to slip away; but the old woman noticed it, and turning, caught the boy by his sleeve. He began to struggle, trying to free himself, but the old woman held on with both hands, knocked his cap off his head, and seized hold of his hair. The boy screamed and the old woman scolded. Martin dropped his awl, not waiting to stick it in its place, and rushed out of the door. Stumbling up the steps, and dropping his spectacles in his hurry, he ran out into the street. The old woman was pulling the boy's hair and scolding him, and threatening to take him to the police. The lad was struggling and protesting, saying, "I did not take it. What are you beating me for? Let me go!"

Martin separated them. He took the boy by the hand and said, "Let him go, Granny. He won't do it again. Let him go for Christ's sake!"

The old woman let go, and the boy wished to run away, but Martin stopped him.

"Ask the Granny's forgiveness!" said he. "And don't do it another time. I saw you take the apple."

The boy began to cry and to beg pardon.

"That's right. And now here's an apple for you," and Martin took an apple from the basket and gave it to the boy, saying, "I will pay you, Granny."

"You will spoil them that way, the young rascals," said the old woman. "He ought to be whipped so that he should remember it for a week."

"Oh, Granny, Granny," said Martin, "that's our way—but it's not God's way. If he should be whipped for stealing an apple, what should be done to us for our sins?"

The old woman was silent.

And Martin told her the parable of the lord who forgave his servant a large debt, and how the servant went out and seized his debtor by the throat. The old woman listened to it all, and the boy, too, stood by and listened.

"God bids us forgive," said Martin, "or else we shall not be forgiven. Forgive every one, and a thoughtless youngster most of all."

The old woman wagged her head and sighed.

"It's true enough," said she, "but they are getting terribly spoilt."

"Then we old ones must show them better ways," Martin replied.

"That's just what I say," said the old woman. "I have had seven of them myself, and only one daughter is left." And the old woman began to tell how and where she was living with her daughter, and how many grandchildren she had. "There now," she said, "I have but little strength left, yet I work hard for the sake of my grandchildren; and nice children they are, too. No one comes out to meet me but the children. Little Annie, now, won't leave me for any one. 'It's grandmother, dear grandmother, darling grandmother.'" And the old woman completely softened at the thought.

"Of course it was only his childishness, God help him," said she, referring to the boy.

As the old woman was about to hoist her sack on her back, the lad sprang forward to her, saying, "Let me carry it for you, Granny. I'm going that way."

The old woman nodded her head, and put the sack on the boy's back, and they went down the street together, the old woman quite forgetting to ask Martin to pay for the apple. Martin stood and watched them as they went along talking to each other.

When they were out of sight Martin went back to the house. Having found his spectacles unbroken on the steps, he picked up his awl and sat down again to work. He worked a little, but could soon not see to pass the bristle through the holes in the leather; and presently he noticed the lamplighter passing on his way to light the street lamps.

"Seems it's time to light up," thought he. So he trimmed his lamp, hung it up, and sat down again to work. He finished off one boot and, turning it about, examined it. It was all right. Then he gathered his tools together, swept up the cuttings, put away the bristles and the thread and the awls, and, taking down the lamp placed it on the table. Then he took the Gospels from the shelf. He meant to open them at the place he had marked the day before with a bit of morocco, but the book opened at another place. As Martin opened it, his yesterday's dream came back to his mind, and no sooner had he thought of it than he seemed to hear footsteps, as though some one were moving behind him. Martin turned round, and it seemed to him as if people were standing in the dark corner, but he could not make out who they were. And a voice whispered in his ear: "Martin, Martin, don't you know me?"

"It is I," said the voice. And out of the dark corner stepped Stepánich, who smiled and vanishing like a cloud was seen no more.

"It is I," said the voice again. And out of the darkness stepped the woman with the baby in her arms, and the woman smiled and the baby laughed, and they too vanished.

"It is I," said the voice once more. And the old woman and the boy with the apple stepped out and both smiled, and then they too vanished.

And Martin's soul grew glad. He crossed himself, put on his spectacles, and began reading the Gospel just where it had opened; and at the top of the page he read:

"I was an hungred, and ye gave me meat: I was thirsty, and ye gave me drink: I was a stranger, and ye took me in."

And at the bottom of the page he read:

"Inasmuch as ye did it unto one of these my brethren, even these least, ye did it unto me" (*Matt. xxv*).

And Martin understood that his dream had come true; and that the Saviour had really come to him that day, and he had welcomed him.

1885.

The Three Hermits

An Old Legend Current in the Volga District

"And in praying use not vain repetitions, as the Gentiles do: for they think that they shall be heard for their much speaking. Be not therefore like unto them: for your Father knoweth what things ye have need of, before ye ask Him."—*Matt* vi. 7, 8.

A Bishop was sailing from Archangel to the Solovétsk Monastery, and on the same vessel were a number of pilgrims on their way to visit the shrines at that place. The voyage was a smooth one. The wind favourable and the weather fair. The pilgrims lay on deck, eating, or sat in groups talking to one another. The Bishop, too, came on deck, and as he was pacing up and down he noticed a group of men standing near the prow and listening to a fisherman, who was pointing to the sea and telling them something. The Bishop stopped, and looked in the direction in which the man was pointing. He could see nothing, however, but the sea glistening in the sunshine. He drew nearer to listen, but when the man saw him, he took off his cap and was silent. The rest of the people also took off their caps and bowed.

"Do not let me disturb you, friends," said the Bishop. "I came to hear what this good man was saying."

"The fisherman was telling us about the hermits," replied one, a tradesman, rather bolder than the rest.

"What hermits?" asked the Bishop, going to the side of the vessel and seating himself on a box.

"Tell me about them. I should like to hear. What were you pointing at?"

"Why, that little island you can just see over there," answered the man, pointing to a spot ahead and a little to the right. "That is the island where the hermits live for the salvation of their souls."

"Where is the island?" asked the Bishop. "I see nothing."

"There, in the distance, if you will please look along my hand. Do you see that little cloud? Below it, and a bit to the left, there is just a faint streak. That is the island."

The Bishop looked carefully, but his unaccustomed eyes could make out nothing but the water shimmering in the sun.

"I cannot see it," he said. "But who are the hermits that live there?"

"They are holy men," answered the fisherman. "I had long heard tell of them, but never chanced to see them myself till the year before last."

And the fisherman related how once, when he was out fishing, he had been stranded at night upon that island, not knowing where he was. In the morning, as he wandered about the island, he came across an earth hut, and met an old man standing near it. Presently two others came out, and after having fed him and dried his things, they helped him mend his boat.

"And what are they like?" asked the bishop.

"One is a small man and his back is bent. He wears a priest's cassock and is very old; he must be more than a hundred, I should say. He is so old that the white of his beard is taking a greenish tinge, but he is always smiling, and his face is as bright as an angel's from heaven. The second is taller, but he also is very old. He wears a tattered, peasant coat. His beard is broad, and of a yellowish grey colour. He is a strong man. Before I had time to help him, he turned my boat over as if it were only a pail. He too is kindly and cheerful. The third is tall, and has a beard as white as snow and reaching

to his knees. He is stern, with overhanging eyebrows; and he wears nothing but a piece of matting tied round his waist."

"And did they speak to you?" asked the Bishop.

"For the most part they did everything in silence, and spoke but little even to one another. One of them would just give a glance, and the others would understand him. I asked the tallest whether they had lived there long. He frowned, and muttered something as if he were angry; but the oldest one took his hand and smiled, and then the tall one was quiet. The oldest one only said: 'Have mercy upon us,' and smiled."

While the fisherman was talking, the ship had drawn nearer to the island.

"There, now you can see it plainly, if your Lordship will please to look," said the tradesman, pointing with his hand.

The Bishop looked, and now he really saw a dark streak—which was the island. Having looked at it a while, he left the prow of the vessel, and going to the stern, asked the helmsman:

"What island is that?"

"That one," replied the man, "has no name. There are many such in this sea."

"Is it true that there are hermits who live there for the salvation of their souls?"

"So it is said, your Lordship, but I don't know if it's true. Fishermen say they have seen them; but of course they may only be spinning yarns."

"I should like to land on the island and see these men," said the Bishop. "How could I manage it?"

"The ship cannot get close to the island," replied the helmsman, "but you might be rowed there in a boat. You had better speak to the captain."

The captain was sent for and came.

"I should like to see these hermits," said the Bishop. "Could I not be rowed ashore?"

The captain tried to dissuade him.

"Of course it could be done," said he, "but we should lose much time. And if I might venture to say so to your Lordship, the old men are not worth your pains. I have heard say that they are foolish old fellows, who understand nothing, and never speak a word, any more than the fish in the sea."

"I wish to see them," said the Bishop, "and I will pay you for your trouble and loss of time. Please let me have a boat."

There was no help for it; so the order was given. The sailors trimmed the sails, the steersman put up the helm, and the ship's course was set for the island. A chair was placed at the prow for the Bishop, and he sat there, looking ahead. The passengers all collected at the prow, and gazed at the island. Those who had the sharpest eyes could presently make out the rocks on it, and then a mud hut was seen. At last one man saw the hermits themselves. The captain brought a telescope and, after looking through it, handed it to the Bishop.

"It's right enough. There are three men standing on the shore. There, a little to the right of that big rock."

The Bishop took the telescope, got it into position, and he saw the three men: a tall one, a shorter one, and one very small and bent, standing on the shore and holding each other by the hand.

The captain turned to the Bishop.

"The vessel can get no nearer in than this, your Lordship. If you wish to go ashore, we must ask you to go in the boat, while we anchor here."

The cable was quickly let out; the anchor cast and the sails furled. There was a jerk, and the vessel shook. Then, a boat having been lowered, the oarsmen jumped in, and the Bishop descended the ladder and took his seat. The men pulled at their oars and the boat moved rapidly towards the island. When they came within a stone's throw, they saw three old men: a tall one with only a piece of matting tied round his waist: a shorter one in a tattered peasant coat, and a very old one bent with age and wearing an old cassock—all three standing hand in hand.

The oarsmen pulled in to the shore, and held on with the boathook while the Bishop got out.

The old men bowed to him, and he gave them his blessing, at which they bowed still lower. Then the Bishop began to speak to them.

"I have heard," he said, "that you, godly men, live here saving your own souls and praying to our Lord Christ for your fellow men. I, an unworthy servant of Christ, am called, by God's mercy, to keep and teach His flock. I wished to see you, servants of God, and to do what I can to teach you, also."

The old men looked at each other smiling, but remained silent.

"Tell me," said the Bishop, "what you are doing to save your souls, and how you serve God on this island."

The second hermit sighed, and looked at the oldest, the very ancient one. The latter smiled, and said:

"We do not know how to serve God. We only serve and support ourselves, servant of God."

"But how do you pray to God?" asked the Bishop.

"We pray in this way," replied the hermit. "Three are ye, three are we, have mercy upon us."

And when the old man said this, all three raised their eyes to heaven, and repeated:

"Three are ye, three are we, have mercy upon us!"

The Bishop smiled.

"You have evidently heard something about the Holy Trinity," said he. "But you do not pray aright. You have won my affection, godly men. I see you wish to please the Lord, but you do not know how to serve Him. That is not the way to pray; but listen to me, and I will teach you. I will teach you, not a way of my own, but the way in which God in the Holy Scriptures has commanded all men to pray to Him."

And the Bishop began explaining to the hermits how God had revealed Himself to men; telling them of God the Father, and God the Son, and God the Holy Ghost.

"God the Son came down on earth," said he, "to save men, and this is how He taught us all to pray. Listen, and repeat after me: 'Our Father.' "

And the first old man repeated after him, "Our Father," and the second said, "Our Father," and the third said, "Our Father."

"Which art in heaven," continued the Bishop.

The first hermit repeated, "Which art in heaven," but the second blundered over the words, and the tall hermit could not say them properly. His hair had grown over his mouth so that he could not speak plainly. The very old hermit, having no teeth, also mumbled indistinctly.

The Bishop repeated the words again, and the old men repeated them after him. The Bishop sat down on a stone, and the old men stood before him, watching his mouth, and repeating the words as he uttered them. And all day long the Bishop laboured, saying a word twenty, thirty, a hundred times over, and the old men repeated it after him. They blundered, and he corrected them, and made them begin again.

The Bishop did not leave off till he had taught them the whole of the Lord's Prayer so that they could not only repeat it after him, but could say it by themselves. The middle one was the first to know it, and to repeat the whole of it alone. The Bishop made him say it again and again, and at last the others could say it too.

It was getting dark and the moon was appearing over the water, before the Bishop rose to return to the vessel. When he took leave of the old men they all bowed down to the ground before him. He raised them, and kissed each of them, telling them to pray as he had taught them. Then he got into the boat and returned to the ship.

And as he sat in the boat and was rowed to the ship he could hear the three voices of the hermits loudly repeating the Lord's Prayer. As the boat drew near the vessel their voices could no longer be heard, but they could still be seen in the moonlight, standing as he had left them on the shore, the shortest in the middle, the tallest on the right, the middle one on the left. As soon as the Bishop had reached the vessel and got on board, the anchor was weighted and the sails unfurled. The wind filled them and the ship sailed away, and the Bishop took a seat in the stern and watched the island they had left. For a time he could still see the hermits, but presently they disappeared from sight, though the island was still visible. At last it too vanished, and only the sea was to be seen, rippling in the moonlight.

The pilgrims lay down to sleep, and all was quiet on deck. The Bishop did not wish to sleep, but sat alone at the stern, gazing at the sea where the island was no longer visible, and thinking of the good old men. He thought how pleased they had been to learn the Lord's Prayer; and he thanked God for having sent him to teach and help such godly men.

So the Bishop sat, thinking, and gazing at the sea where the island had disappeared. And the moonlight flickered before his eyes, sparkling, now here, now there, upon the waves. Suddenly he saw something white and shining, on the bright path which the moon cast across the sea. Was it a seagull, or the little gleaming sail of some small boat? The Bishop fixed his eyes on it, wondering.

"It must be a boat sailing after us," thought he, "but it is overtaking us very rapidly. It was far, far away a minute ago, but now it is much nearer. It cannot be a boat, for I can see no sail; but whatever it may be, it is following us and catching us up."

And he could not make out what it was. Not a boat, nor a bird, nor a fish! It was too large for a man, and besides a man could not be out there in the midst of the sea. The Bishop rose, and said to the helmsman:

"Look there, what is that, my friend? What is it?" the Bishop repeated, though he could now see plainly what it was—the three hermits running upon the water, all gleaming white, their grey beards shining, and approaching the ship as quickly as though it were not moving.

The steersman looked, and let go the helm in terror.

"Oh Lord! The hermits are running after us on the water as though it were dry land!"

The passengers, hearing him, jumped up and crowded to the stern. They saw the hermits coming along hand in hand, and the two outer ones beckoning the ship to stop. All three were gliding along upon the water without moving their feet. Before the ship could be stopped, the hermits had reached it, and raising their heads, all three as with one voice, began to say:

"We have forgotten your teaching, servant of God. As long as we kept repeating it we remembered, but when we stopped saying it for a time, a word dropped out, and now it has all gone to pieces. We can remember nothing of it. Teach us again."

The Bishop crossed himself, and learning over the ship's side, said:

"Your own prayer will reach the Lord, men of God. It is not for me to teach you. Pray for us sinners."

And the Bishop bowed low before the old men; and they turned and went back across the sea. And a light shone until daybreak on the spot where they were lost to sight.

1886.

Questions

1. If we regard *morality* as human conduct conforming to a conception of right and wrong and *ethics* as the study of the principles upon which that conduct is based, do these episodes display any moral principles that could be used to construct a Christian ethic?

2. Consider all three stories. Is there a common theme present? If so, what is it? Could it serve as the basis for an ethical code? Explain.

3. What is the view of "man" that underlies these stories? Explain.

4. Is justice done in "God Sees the Truth, but Waits"? If not, why not? If so, what *sort* of justice? Contrast this view of justice with those in chapters three, fourteen, and seventeen of this book.

5. What is the *nature* of Martin's change in "Where Love Is, God Is"? This story seems to suggest *how* the Scriptures are to be understood. What is the suggestion? Explain.

6. Do the three hermits know or understand something that the bishop does not? What does the bishop learn? Could this be taught any other way?

13

Pleasure Seekers

The Stricken Doe

After dining at Brantes, at the Deux Cou-ronnes, the three men made ready to get into their motor-car. Suddenly a little servant-girl appeared: Béville had left his camera behind in the dining-room: she handed it to him without a word and went back into the hotel.

"She's not very talkative!" he observed.

"Oh!" said the garage attendant, "that's the Breton girl. She only arrived here from Brittany two days ago and she doesn't know a word of French yet."

"The Breton girl?" echoed Béville.

"Why, doesn't Monsieur know?" asked the fellow with a snigger. "In hotels like this, small-town hotels, they always get hold of a Breton girl. For the travellers, in case . . ."

The three laughed. The car started, and a few moments later they were in the open country.

"The Stricken Doe" by Pierre Mille, translated by Vyvyan Holland, from *Tellers of Tales*, selected by W. Somerset Maugham. Copyright 1937 by Doubleday & Company, Inc. Reprinted by permission of the Publisher.

"Do you notice the smell of the air; isn't it delightful?" Béville asked the man next to him.

"Yes," replied Bottiaux. "That's because it's been raining and the earth is still warm and the car is going very fast, so that the air is full of fragrance."

Béville spread himself out, half asleep, a little intoxicated from the champagne he had drunk at dinner and intoxicated, too, by the brisk, warm night air which bathed him, buffeted him, impregnated his body and gave him a feeling of lazy, languid voluptuousness. He was no longer on earth, but floated above it, and from time to time he stretched out his arms as though trying to seize some delectable object of his thoughts.

"Pity there are no women, eh, Jalin?"

But Jalin, the owner of the car, who was driving, did not even turn his head. He had quite enough to do to steer the formidable machine over the road along which they sped, whitened by the light of the huge headlights, and on either side of which the straight lines of the trees formed, as it

were, two solid walls, so fast were they travelling.

He merely growled:

"Women? Certainly not!"

All his virility, all his vigour, all his
strength as a male and as an intelligent ath-
lete were now concentrated in his brain and
in his hands. But, like the others, he spread
his nostrils to inhale the perfumes of the
summer night, those of the limes, of the
mountain-ash and of thousands of little
herbs, whose names no one knows, which
have been fertilized by the sun-lit hours
and during the night enjoy the raptures of
that contact within their closed petals. That
was enough for him. He merely murmured:

"It's lovely, isn't it?"

Rabbits, roused by the roar of the car,
blinded by the headlights and crazy with
fear, ran out of the ditches beside the road
and sped like black bullets across their
path. But suddenly the road was plunged
into darkness and the branches above their
heads were interspersed with patches of
sky. One second before, this machine, this
meteor, this furious rushing object seemed
to be the sole source of light in the world;
and now it was nothing but the centre of a
world of darkness, while other objects
sprang into life again in the gloom. It was
staggeringly sudden and unexpected. Jalin
explained:

"Good Heavens, the lights have gone
out!"

"Light them again, then," said Bottiaux.

Jalin shrugged his shoulders.

"I'm afraid they're short-circuited. I can't
do anything about it."

"Well then, drive by the side-lights."

"Yes, but they're really only parking
lights!" replied Jalin.

"They're quite enough for the police.
Anyway, drive on! We must get to Paris. I
want to sleep in Paris."

Jalin nodded his head. An eighty horse-
power car is no more capable of travelling
slowly than a race-horse on a track or a
destroyer on the seas. However much one
tries to hold it back it leaps forward and
takes matters into its own hands. Jalin knew

the folly of travelling blindly at sixty miles
an hour when in two seconds one is upon
an object which one first sees sixty yards
away. Yet he consented. Like the other two
he was feeling too happy, too impetuous,
too much lifted out of himself, and too
much carried away by the movement of
which he thought himself master. It is the
same in a cavalry charge: one goes straight
to one's death and one cannot prevent oneself from doing so.

The gloom above them and on each side
of the road became more intense. They
were travelling through a wood, a dark confused mass of serried trees whose trunks
and branches seemed to be intertwined. It
was dark, so dark that it almost hurt their
eyes, and made them want to shade them
with their hands, as though to protect them
from a sudden shock. And at that very moment, when this alarming condition
seemed at its worst, Jalin thought he could
distinguish something in front of him, a
shadow even darker than the prevailing
gloom, a living, terrified shadow. He
wrenched his steering-wheel and jammed
on the brakes. Anyone who knows about
the modern machine has experienced the
physical consequences of that sudden stop-
ping, that abrupt deviation of a projectile
meant to travel in a straight line; the whole
of one's inside seems to displace itself, and
one has a sort of bitter forecast of the agony
of death. But the car was wide and low-
sprung, so it did not turn over but obeyed
as best it could, mounted a heap of stones
and came shudderingly to a standstill.

"What's the matter?" asked Béville, who
had gone quite grey.

Bottiaux jumped out and joined Jalin
who was mopping his forehead and kneeling before a pathetic object which still quivered as it lay stretched on the ground,
dimly lit by one of the side-lights of the car.

"What a bit of luck," observed Béville
who had also got out of the car. "It's only
a doe!"

The three men sighed deeply and their
voices echoed among the trees as they expressed their relief. With their heavy over-

coats, caps and goggles they were strangely alike: fine-looking men, all three bearded, and with an air of wealth, vigour and strength.

"What a bit of luck!" repeated Jalin.

But his laughter, which mingled with that of the others, suddenly ceased. He had just noticed the doe's eyes: they were so soft, so sad and so frightened, full of the puzzled terror of not knowing why it was there and of what had struck it in the night. Poor pretty little thing! Poor little woodland beast, so wild and innocent! They had all killed many others when they were out hunting with horses and hounds and beaters. But not like that. It lay mangled, wounded and dying, and quivering so painfully, with that despairing look still in its suffering eyes.

"We'll have to go back to Brantes," said Jalin. "I can't go on without my headlights. We can sleep at the hotel where we dined."

He turned the car and they returned to Brantes as slowly as they could.

Gradually the memory of the slaughtered animal was obliterated from their minds. It might have been a human being, they might themselves have been killed, indeed they had for a moment been faced by the fear of death. But they were alive, their blood coursed healthily through their veins and the world would still be theirs for years and years to come. The future stretched before them like a colonnade which one can follow endlessly with one's eyes, in an atmosphere of pure happiness.

The door of the Hôtel des Deux Couronnes was shut. Everyone was asleep. They knocked for a long time before a light appeared. Even then they had to wait a little longer, because in small towns people have to be cautious: they want to know with whom they are dealing.

"Look," said Bottiaux, when the door opened at last, "it's the Breton girl."

In her hand she held one of those tiny lamps, the wicks of which are protected by small globes, and which for the past twenty years have taken the place of night-lights. This feeble light gave a pink tinge to one side of her soft, childish, homely face, and everything else, her dressing-jacket hurriedly thrown over her rough night-dress, her linen petticoat, her bare slippered feet were lost in shadow. All that was visible was her sensitive little face, suspended in the air like a disembodied soul.

"Room?" she asked in rather a husky voice, in the way people do when they speak a foreign language.

"Yes, sleep; beds, eh? Good beds!" explained Bottiaux.

She lit candles for them, smiled, showed them to their rooms and retired.

But when Béville got to bed he found that he was unable to sleep. He was feeling too shattered, and still too excited by the fragrance of the night, by the speed of the car and by that strong feeling of gratitude towards life which infects everyone who has just escaped a great danger. Then he remembered the words of the garage attendant: "The Breton girl? That's what she's there for!" and he left his room, barefooted, and crept noiselessly along the passage.

Béville had noticed where the Breton girl slept; in a kind of lean-to, a cupboard fixed up on the staircase, between the ground floor and the first floor. He went straight there, shading his candle with his hand. Yes, that was the right place: she was sleeping on a common iron bedstead, her hair loose about her shoulders and one hand beneath her head to raise it as she had no pillow. All that could be seen of her body was a rounded neck and the delicate swell of a very young breast. Béville put his hand on her shoulder and kissed her. He had blown out the candle. The girl woke with a start and put her hands out in an instictive gesture of self-protection:

"*Ma Doué*," she said.

But Béville already had her in his arms and she felt his mouth upon hers again. Yes, it was true, she was the Breton girl, she was employed for that, paid for that, thirty francs a month in addition to presents from the guests. And besides, this man was a gentleman. Centuries of domination, almost of slavery, had taught her race that one must always obey "gentlemen," the leaders, the masters; their men followed them to war, their women to bed. So she must submit. Her poor little servile soul dared not protest. Only her body recoiled in horror, because it was still pure. Every virgin defends herself, every virgin is afraid. No doubt this is an instinct which nature has given her so that she must need courage to give herself and that thus she should only give herself from choice and, as it were, as a sacrifice to the man she loves. The Breton girl, humble savage, sold as in ancient days, but even more basely, experienced a feeling of terror. She implored him to let her go, in confused hurried words, in her obscure language, the language spoken on the shores of western seas, the only one she knew; but Béville did not understand.

He never knew why the girl did not return the kisses he gave her before possessing her. Neither did he understand when, a satisfied and yet sadly disappointed male—for such is the punishment of careless, brutal males that his only thought was to leave an offering and to get away—he never understood why a mouth had brushed, not his lips, she would not have dared, but his cheek and his forehead: the caress of a timid child who wanted so much, yes, so much, to be able to imagine the memory of the shadow of true tenderness after the horror of her ravishment. But there was nothing. He just went away and that was all.

Next day at dawn Jalin came and woke his two friends. When Béville came down he had almost forgotten. Happy men have, as it were, no memories. They live in advance and discount their future pleasures daily. If he had thought at all about the events of the night he would merely have felt that he had been rather unkind and, as he knew this, he took care to divert his thoughts into other channels. Moreover, Jalin had already got everything ready for their departure. The bill was paid and the engine of the car was running. He threw his two companions their coats and caps.

"Off we go!"

He backed into the hotel courtyard to enable him to turn before the front door. And at that moment there appeared in the doorway the misused slave who had let them in the previous night. She had just come out of her room where she had no doubt lain awake for hours, alone and defiled. She was wearing the same clothes, humble to the point of abjectness, a rough chemise and a shapeless jacket. She had not done her hair, she was not pretty, even her youth seemed to have become tarnished, and she stared at the three men hopelessly, her eyes full of misery. For the appalling thing that had happened to her and had perhaps left a living result within her, had taken place in inky darkness and she could not tell *which* of the three men it had been. Nor would she ever know.

The motor-car turned, well under control, and shot off. Bottiaux remarked musingly:

"That Breton girl's eyes. . . . What did they remind me of? Oh! yes, they were just like those of that doe last night. Did you see them?"

"No," replied Béville, "I didn't notice."

Questions

1. Is there a point in the story at which any of these men might be able to seriously consider their own morality? If so, who and where? If not, why not?

2. What does it mean that Jalin was "lifted out of himself"? Contrast this with Socrates saying that "the unexamined life is not worth living." What is the difference between getting out of oneself and examining oneself?

3. What is meant by the following?

> Every virgin defends herself, every virgin is afraid. No doubt this is an instinct which nature has given her so that she must need courage to give herself and that thus she should only give herself from choice and, as it were, as a sacrifice to the man she loves.

Analyze the concept of *human being* which gives rise to this characterization of virginity, giving special attention to the concepts of "instinct" and "sexuality." (Contrast this view of human being, for example, with the simpleminded notions we often express in the propositions "Man is instinctual" and "It's my body and I'll do what I like with it.")

4. If you are working with a text of ethical theories, describe this episode in terms of the theories you have studied. It might be particularly helpful to evaluate it from the perspectives of Plato, Kant, Mill, Nietzsche, and Moore.

5. Suppose that you are Epicurus, and suppose further that the men in this selection call themselves "Epicureans." What would (could?) you say to them?

14

Justice Outside the Law?

The Adventure of the Devil's Foot

In recording from time to time some of the curious experiences and interesting recollections which I associate with my long and intimate friendship with Mr. Sherlock Holmes, I have continually been faced by difficulties caused by his own aversion to publicity. To his sombre and cynical spirit all popular applause was always abhorrent, and nothing amused him more at the end of a successful case than to hand over the actual exposure to some orthodox official, and to listen with a mocking smile to the general chorus of misplaced congratulation. It was indeed this attitude upon the part of my friend and certainly not any lack of interesting material which has caused me of late years to lay very few of my records before the public. My participation in some of his adventures was always a privilege which entailed discretion and reticence upon me.

From *His Last Bow* by Sir Arthur Conan Doyle. Reprinted by permission of International Creative Management on behalf of the Doyle estate.

It was, then, with considerable surprise that I received a telegram from Holmes last Tuesday—he has never been known to write where a telegram would serve—in the following terms:

Why not tell them of the Cornish horror—strangest case I have handled.

I have no idea what backward sweep of memory had brought the matter fresh to his mind, or what freak had caused him to desire that I should recount it; but I hasten, before another cancelling telegram may arrive, to hunt out the notes which give me the exact details of the case and to lay the narrative before my readers.

It was, then, in the spring of the year 1897 that Holmes's iron constitution showed some symptoms of giving way in the face of constant hard work of a most exacting kind, aggravated, perhaps, by occasional indiscretions of his own. In March of that year Dr. Moore Agar, of Harley Street, whose dramatic introduction to Holmes I may some day recount, gave positive injunctions that the famous private agent lay aside all his cases and surrender himself to complete rest if he wished to avert an absolute breakdown. The state of his health was not a matter in which he himself took the faintest interest, for his mental detachment was absolute, but he was induced at last, on the threat of being permanently disqualified from work, to give himself a complete change of scene and air. Thus it was that in the early spring of that year we found ourselves together in a small cottage near Poldhu Bay, at the further extremity of the Cornish peninsula.

It was a singular spot, and one peculiarly well suited to the grim humour of my patient. From the windows of our little whitewashed house, which stood high upon a grassy headland, we looked down upon the whole sinister semicircle of Mounts Bay, that old death trap of sailing vessels, with its fringe of black cliffs and surge-swept reefs on which innumerable seamen have met their end. With a northerly breeze it lies placid and sheltered, inviting the storm-tossed craft to tack into it for rest and protection.

Then come the sudden swirl round of the wind, the blustering gale from the southwest, the dragging anchor, the lee shore, and the last battle in the creaming breakers. The wise mariner stands far out from that evil place.

On the land side our surroundings were as sombre as on the sea. It was a country of rolling moors, lonely and dun-coloured, with an occasional church tower to mark the site of some old-world village. In every direction upon these moors there were traces of some vanished race which had passed utterly away, and left as its sole record strange monuments of stone, irregular mounds which contained the burned ashes of the dead, and curious earthworks which hinted at prehistoric strife. The glamour and mystery of the place, with its sinister atmosphere of forgotten nations, appealed to the imagination of my friend, and he spent much of his time in long walks and solitary meditations upon the moor. The ancient Cornish language had also arrested his attention, and he had, I remember, conceived the idea that it was akin to the Chaldean, and had been largely derived from the Phœnician traders in tin. He had received a consignment of books upon philology and was settling down to develop this thesis when suddenly, to my sorrow and to his unfeigned delight, we found ourselves, even in that land of dreams, plunged into a problem at our very doors which was more intense, more engrossing, and infinitely more mysterious than any of those which had driven us from London. Our simple life and peaceful, healthy routine were violently interrupted, and we were precipitated into the midst of a series of events which caused the utmost excitement not only in Cornwall but throughout the whole west of England. Many of my readers may retain some recollection of what was called at the time "The Cornish Horror," though a most imperfect account of the matter reached the London press. Now, after thirteen years, I will give the true details of this inconceivable affair to the public.

I have said that scattered towers marked the villages which dotted this part of Cornwall. The nearest of these was the hamlet of Tredannick Wollas, where the cottages of a couple of hundred inhabitants clustered round an ancient, moss-grown church. The vicar of the parish, Mr. Roundhay, was something of an archæologist, and as such Holmes had made his acquaintance. He was a middle-aged man, portly and affable, with a considerable fund of local lore. At his invitation we had taken tea at the vicarage and had come to know, also, Mr. Mortimer Tregennis, an independent gentleman, who increased the clergyman's scanty resources by taking rooms in his large, straggling house. The vicar, being a bachelor, was glad to come to such an arrangement, though he had little in common with his lodger, who was a thin, dark, spectacled man, with a stoop which gave the impression of actual, physical deformity. I remember that during our short visit we found the vicar garrulous, but his lodger strangely reticent, a sad-faced, introspective man, sitting with averted eyes, brooding apparently upon his own affairs.

These were the two men who entered abruptly into our little sitting-room on Tuesday, March the 16th, shortly after our breakfast hour, as we were smoking together, preparatory to our daily excursion upon the moors.

"Mr. Holmes," said the vicar in an agitated voice, "the most extraordinary and tragic affair has occurred during the night. It is the most unheard-of business. We can only regard it as a special Providence that you should chance to be here at the time, for in all England you are the one man we need."

I glared at the intrusive vicar with no very friendly eyes; but Holmes took his pipe from his lips and sat up in his chair like an old hound who hears the view-halloa. He waved his hand to the sofa, and our palpitating visitor with his agitated companion sat side by side upon it. Mr. Mortimer Tregennis was more self-contained than the clergyman, but the twitching of his thin hands and the brightness of his dark eyes showed that they shared a common emotion.

"Shall I speak or you?" he asked of the vicar.

"Well, as you seem to have made of the discovery, whatever it may be, and the vicar to have had it second-hand, perhaps you had better do the speaking," said Holmes.

I glanced at the hastily clad clergyman, with the formally dressed lodger seated beside him, and was amused at the surprise which Holmes's simple deduction had brought to their faces.

"Perhaps I had best say a few words first," said the vicar, "and then you can judge if you will listen to the details from Mr. Tregennis, or whether we should not hasten at once to the scene of this mysterious affair. I may explain, then, that our friend here spent last evening in the company of his two brothers, Owen and George, and of his sister Brenda, at their house of Tredannick Wartha, which is near the old stone cross upon the moor. He left them shortly after ten o'clock, playing cards round the dining-room table, in excellent health and spirits. This morning, being an early riser, he walked in that direction before breakfast and was overtaken by the carriage of Dr. Richards, who explained that he had just been sent for on a most urgent call to Tredannick Wartha. Mr. Mortimer Tregennis naturally went with him. When he arrived at Tredannick Wartha he found an extraordinary state of things. His two brothers and his sister were seated round the table exactly as he had left them, the cards still spread in front of them and the candles burned down to their sockets. The sister lay back stone-dead in her chair, while the two brothers sat on each side of her laughing, shouting, and singing, the senses stricken clean out of them. All three of them, the dead woman and the two demented men, retained upon their faces an expression of the utmost horror—a convulsion of terror which was dreadful to look upon. There was no sign of the presence of anyone in the house, except Mrs. Porter, the old cook and housekeeper, who declared that she had slept deeply and heard no sound during the night. Nothing had been stolen or disarranged, and there is absolutely no explanation of what the horror can be which has frightened a woman to death and two strong men out of their senses. There is the situation, Mr. Holmes, in a nutshell, and if you can help us to clear it up you will have done a great work."

I had hoped that in some way I could coax my companion back into the quiet which had been the object of our journey; but one glance at his intense face and contracted eyebrows told me how vain was now the expectation. He sat for some little time in silence, absorbed in the strange drama which had broken in upon our peace.

"I will look into this matter," he said at last. "On the face of it, it would appear to be a case of a very exceptional nature. Have you been there yourself, Mr. Roundhay?"

"No, Mr. Holmes. Mr. Tregennis brought back the account to the vicarage, and I at once hurried over with him to consult you."

"How far is it to the house where this singular tragedy occurred?"

"About a mile inland."

"Then we shall walk over together. But before we start I must ask you a few questions, Mr. Mortimer Tregennis."

The other had been silent all this time, but I had observed that his more controlled excitement was even greater than the obtrusive emotion of the clergyman. He sat with a pale, drawn face, his anxious gaze fixed upon Holmes, and his thin hands clasped convulsively together. His pale lips quivered as he listened to the dreadful experience which had befallen his family, and his dark eyes seemed to reflect something of the horror of the scene.

"Ask what you like, Mr. Holmes," said he eagerly. "It is a bad thing to speak of, but I will answer you the truth."

"Tell me about last night."

"Well, Mr. Holmes, I supped there, as the vicar has said, and my elder brother George proposed a game of whist afterwards. We sat down about nine o'clock. It was a quarter-past ten when I moved to go. I left them all round the table, as merry as could be."

"Who let you out?"

"Mrs. Porter had gone to bed, so I let myself out. I shut the hall door behind me. The window of the room in which they sat was closed, but the blind was not drawn down. There was no change in door or window this morning, nor any reason to think that any stranger had been to the house. Yet there they sat, driven clean mad with terror, and Brenda lying dead of fright, with her head hanging over the arm of the chair. I'll never get the sight of that room out of my mind so long as I live."

"The facts, as you state them, are certainly most remarkable," said Holmes. "I take it that you have no theory yourself which can in any way account for them?"

"It's devilish, Mr. Holmes, devilish!" cried Mortimer Tregennis. "It is not of this world. Something has come into that room which has dashed the light of reason from their minds. What human contrivance could do that?"

"I fear," said Holmes, "that if the matter is beyond humanity it is certainly beyond me. Yet we must exhaust all natural explanations before we fall back upon such a theory as this. As to yourself, Mr. Tregennis, I take it you were divided in some way from your family, since they lived together and you had rooms apart?"

"That is so, Mr. Holmes, though the matter is past and done with. We were a family of tin-miners at Redruth, but we sold out our venture to a company, and so retired with enough to keep us. I won't deny that there was some feeling about the division of the money and it stood between us for a time, but it was all forgiven and forgotten, and we were the best of friends together.

"Looking back at the evening which you spent together, does anything stand out in your memory as throwing any possible light upon the tragedy? Think carefully, Mr. Tregennis, for any clue which can help me."

"There is nothing at all, sir."

"Your people were in their usual spirits?"

"Never better."

"Were they nervous people? Did they ever show any apprehension of coming danger?"

"Nothing of the kind."

"You have nothing to add then, which could assist me?"

Mortimer Tregennis considered earnestly for a moment.

"There is one thing occurs to me," said he at last. "As we sat at the table my back was to the window, and my brother George, he being my partner at cards, was facing it. I saw him once look hard over my shoulder, so I turned round and looked also. The blind was up and the window shut, but I could just make out the bushes on the lawn, and it seemed to me for a moment that I saw something moving among them. I couldn't even say if it was man or animal, but I just thought there was something there. When I asked him what he was looking at, he told me that he had the same feeling. That is all that I can say."

"Did you not investigate?"

"No; the matter passed as unimportant."

"You left them, then, without any premonition of evil?"

"None at all."

"I am not clear how you came to hear the news so early this morning."

"I am an early riser and generally take a walk before breakfast. This morning I had hardly started when the doctor in his carriage overtook me. He told me that old Mrs. Porter had sent a boy down with an urgent message. I sprang in beside him and we drove on. When we got there we looked into that dreadful room. The candles and the fire must have burned out hours before, and they had been sitting there in the dark until dawn had broken. The doctor said Brenda must have been dead at least six hours. There were no signs of violence. She just lay across the arm of the chair with that look on her face. George and Owen were singing snatches of songs and gibbering like two great apes. Oh, it was awful to see! I couldn't stand it, and the doctor was as white as a sheet. Indeed, he fell into a chair in a sort of faint, and we nearly had him on our hands as well."

"Remarkable—most remarkable!" said Holmes, rising and taking his hat. "I think, perhaps, we had better go down to Tredannick Wartha without further delay. I confess that I have seldom known a case which at first sight presented a more singular problem."

Our proceedings of that first morning did little to advance the investigation. It was marked, however, at the outset by an incident which left the most sinister impression upon my mind. The approach to the spot at which the tragedy occurred is down a narrow, winding, country lane. While we made our way along it we heard the rattle of a carriage coming towards us

and stood aside to let it pass. As it drove by us I caught a glimpse through the closed window of a horribly contorted, grinning face glaring out at us. Those staring eyes and gnashing teeth flashed past us like a dreadful vision.

"My brothers!" cried Mortimer Tregennis, white to his lips. "They are taking them to Helston."

We looked with horror after the black carriage, lumbering upon its way. Then we turned our steps towards this ill-omened house in which they had met their strange fate.

It was a large and bright dwelling, rather a villa than a cottage, with a considerable garden which was already, in that Cornish air, well filled with spring flowers. Towards this garden the window of the sitting-room fronted, and from it, according to Mortimer Tregennis, must have come that thing of evil which had by sheer horror in a single instant blasted their minds. Holmes walked slowly and thoughtfully among the flower-plots and along the path before we entered the porch. So absorbed was he in his thoughts, I remember, that he stumbled over the watering-pot, upset its contents, and deluged both our feet and the garden path. Inside the house we were met by the elderly Cornish housekeeper, Mrs. Porter, who, with the aid of a young girl, looked after the wants of the family. She readily answered all Holmes's questions. She had heard nothing in the night. Her employers had all been in excellent spirits lately, and she had never known them more cheerful and prosperous. She had fainted with horror upon entering the room in the morning and seeing that dreadful company round the table. She had, when she recovered, thrown open the window to let the morning air in, and had run down to the lane, whence she sent a farm-lad for the doctor. The lady was on her bed upstairs if we cared to see her. It took four strong men to get the brothers into the asylum carriage. She would not herself stay in the house another day and was starting that very afternoon to rejoin her family at St. Ives.

We ascended the stairs and viewed the body. Miss Brenda Tregennis had been a very beautiful girl, though now verging upon middle age. Her dark, clear-cut face was handsome, even in death, but there still lingered upon it something of that convulsion of horror which had been her last human emotion. From her bedroom we descended to the sitting-room, where this strange tragedy had actually occurred. The charred ashes of the overnight fire lay in the grate. On the table were the four guttered and burned-out candles, with the cards scattered over its surface. The chairs had been moved back against the walls, but all else was as it had been the night before. Holmes paced with light, swift steps about the room; he sat in the various chairs, drawing them up and reconstructing their positions. He tested how much of the garden was visible; he examined the floor, the ceiling, and the fireplace; but never once did I see that sudden brightening of his eyes and the tightening of his lips which would have told me that he saw some gleam of light in this utter darkness.

"Why a fire?" he asked once. "Had they always a fire in this small room on a spring evening?"

Mortimer Tregennis explained that the night was cold and damp. For that reason, after his arrival, the fire was lit. "What are you going to do now, Mr. Holmes?" he asked.

My friend smiled and laid his hand upon my arm. "I think, Watson, that I shall resume that course of tobacco-poisoning which you have so often and so justly condemned," said he. "With your permission, gentlemen, we will now return to our cottage, for I am not aware that any new factor is likely to come to our notice here. I will turn the facts over in my mind, Mr. Tregennis, and should anything occur to me I will certainly communicate with you and the vicar. In the meantime I wish you both good-morning."

It was not until long after we were back in Poldhu Cottage that Holmes broke his complete and absorbed silence. He sat coiled in his armchair, his haggard and ascetic face hardly visible amid the blue swirl of his tobacco smoke, his black brows drawn down, his forehead contracted, his eyes vacant and far away. Finally he laid down his pipe and sprang to his feet.

"It won't do, Watson!" said he with a laugh. "Let us walk along the cliffs together and search for flint arrows. We are more likely to find them than clues to this problem. To let the brain work without sufficient material is like racing an engine. It racks itself to pieces. The sea air, sunshine, and patience, Watson—all else will come.

"Now, let us calmly define our position, Watson," he continued as we skirted the cliffs together. "Let us get a firm grip of the very little which we *do* know, so that when fresh facts arise we may be ready to fit them into their places. I take it, in the first place, that neither of us is prepared to admit diabolical intrusions into the affairs of men. Let us begin by ruling that entirely out of our minds. Very good. There remain three persons who have been grievously striken by some conscious or unconscious human agency. That is firm ground. Now, when did this occur? Evidently, assuming his narrative to be true, it was immediately after Mr. Mortimer Tregennis had left the room. That is a very important point. The presumption is that it was within a few minutes afterwards. The cards still lay upon the table. It was already past their usual hour for bed. Yet they had not changed their position or pushed back their chairs. I repeat, then, that the occurrence was immediately after his departure, and not later than eleven o'clock last night.

"Our next obvious step is to check, so far as we can, the movements of Mortimer Tregennis after he left the room. In this there is no difficulty, and they seem to be above suspicion. Knowing my methods as you do, you were, of course, conscious of the somewhat clumsy water-pot expedient by which I obtained a clearer impress of his foot than might otherwise have been possible. The wet, sandy path took it admirably. Last night was also wet, you will remember, and it was not difficult—having obtained a sample print—to pick out his track among others and to follow his movements. He appears to have walked away swiftly in the direction of the vicarage.

"If, then, Mortimer Tregennis disappeared from the scene, and yet some outside person affected the cardplayers, how can we reconstruct that person, and how was such an impression of horror conveyed? Mrs. Porter may be eliminated. She is evidently harmless. Is there any evidence that someone crept up to the garden window and in some manner produced so terrific an effect that he drove those who saw it out of their senses? The only suggestion in this direction comes from Mortimer Tregennis himself, who says that his brother spoke about some movement in the garden. That is certainly remarkable, as the night was rainy, cloudy, and dark. Anyone who had the design to alarm these people would be compelled to place his very face against the glass before he could be seen. There is a three-foot flower-border outside this window, but no indication of a footmark. It is difficult to imagine, then, how an outsider could have made so terrible an impression upon the company, nor have we found any possible motive for so strange and elaborate an attempt. You perceive our difficulties, Watson?"

"They are only too clear," I answered with conviction.

"And yet, with a little more material, we may prove that they are not insurmountable," said Holmes. "I fancy that among your extensive archives, Watson, you may find some which were nearly as obscure. Meanwhile, we shall put the case aside until more accurate data are available, and devote the rest of our morning to the pursuit of neolithic man."

I may have commented upon my friend's power of mental detachment, but never have I wondered at it more than upon that spring morning in Cornwall when for two hours he discoursed upon celts, arrowheads, and shards, as lightly as if no sinister mystery were waiting for his solution. It was not until we had returned in the afternoon to our cottage that we found a visitor awaiting us, who soon brought our minds back to the matter in hand. Neither of us needed to be told who that visitor was. The huge body, the craggy and deeply seamed face with the fierce eyes and hawk-like nose, the grizzled hair which nearly brushed our cottage ceiling, the beard—golden at the fringes and white near the lips, save for the nicotine stain from his perpetual cigar—all these were as well known in London as in Africa, and could only be associated with the tremendous personality of Dr. Leon Sterndale, the great lion-hunter and explorer.

We had heard of his presence in the district and had once or twice caught sight of his tall figure upon the moorland paths. He made no advances to us, however, nor would we have dreamed of doing so to him, as it was well known that it was his love of seclusion which caused him to spend the greater part of the intervals between his journeys in a small bungalow buried in the lonely wood of Beauchamp Arriance. Here, amid his books and his maps, he lived an absolutely lonely life, attending to his own simple wants and paying little apparent heed to the affairs of his neighbours. It was a surprise to me, therefore, to hear him asking Holmes in an eager voice whether he had made any advance in his reconstruction of this mysterious episode. "The county police are utterly at fault," said he, "but perhaps your wider experience has suggested some conceivable explanation. My only claim to being taken into your confidence is that during my many residences here I have come to know this family of Tregennis very well—indeed, upon my Cornish mother's side I could call them cousins—and their strange fate has naturally been a great shock to me. I may tell you that I had got as far as Plymouth upon my way to Africa, but the news reached me this morning, and I came straight back again to help in the inquiry."

Holmes raised his eyebrows.

"Did you lose your boat through it?"

"I will take the next."

"Dear me! that is friendship indeed."

"I tell you they were relatives."

"Quite so—cousins of your mother. Was your baggage aboard the ship?"

"Some of it, but the main part at the hotel."

"I see. But surely this event could not have found its way into the Plymouth morning papers."

"No, sir; I had a telegram."

"Might I ask from whom?"

A shadow passed over the gaunt face of the explorer.

"You are very inquisitive, Mr. Holmes."

"It is my business."

With an effort Dr. Sterndale recovered his ruffled composure.

"I have no objection to telling you," he said. "It was Mr. Roundhay, the vicar, who sent me the telegram which recalled me."

"Thank you," said Holmes. "I may say in answer to your original question that I have not cleared my mind entirely on the subject of this case, but that I have every hope of reaching some conclusion. It would be premature to say more."

"Perhaps you would not mind telling me if your suspicions point in any particular direction?"

"No, I can hardly answer that."

"Then I have wasted my time and need not prolong my visit." The famous doctor strode out of our cottage in considerable ill-humour, and within five minutes Holmes had followed him. I saw him no more until the evening, when he returned with a slow step and haggard face which assured me that he had made no great progress with his investigation. He glanced at a telegram which awaited him and threw it into the grate.

"From the Plymouth hotel, Watson," he said. "I learned the name of it from the vicar, and I wired to make certain that Dr. Leon Sterndale's account was true. It appears that he did indeed spend last night there, and that he has actually allowed some of his baggage to go on to Africa, while he returned to be present at this investigation. What do you make of that, Watson?"

"He is deeply interested."

"Deeply interested—yes. There is a thread here which we have not yet grasped and which might lead us through the tangle. Cheer up, Watson, for I am very sure that our material has not yet all come to hand. When it does we may soon leave our difficulties behind us."

Little did I think how soon the words of Holmes would be realized, or how strange and sinister would be that new development which opened up an entirely fresh line of investigation. I was shaving at my window in the morning when I heard the rattle of hoofs and, looking up, saw a dog-cart coming at a gallop down the road. It pulled up at our door, and our friend, the vicar, sprang from it and rushed up our garden path. Holmes was already dressed, and we hastened down to meet him.

Our visitor was so excited that he could hardly articulate, but at last in gasps and bursts his tragic story came out of him.

"We are devil-ridden, Mr. Holmes! My poor parish is devil-ridden!" he cried. "Satan himself is loose in it! We are given over into his hands!" He danced about in his agitation, a ludicrous object if it were not for his ashy face and startled eyes. Finally he shot out his terrible news.

"Mr. Mortimer Tregennis died during the night, and with exactly the same symptoms as the rest of his family."

Holmes sprang to his feet, all energy in an instant.

"Can you fit us both into your dogcart?"

"Yes, I can."

"Then, Watson, we will postpone our breakfast. Mr. Roundhay, we are entirely at your disposal. Hurry—hurry, before things get disarranged."

The lodger occupied two rooms at the vicarage, which were in an angle by themselves, the one above the other. Below was a large sitting-room; above, his bedroom. They looked out upon a croquet lawn which came up to the windows. We had arrived before the doctor or the police, so

that everything was absolutely undisturbed. Let me describe exactly the scene
as we saw it upon that misty March morning. It has left an impression which can
never be effaced from my mind.

The atmosphere of the room was of a
horrible and depressing stuffiness. The servant who had first entered had thrown up
the window, or it would have been even
more intolerable. This might partly be due
to the fact that a lamp stood flaring and
smoking on the centre table. Beside it sat
the dead man, leaning back in his chair, his
thin beard projecting, his spectacles
pushed up on to his forehead, and his lean
dark face turned towards the window and
twisted into the same distortion of terror
which had marked the features of his dead
sister. His limbs were convulsed and his
fingers contorted as though he had died in
a very paroxysm of fear. He was fully
clothed, though there were signs that his
dressing had been done in a hurry. We had
already learned that his bed had been slept
in, and that the tragic end had come to him
in the early morning.

One realized the red-hot energy which
underlay Holmes's phlegmatic exterior
when one saw the sudden change which
came over him from the moment that he
entered the fatal apartment. In an instant
he was tense and alert, his eyes shining, his
face set, his limbs quivering with eager activity. He was out on the lawn, in through
the window, round the room, and up into
the bedroom, for all the world like a dash-
ing foxhound drawing a cover. In the bedroom he made a rapid cast around and
ended by throwing open the window, which
appeared to give him some fresh cause for
excitement, for he leaned out of it with loud
ejaculations of interest and delight. Then
he rushed down the stair, out through the
open window, threw himself upon his face
on the lawn, sprang up and into the room
once more, all with the energy of the hunter
who is at the very heels of his quarry. The
lamp, which was an ordinary standard, he
examined with minute care, making certain
measurements upon its bowl. He carefully

scrutinized with his lens the talc shield
which covered the top of the chimney and
scraped off some ashes which adhered to its
upper surface, putting some of them into
an envelope, which he placed in his pocket-
book. Finally, just as the doctor and the
official police put in an appearance, he
beckoned to the vicar and we all three went
out upon the lawn.

"I am glad to say that my investigation
has not been entirely barren," he remarked. "I cannot remain to discuss the
matter with the police, but I should be exceedingly obliged, Mr. Roundhay, if you
would give the inspector my compliments
and direct his attention to the bed-room
window and to the sitting-room lamp. Each
is suggestive, and together they are almost
conclusive. If the police would desire further information I shall be happy to see any
of them at the cottage. And now, Watson,
I think that, perhaps, we shall be better employed elsewhere."

It may be that the police resented the
intrusion of an amateur, or that they imagined themselves to be upon some hopeful
line of investigation; but it is certain that we
heard nothing from them for the next two
days. During this time Holmes spent some
of his time smoking and dreaming in the
cottage; but a greater portion in country
walks which he undertook alone, returning
after many hours without remark as to
where he had been. One experiment served
to show me the line of his investigation. He
had bought a lamp which was the duplicate
of the one which had burned in the room of
Mortimer Tregennis on the morning of the
tragedy. This he filled with the same oil as
that used at the vicarage, and he carefully
timed the period which it would take to be
exhausted. Another experiment which he
made was of a more unpleasant nature, and
one which I am not likely ever to forget.

"You will remember, Watson," he remarked one afternoon, "that there is a single common point of resemblance in the
varying reports which have reached us.
This concerns the effect of the atmosphere
of the room in each case upon those who

had first entered it. You will recollect that Mortimer Tregennis, in describing the episode of his last visit to his brother's house, remarked that the doctor on entering the room fell into a chair? You had forgotten? Well, I can answer for it that it was so. Now, you will remember also that Mrs. Porter, the housekeeper, told us that she herself fainted upon entering the room and had afterwards opened the window. In the second case—that of Mortimer Tregennis himself—you cannot have forgotten the horrible stuffiness of the room when we arrived, though the servant had thrown open the window. That servant, I found upon inquiry, was so ill that she had gone to her bed. You will admit, Watson, that these facts are very suggestive. In each case there is evidence of a poisonous atmosphere. In each case, also, there is combustion going on in the room—in the one case a fire, in the other a lamp. The fire was needed, but the lamp was lit—as a comparison of the oil consumed will show—long after it was broad daylight. Why? Surely because there is some connection between three things— the burning, the stuffy atmosphere, and, finally, the madness or death of those unfortunate people. That is clear, is it not?"

"It would appear so."

"At least we may accept it as a working hypothesis. We will suppose, then, that something was burned in each case which produced an atmosphere causing strange toxic effects. Very good. In the first instance—that of the Tregennis family—this substance was placed in the fire. Now the window was shut, but the fire would naturally carry fumes to some extent up the chimney. Hence one would expect the effects of the poison to be less than in the second case, where there was less escape for the vapour. The result seems to indicate that it was so, since in the first case only the woman, who had presumably the more sensitive organism, was killed, the others exhibiting that temporary or permanent lunacy which is evidently the first effect of the drug. In the second case the result was complete. The facts, therefore, seem to bear out the theory of a poison which worked by combustion.

"With this train of reasoning in my head I naturally looked about in Mortimer Tregennis's room to find some remains of this substance. The obvious place to look was the talc shield or smoke-guard of the lamp. There, sure enough, I perceived a number of flaky ashes, and round the edges a fringe of brownish powder, which had not yet been consumed. Half of this I took, as you saw, and I placed it in an envelope."

"Why half, Holmes?"

"It is not for me, my dear Watson, to stand in the way of the official police force. I leave them all the evidence which I found. The poison still remained upon the talc had they the wit to find it. Now, Watson, we will light our lamp; we will, however, take the precaution to open our window to avoid the premature decease of two deserving members of society, and you will seat yourself near that open window in an armchair unless, like a sensible man, you determine to have nothing to do with the affair. Oh, you will see it out, will you? I thought I knew my Watson. This chair I will place opposite yours, so that we may be the same distance from the poison and face to face. The door we will leave ajar. Each is now in a position to watch the other and to bring the experiment to an end should the symptoms seem alarming. Is that all clear? Well, then, I take our powder—or what remains of it—from the envelope, and I lay it above the burning lamp. So! Now, Watson, let us sit down and await developments."

They were not long in coming. I had hardly settled in my chair before I was conscious of a thick, musky odour, subtle and nauseous. At the very first whiff of it my brain and my imagination were beyond all control. A thick, black cloud swirled before my eyes, and my mind told me that in this cloud, unseen as yet, but about to spring out upon my appalled senses, lurked all that was vaguely horrible, all that was monstrous and inconceivably wicked in the universe. Vague shapes swirled and swam amid the dark cloud-bank, each a menace and a warning of something coming, the advent of some unspeakable dweller upon the threshold, whose very shadow would blast my soul. A freezing horror took possession of me. I felt that my hair was rising, that my eyes were protruding, that my mouth was opened, and my tongue like leather. The turmoil within my brain was such that something must surely snap. I tried to scream and was vaguely aware of some hoarse croak which was my own voice, but distant and detached from myself. At the same moment, in some effort of escape, I broke through that cloud of despair and had a glimpse of Holmes's face, white, rigid, and drawn with horror—the very look which I had seen upon the features of the dead. It was that vision which gave me an instant of sanity and of strength. I dashed from my chair, threw my arms round Holmes, and together we lurched through the door, and an instant afterwards had thrown ourselves down upon the grass plot and were lying side by side, conscious only of the glorious sunshine which was bursting its way through the hellish cloud of terror which had girt us in. Slowly it rose from our souls like the mists from a landscape until peace and reason had returned, and we were sitting upon the grass, wiping our clammy foreheads, and looking with apprehension at each other to mark the last traces of that terrific experience which we had undergone.

"Upon my word, Watson!" said Holmes at last with an unsteady voice, "I owe you both my thanks and an apology. It was an unjustifiable experiment even for one's self, and doubly so for a friend. I am really very sorry."

"You know," I answered with some emotion, for I had never seen so much of Holmes's heart before, "that it is my greatest joy and privilege to help you."

He relapsed at once into the half-humorous, half-cynical vein which was his habitual attitude to those about him. "It would be superfluous to drive us mad, my dear Watson," said he. "A candid observer would certainly declare that we were so already before we embarked upon so wild an experiment. I confess that I never imagined that the effect could be so sudden and so severe." He dashed into the cottage, and, reappearing with the burning lamp held at full arm's length, he threw it among a bank of brambles. "We must give the room a little time to clear. I take it, Watson, that you have no longer a shadow of a doubt as to how these tragedies were produced?"

"None whatever."

"But the cause remains as obscure as before. Come into the arbour here and let us discuss it together. That villainous stuff seems still to linger round my throat. I think we must admit that all the evidence points to this man, Mortimer Tregennis, having been the criminal in the first tragedy, though he was the victim in the second one. We must remember, in the first place, that there is some story of a family quarrel, followed by a reconciliation. How bitter that quarrel may have been, or how hollow the reconciliation we cannot tell. When I think of Mortimer Tregennis, with the foxy face and the small shrewd, beady eyes behind the spectacles, he is not a man whom I should judge to be of a particularly forgiving disposition. Well, in the next place, you will remember that this idea of someone moving in the garden, which took our attention for a moment from the real cause of the tragedy, emanated from him. He had a motive in misleading us. Finally, if he did not throw this substance into the fire at the moment of leaving the room, who did do so? The affair happened immediately after his departure. Had anyone else come in, the family would certainly have risen from the table. Besides, in peaceful Cornwall, visitors do not arrive after ten o'clock at night. We may take it, then, that all the evidence points to Mortimer Tregennis as the culprit."

"Then his own death was suicide!"

"Well, Watson, it is on the face of it a not impossible supposition. The man who had the guilt upon his soul of having brought such a fate upon his own family might well be driven by remorse to inflict it upon himself. There are, however, some cogent reasons against it. Fortunately, there is one man in England who knows all about it, and I have made arrangements by which we shall hear the facts this afternoon from his own lips. Ah! he is a little before his time. Perhaps you would kindly step this way, Dr. Leon Sterndale. We have been conducting a chemical experiment indoors which has left our little room hardly fit for the reception of so distinguished a visitor."

I had heard the click of the garden gate, and now the majestic figure of the great African explorer appeared upon the path. He turned in some surprise towards the rustic arbour in which we sat.

"You sent for me, Mr. Holmes. I had your note about an hour ago, and I have come, though I really do not know why I should obey your summons."

"Perhaps we can clear the point up before we separate," said Holmes. "Meanwhile, I am much obliged to you for your courteous acquiescence. You will excuse this informal reception in the open air, but my friend Watson and I have nearly furnished an additional chapter to what the papers call the Cornish Horror, and we prefer a clear atmosphere for the present. Perhaps, since the matters which we have to discuss will affect you personally in a very intimate fashion, it is as well that we should talk where there can be no eavesdropping."

The explorer took his cigar from his lips and gazed sternly at my companion.

"I am at a loss to know, sir," he said, "what you can have to speak about which affects me personally in a very intimate fashion."

"The killing of Mortimer Tregennis," said Holmes.

For a moment I wished that I were armed. Sterndale's fierce face turned to a dusky red, his eyes glared, and the knotted, passionate veins started out in his forehead, while he sprang forward with clenched hands towards my companion. Then he stopped, and with a violent effort he resumed a cold, rigid calmness, which was, perhaps, more suggestive of danger than his hot-headed outburst.

"I have lived so long among savages and beyond the law," said he, "that I have got into the way of being a law to myself. You would do well, Mr. Holmes, not to forget it, for I have no desire to do you an injury."

"Nor have I any desire to do you an injury, Dr. Sterndale. Surely the clearest proof of it is that, knowing what I know, I have sent for you and not for the police."

Sterndale sat down with a gasp, overawed for, perhaps, the first time in his adventurous life. There was a calm assurance of power in Holmes's manner which could not be withstood. Our visitor stammered for a moment, his great hands opening and shutting in his agitation.

"What do you mean?" he asked at last. "If this is bluff upon your part, Mr. Holmes, you have chosen a bad man for your experiment. Let us have no more beating about the bush. What *do* you mean?"

"I will tell you," said Holmes, "and the reason why I tell you is that I hope frankness may beget frankness. What my next step may be will depend entirely upon the nature of your own defence."

"My defence?"

"Yes, sir."

"My defence against what?"

"Against the charge of killing Mortimer Tregennis."

Sterndale mopped his forehead with his handkerchief. "Upon my word, you are getting on," said he. "Do all your successes depend upon this prodigious power of bluff?"

"This bluff," said Holmes sternly, "is upon your side, Dr. Leon Sterndale, and not upon mine. As a proof I will tell you some of the facts upon which my conclusions are based. Of your return from Plymouth, allowing much of your property to go on to Africa, I will say nothing save that it first informed me that you were one of the factors which had to be taken into account in restructuring this drama——"

"I came back——"

"I have heard your reasons and regard them as unconvincing and inadequate. We will pass that. You came down here to ask me whom I suspected. I refused to answer you. You then went to the vicarage, waited outside it for some time, and finally returned to your cottage."

"How do you know that?"

"I followed you."

"I saw no one."

"That is what you may expect to see when I follow you. You spent a restless night at your cottage, and you formed certain plans, which in the early morning you proceeded to put into execution. Leaving your door just as day was breaking, you filled your pocket with some reddish gravel that was lying heaped beside your gate."

Sterndale gave a violent start and looked at Holmes in amazement.

"You then walked swiftly for the mile which separated you from the vicarage. You were wearing, I may remark, the same pair of ribbed tennis shoes which are at the present moment upon your feet. At the vicarage you passed through the orchard and the side hedge, coming out under the window of the lodger Tregennis. It was now daylight, but the household was not yet stirring. You drew some of the gravel from your pocket, and you threw it up at the window above you."

Sterndale sprang to his feet.

"I believe that you are the devil himself!" he cried.

Holmes smiled at the compliment. "It took two, or possibly three, handfuls before the lodger came to the window. You beckoned him to come down. He dressed hurriedly and descended to his sitting-room. You entered by the window. There was an interview—a short one—during which you walked up and down the room. Then you passed out and closed the window, standing on the lawn outside smoking a cigar and watching what occurred. Finally, after the death of Tregennis, you withdrew as you

had come. Now, Dr. Sterndale, how do you justify such conduct, and what were the motives for your actions? If you prevaricate or trifle with me, I give you my assurance that the matter will pass out of my hands forever."

Our visitor's face had turned ashen gray as he listened to the words of his accuser. Now he sat for some time in thought with his face sunk in his hands. Then with a sudden impulsive gesture he plucked a photograph from his breast-pocket and threw it on the rustic table before us.

"That is why I have done it," said he.

It showed the bust and face of a very beautiful woman. Holmes stooped over it.

"Brenda Tregennis," said he.

"Yes, Brenda Tregennis," repeated our visitor. "For years I have loved her. For years she has loved me. There is the secret of that Cornish seclusion which people have marvelled at. It has brought me close to the one thing on earth that was dear to me. I could not marry her, for I have a wife who has left me for years and yet whom, by the deplorable laws of England, I could not divorce. For years Brenda waited. For years I waited. And this is what we have waited for." A terrible sob shook his great frame, and he clutched his throat under his brindled beard. Then with an effort he mastered himself and spoke on:

"The vicar knew. He was in our confidence. He would tell you that she was an angel upon earth. That was why he telegraphed to me and I returned. What was my baggage or Africa to me when I learned that such a fate had come upon my darling? There you have the missing clue to my action, Mr. Holmes."

"Proceed," said my friend.

Dr. Sterndale drew from his pocket a paper packet and laid it upon the table. On the outside was written *"Radix pedis diaboli"* with a red poison label beneath it. He pushed it towards me. "I understand that you are a doctor, sir. Have you ever heard of this preparation?"

"Devil's-foot root! No, I have never heard of it."

"It is no reflection upon your professional knowledge," said he, "for I believe that, save for one sample in a laboratory at Buda, there is no other specimen in Europe. It has not yet found its way either into the pharmacopœia or into the literature of toxicology. The root is shaped like a foot, half human, half goatlike; hence the fanciful name given by a botanical missionary. It is used as an ordeal poison by the medicine-men in certain districts of West Africa and is kept as a secret among them. This particular specimen I obtained under very extraordinary circumstances in the Ubanghi country." He opened the paper as he spoke and disclosed a heap of reddish-brown, snuff-like powder.

"Well, sir?" asked Holmes sternly.

"I am about to tell you, Mr. Holmes, all that actually occurred, for you already know so much that it is clearly to my interest that you should know all. I have already explained the relationship in which I stood to the Tregennis family. For the sake of the sister I was friendly with the brothers. There was a family quarrel about money which estranged this man Mortimer, but it was supposed to be made up, and I afterwards met him as I did the others. He was a sly, subtle, scheming man, and several things arose which gave me a suspicion of him, but I had no cause for any positive quarrel.

"One day, only a couple of weeks ago, he came down to my cottage and I showed him some of my African curiosities. Among other things I exhibited this powder, and I told him of its strange properties, how it stimulates those brain centres which control the emotion of fear, and how either madness or death is the fate of the unhappy native who is subjected to the ordeal by the priest of his tribe. I told him also how powerless European science would be to detect it. How he took it I cannot say, for I never left the room, but there is no doubt that it was then, while I was opening cabinets and stooping to boxes, that he managed to abstract some of the devil's-foot root. I well remember how he plied me with questions as to the amount and the time that was needed for its effect, but I little dreamed that he could have a personal reason for asking.

"I thought no more of the matter until the vicar's telegram reached me at Plymouth. This villain had thought that I would be at sea before the news could reach me, and that I should be lost for years in Africa. But I returned at once. Of course, I could not listen to the details without feeling assured that my poison had been used. I came round to see you on the chance that some other explanation had suggested itself to you. But there could be none. I was convinced that Mortimer Tregennis was the murderer; that for the sake of money, and with the idea, perhaps, that if the other members of his family were all insane he would be the sole guardian of their joint property, he had used the devil's-foot powder upon them, driven two of them out of their senses, and killed his sister Brenda, the one human being whom I have ever loved or who has ever loved me. There was his crime; what was to be his punishment?

"Should I appeal to the law? Where were my proofs? I knew that the facts were true, but could I help to make a jury of countrymen believe so fantastic a story? I might or I might not. But I could not afford to fail. My soul cried out for revenge. I have said to you once before, Mr. Holmes, that I have spent much of my life outside the law, and that I have come at last to be a law to myself. So it was now. I determined that the fate which he had given to others should be shared by himself. Either that or I would do justice upon him with my own hand. In all England there can be no man who sets less value upon his own life than I do at the present moment.

"Now I have told you all. You have yourself supplied the rest. I did, as you say, after a restless night, set off early from my cottage. I foresaw the difficulty of arousing him, so I gathered some gravel from the pile which you have mentioned, and I used it to throw up to his window. He came down and admitted me through the window of the sitting-room. I laid his offence before him. I told him that I had come both as judge and executioner. The wretch sank into a chair, paralyzed at the sight of my revolver. I lit the lamp, put the powder above it, and stood outside the window, ready to carry out my threat to shoot him should he try to leave the room. In five minutes he died. My God! how he died! But my heart was flint, for he endured nothing which my innocent darling had not felt before him. There is my story, Mr. Holmes. Perhaps, if you loved a woman, you would have done as much yourself. At any rate, I am in your hands. You can take what steps you like. As I have already said, there is no man living who can fear death less than I do."

Holmes sat for some little time in silence.

"What were your plans?" he asked at last.

"I had intended to bury myself in central Africa. My work there is but half finished."

"Go and do the other half," said Holmes. "I, at least, am not prepared to prevent you."

Dr. Sterndale raised his giant figure, bowed gravely, and walked from the arbour. Holmes lit his pipe and handed me his pouch.

"Some fumes which are not poisonous would be a welcome change," said he. "I think you must agree, Watson, that it is not a case in which we are called upon to interfere. Our investigation has been independent, and our action shall be so also. You would not denounce the man?"

"Certainly not," I answered.

"I have never loved, Watson, but if I did and if the woman I loved had met such an end, I might act even as our lawless lion-hunter has done. Who knows? Well, Watson, I will not offend your intelligence by explaining what is obvious. The gravel upon the window-sill was, of course, the starting-point of my research. It was unlike anything in the vicarage garden. Only when my attention had been drawn to Dr. Sterndale and his cottage did I find its counterpart. The lamp shining in broad daylight and the remains of powder upon the shield were successive links in a fairly obvious chain. And now, my dear Watson, I think we may dismiss the matter from our mind and go back with a clear conscience to the study of those Chaldean roots which are surely to be traced in the Cornish branch of the great Celtic speech."

Questions

1. Is justice done in this case?

2. Consider Holmes' silence. Is it morally right for him to remain silent? If your answer is yes, how is that answer justified? For example, how is silence justified in regard to legal responsibilities? Is it a matter of justification?

3. Is it possible to specify *a priori* when one is not obliged to obey the law? To what standard can one appeal?

4. Suppose that Sterndale is brought to trial and you are a member of the jury. What do you do? Consider this problem from the perspectives of defense attorney, prosecutor, and judge. At what point would legal and professional responsibilities be satisfied? Does a moral problem remain?

5. How are morality and motives related? What do Dr. Sterndale's motives have to do with Holmes' decision?

6. If you are working with a text of ethical theories, describe this episode in terms of the theories you have studied. It might be particularly helpful to evaluate it from the perspectives of Aristotle, Kant, Mill, and Prichard.

15

Doing What
Everyone Else Does

Saturday Afternoon

Tom Denny shoved the hunk of meat out of his way and stretched out on the meat block. He wanted to lie on his back and rest. The meat block was the only comfortable place in the butchershop where a man could stretch out and Tom just had to rest every once in a while. He could prop his foot on the edge of the block, swing the other leg across his knee and be fairly comfortable with a hunk of rump steak under his head. The meat was nice and cool just after it came from the icehouse. Tom did that. He wanted to rest himself a while and he had to be comfortable on the meat block. He kicked off his shoes so he could wiggle his toes.

Tom's butchershop did not have a very pleasant smell. Strangers who went in to buy Tom's meat for the first time were always asking him what it was that had died between the walls. The smell got worse and worse year after year.

From *The Complete Stories of Erskine Caldwell* by Erskine Caldwell. Copyright 1930, © 1958 by Erskine Caldwell, by permission of Little, Brown and Co.

Tom bit off a chew of tobacco and made himself comfortable on the meat block.

There was a swarm of flies buzzing around the place: those lazy, stinging, fat and greasy flies that lived in Tom's butchershop. A screen door at the front kept out some of them that tried to get inside, but if they were used to coming in and filling up on the fresh blood on the meat block they knew how to fly around to the back door where there had never been a screen.

Everybody ate Tom's meat, and liked it. There was no other butchershop in town. You walked in and said, "Hello, Tom. How's everything today?" "Everything's slick as a whistle with me, but my old woman's got the chills and fever again." Then after Tom had finished telling how it felt to have chills and fever, you said, "I want a pound of pork chops, Tom." And Tom said, "By gosh, I'll git it for you right away." While you stood around waiting for the chops Tom turned the hunk of beef over two or three times businesslike and hacked off a pound of pork for you. If you wanted veal it was all the same to Tom. He slammed the hunk of beef around several times making a great to-do, and got the veal for you. He pleased everybody. Ask Tom for any kind of meat you could name, and Tom had it right there on the meat block waiting to be cut off and weighed.

Tom brushed the flies off his face and took a little snooze. It was midday. The country people had not yet got to town. It was laying-by season and everybody was working right up to twelve-o'clock sun time, which was half an hour slower than railroad time. There was hardly anybody in town at this time of day, even though it was Saturday. All the town people who had wanted some of Tom's meat for dinner had already got what they needed, and it was too early in the day to buy Sunday meat. The best time of day to get meat from Tom if it was to be kept over until Sunday was about ten o'clock Saturday night. Then you could take it home and be fairly certain that it would not turn bad before noon the next day—if the weather was not too hot.

The flies buzzed and lit on Tom's mouth and nose and Tom knocked them away with his hand and tried to sleep on the meat block with the cool hunk of rump steak under his head. The tobacco juice kept trying to trickle down his throat and Tom had to keep spitting it out. There was a cigar box half full of sawdust in the corner behind the showcase where livers and brains were kept for display, but he could not quite spit that far from the position he was in. The tobacco juice splattered on the floor midway between the meat block and the cigar box. What little of it dripped on the piece of rump steak did not really matter: most people cleaned their meat before they cooked and ate it, and it would all wash off.

But the danged flies! They kept on buzzing and stinging as mean as ever, and there is nothing any meaner than a lazy, well-fed, butchershop fly in the summertime, anyway. Tom knocked them off his face and spat them off his mouth the best he could without having to move too much. After a while he let them alone.

Tom was enjoying a good little snooze when Jim Baxter came running through the back door from the barbershop on the corner. Jim was Tom's partner and he came in sometimes on busy days to help out. He was a great big man, almost twice as large as Tom. He always wore a big wide-brimmed black hat and a blue shirt with the sleeves rolled up above his elbows. He had a large egg-shaped belly over which his breeches were always slipping down. When he walked he tugged at his breeches all the time, pulling them up over the top of his belly. But they were always working down until it looked as if they were ready to drop to the ground any minute and trip him. Jim would not wear suspenders. A belt was more sporty-looking.

Tom was snoozing away when Jim ran in the back door and grabbed him by the shoulders. A big handful of flies had gone to sleep on Tom's mouth. Jim shooed them off.

"Hey, Tom, Tom!" Jim shouted breathlessly. "Wake up, Tom! Wake up quick!"

Tom jumped to the floor and pulled on his shoes. He had become so accustomed to people coming in and waking him up to buy a quarter's worth of steak or a quarter's worth of ham that he had mistaken Jim for a customer. He rubbed the back of his hands over his mouth to take away the fly stings.

"What the hell!" he sputtered, looking up and seeing Jim standing there beside him. "What you want?"

"Come on, Tom! Git your gun! We're going after a nigger down the creek a ways."

"God Almighty, Jim!" Tom shouted, now fully awake. He clutched Jim's arm and begged: "You going to git a nigger, sure enough?"

"You're damn right, Tom. You know that gingerbread nigger what used to work on the railroad a long time back? Him's the nigger we're going to git. And we're going to git him good and proper, the yellow-faced coon. He said something to Fred Jackson's oldest gal down the road yonder about an hour ago. Fred told us all about it over at the barbershop. Come on, Tom. We got to hurry. I expect we'll jerk him up pretty soon now.''

Tom tied on his shoes and ran across the street behind Jim. Tom had his shotgun under his arm, and Jim had pulled the cleaver out of the meat block. They'd get the Goddamn nigger all right—God damn his yellow hide to hell!

Tom climbed into an automobile with some other men. Jim jumped on the running board of another car just as it was leaving. There were thirty or forty cars headed for the creek bottom already and more getting ready to start.

They had a place already picked out at the creek. There was a clearing in the woods by the road and there was just enough room to do the job like it should be done. Plenty of dry brushwood near by and a good-sized sweetgum tree in the middle of the clearing. The automobiles stopped and the men jumped out in a hurry. Some others had gone for Will Maxie. Will was the gingerbread Negro. They would probably find him at home laying-by his cotton. Will could grow good cotton. He cut out all the grass first, and then he banked his rows with earth. Everybody else laid-by his cotton without going to the trouble of taking out the grass. But Will was a pretty smart Negro. And he could raise a lot of corn too, to the acre. He always cut out the grass before· he laid-by his corn. But nobody liked Will. He made too much money by taking out the grass before laying-by his cotton and corn. He made more money than Tom and Jim made in the butchershop selling people meat.

Doc Cromer had sent his boy down from the drugstore with half a dozen cases of Coca-Cola and a piece of ice in a washtub. The tub had some muddy water put in it from the creek, then the chunk of ice, and then three cases of Coca-Cola. When they were gone the boy would put the other three cases in the tub and give the dopes a chance to cool. Everybody likes to drink a lot of dopes when they are nice and cold.

Tom went out in the woods to take a drink of corn with Jim and Hubert Wells. Hubert always carried a jug of corn with him wherever he happened to be going. He made the whisky himself at his own still and got a fairly good living by selling it around the courthouse and the barbershop. Hubert made the best corn in the county.

Will Maxie was coming up the big road in a hurry. A couple of dozen men were behind him poking him with sticks. Will was getting old. He had a wife and three grown daughters, all married and settled. Will was a pretty good Negro too, minding his own business, stepping out of the road when he met a white man, and otherwise behaving himself. But nobody liked Will. He made too much money by taking the grass out of his cotton before it was laid-by.

Will came running up the road and the men steered him into the clearing. It was all fixed. There was a big pile of brushwood and a trace-chain for his neck and one for his feet. That would hold him. There were two or three cans of gasoline, too.

Doc Cromer's boy was doing a good business with his Coca-Colas. Only five or six bottles of the first three cases were left in the washtub. He was getting ready to put the other cases in now and give the dopes a chance to get nice and cool. Everybody likes to have a dope every once in a while.

The Cromer boy would probably sell out and have to go back to town and bring back several more cases. And yet there was not such a big crowd today, either. It was the hot weather that made people have to drink a lot of dopes to stay cool. There were only a hundred and fifty or seventy-five there today. There had not been enough time for the word to get passed around. Tom would have missed it if Jim had not run in and told him about it while he was taking a nap on the meatblock.

Will Maxie did not drink Coca-Cola. Will never spent his money on anything like that. That was what was wrong with him. He was too damn good for a Negro. He did not drink corn whiskey, nor make it; he did not carry a knife, nor a razor; he bared his head when he met a white man, and he lived with his own wife. But they had him now! God damn his gingerbread hide to hell! They had him where he could not take any more grass out of his cotton before laying it by. They had him tied to a sweet-gum tree in the clearing at the creek with a trace-chain around his neck and another around his knees. Yes, sir, they had Will Maxie now, the yellow-faced coon! He would not take any more grass out of his cotton before laying it by!

Tom was feeling good. Hubert gave him another drink in the woods. Hubert was all right. He made good corn whiskey. Tom liked him for that. And Hubert always took his wife a big piece of meat Saturday night to use over Sunday. Nice meat, too. Tom cut off the meat and Hubert took it home and made a present of it to his wife.

Will Maxie was going up in smoke. When he was just about gone they gave him the lead. Tom stood back and took good aim and fired away at Will with his shotgun as fast as he could breech it and put in a new load. About forty or more of the other men had shotguns too. They filled him so full of lead that his body sagged from his neck where the trace-chain held him up.

The Cromer boy had sold completely out. All of his ice and dopes were gone. Doc Cromer would feel pretty good when his boy brought back all that money. Six whole cases he sold, at a dime a bottle. If he had brought along another case or two he could have sold them easily enough. Everybody likes Coca-Cola. There is nothing better to drink on a hot day, if the dopes are nice and cool.

After a while the men got ready to draw the body up in the tree and tie it to a limb so it could hang there, but Tom and Jim could not wait and they went back to town the first chance they got to ride. They were in a big hurry. They had been gone several hours and it was almost four o'clock. A lot of people came downtown early Saturday afternoon to get their Sunday meat before it was picked over by the country people. Tom and Jim had to hurry back and open up the meat-market and get to work slicing

steaks and chopping soup bones with the cleaver on the meatblock. Tom was the butcher. He did all the work with the meat. He went out and killed a cow and quartered her. Then he hauled the meat to the butcher-shop and hung it on the hooks in the icehouse. When somebody wanted to buy some meat, he took one of the quarters from the hook and threw it on the meatblock and cut what you asked for. You told Tom what you wanted and he gave it to you, no matter what you asked for.

Then you stepped over to the counter and paid Jim the money for it. Jim was the cashier. He did all the talking, too. Tom had to do the cutting and weighing. Jim's egg-shaped belly was too big for him to work around the meatblock. It got in his way when he tried to slice you a piece of tenderloin steak, so Tom did that and Jim took the money and put it into the cashbox under the counter.

Tom and Jim got back to town just in time. There was a big crowd standing around on the street getting ready to do their weekly trading, and they had to have some meat. You went in the butcher-shop and said, "Hello, Tom. I want two pounds and a half of pork chops." Tom said, "Hello, I'll get it for you right away." While you were waiting for Tom to cut the meat off the hunk of rump steak you asked him how was everything.

"Everything's slick as a whistle," he said, "except for my old woman's got the chills and fever pretty bad again."

Tom weighed the pork chops and wrapped them up for you and then you stepped over to Jim and paid him the money. Jim was the cashier. His egg-shaped belly was too big for him to work around the meatblock. Tom did that part, and Jim took the money and put it into the cashbox under the counter.

Questions

1. Given the brief picture of Tom Denny, describe the kind of character he has. Give special attention to the question of what his concerns have

been up to this time. For how much of this attitude is he responsible?

2. Analyze Tom Denny's character making use of the terms the author uses to describe the flies. Contrast this with Socrates' view of "human excellence." ·

3. Hubert Wells "made the whisky himself at his own still and got a fairly good living by selling it around the courthouse and the barber shop." Contrast the view of the law implied here (and in the rest of the story) with that of Socrates (especially in chapter three of this book). Contrast both these views with that of Holmes (in chapter fourteen of this book).

4. Analyze the similarities and differences between Socrates and Will Maxie. Give special

attention to the part that prejudice has in their deaths.

5. Some anthropologists, who subscribe to William Graham Sumners views, have defined morality as "folkways" (i.e., whatever is commonly done) formalized by philosophical or religious systems. If shooting and burning people of minority races or beliefs *is* done in some locations and times, does this make it *morally* acceptable? If your answer is no, respond to the apparent claim in this line of thinking that such acts could be right for others if not right for you.

6. Is it possible to be moral in a group? That is, can morality be ascribed to the practice of a group, or is it only intelligible in terms of *individuals'* lives, conduct, and commitments?

16

Doing What One Wants

I Got Up, Stiff from Sleeping in the Chair

[At this point in the story, Jacob Horner has recently been interviewed for a position in the English Department at Wicomico State Teachers College where Joe Morgan is on the history faculty. Having been a member of the interviewing committee, Joe and his wife Rennie had Horner to supper last night.

editor]

I got up, stiff from sleeping in the chair, showered, changed my clothes, and went out for breakfast. Perhaps because the previous day had been, for me, so unusually eventful, or perhaps because I'd had relatively little sleep (I must say I take no great interest in causes), my mind was empty. All the way to the restaurant, all through the meal, all the way home, it was as though there were no Jacob Horner today. After I'd eaten I returned to my room, sat in my

From *The End of the Road* by John Barth. Copyright © 1958, 1967 by John Barth. Reprinted by permission of Doubleday & Company, Inc.

rocker, and rocked, barely sentient, for a long time, thinking of nothing.

Once I had a dream in which it became a matter of some importance to me to learn the weather prediction for the following day. I searched the newspapers for the weather report, but couldn't find it in its usual place. I turned the radio on, but the news broadcasters made no mention of tomorrow's weather. I dialed the Weather number on the telephone (this dream took place in Baltimore), but although the recording described the current weather conditions it told me nothing about the forecast for the next day. Finally I called the Weather Bureau directly, but it was late at night and no one answered. I happened to know the chief meteorologist's name, and so I called his house. The telephone rang many times before he answered; it seemed to me that I detected an uneasiness in his voice.

"What is it?" he asked.

"I want to know what weather we'll be having tomorrow," I demanded. "It's terribly important."

"There's no use your trying to impress me," the meteorologist said. "No use at all. What made you suspicious?"

"I assure you, sir, I just want to know what the weather will be tomorrow. I can't say I see anything suspicious in that question."

"There isn't going to be any weather tomorrow."

"What?"

"You heard me. There isn't going to be any weather tomorrow. All our instruments agree. No weather."

"But that's impossible!"

"I've said what I've said," the weatherman grumbled. "No weather tomorrow, and that's that. Leave me alone; I have to sleep."

That was the end of the dream, and I woke up very much upset. I tell it now to illustrate a difference between moods and the weather, their usual analogy: a day without weather is unthinkable, but for me at least there were frequently days without any mood at all. On these days Jacob Horner, except in a meaningless metabolistic sense, ceased to exist, for I was without a personality. Like those microscopic specimens that biologists must dye in order to make them visible at all, I had to be colored with some mood or other if there was to be a recognizable self to me. The fact that my successive and discontinuous selves were linked to one another by the two unstable threads of body and memory; the fact that in the nature of Western languages the word *change* presupposes something upon which the changes operate; the fact that although the specimen is invisible without the dye, the dye is not the specimen—these are considerations of which I was aware, but in which I had no interest.

On my weatherless days my body sat in a rocking chair and rocked and rocked and rocked, and my mind was as nearly empty as interstellar space. Such was the day after the Morgans' visit: I sat and rocked from eight-thirty in the morning until perhaps two in the afternoon. If I looked at Laocoön at all, it was without recognition. But at two

o'clock the telephone rang and startled into being a Jacob Horner, who jumped from the chair and answered it.

"Hello?"

"Jacob? This is Rennie Morgan. Will you have dinner with us tonight?"

"*Why,* for God's sake?" This Jacob Horner was an irritable type.

"Why?"

"Yes. Why the hell are you all so anxious to feed me dinner?"

"Are you angry?"

"No, I'm not angry. I just want to know why you're all so anxious to feed me a dinner."

"Don't you want to come?"

"I didn't say that. Why are you all so anxious to feed me a dinner? That's all I asked."

There was a pause. Rennie was one who took all questions seriously; she would not offer an answer simply to terminate a situation, but must search herself for the truth. This, I take it, was Joe's doing. Another person would have asked pettishly, "Why does anybody ask anybody for dinner?" and thereby cloaked ignorance in the garb of self-evidence. After a minute she replied in a careful voice, as though examining her answer as she spoke.

"Well, I think it's because Joe's pretty much decided that he wants to get to know you well. He enjoyed the conversation last night."

"Didn't you?" I interrupted out of curiosity. I didn't really see how she could have, for we had talked of nothing but abstract ideas, and Rennie's determined but limited participation had been under what struck me as a tacit but very careful scrutiny from her husband. I don't mean to suggest that there was anything ungenuine in Rennie's interest, though it was awfully *deliberate,* or anything of the husband embarrassed by his wife's opinions in Joe's concern about her statements; his attention was that of a tutor listening to his favorite protégé, and when he questioned her opinions he did so in an entirely impersonal, unarrogant, and unpedantic manner. Joe was not a pedant.

"Yes, I believe I did. Do you think that there ought to be a kind of waiting period between visits, Jacob?"

I was amazed. "What do *you* think?"

Again a short pause, and then a solemn opinion.

"It seems to me that there wouldn't be any reason for it unless one of us just happened to feel like not seeing the other for a while. I think sometimes a person feels that way. Is that how you feel, Jake?"

"Well, now, let me see," I said soberly, and paused. "It seems to me that you do right to question the validity of social conventions, like waiting a certain time between visits, but you have to keep in mind that they're all ultimately unjustifiable. But it doesn't follow that because a thing is unjustifiable it's without value. And you have to remember that *dispensing* with a convention, even a silly one, always involves the risk of being made to feel unreasonably guilty, simply because the conventions *do* happen to be conventions. Take drinking beer for breakfast, for instance, or going through red lights late at night, or committing adultery with your husband's approval, or performing a euthanasia . . ."

"Are you making fun of me?" Rennie demanded mildly, as though asking purely for information.

"I am indeed!"

"You know, it seems to me that lots of times a person makes fun of another person because the other person's opinions make him uncomfortable but he doesn't really know how to refute them. He feels that he *ought* to know how, but he doesn't, and instead of admitting that to himself and studying the problem and working out a real refutation, he just sneers at the other person's argument. It's too easy to sneer at an argument. I feel that way a lot about you, Jake."

"Yes. Joe said the same thing."

"Now you *are* making fun of me, aren't you?"

I was resolved not to let Mrs. Rennie Morgan make me uncomfortable again. That was too easy.

"Listen, I'll come eat your dinner tonight. I'll come at six o'clock, after you've put your kids to bed, as you said."

"We neither one want you to come if you don't feel like it, Jake. You have to be—"

"Now wait a minute. *Why* don't you want me to come even if I don't feel like it?"

"What?"

"I said why don't you want me to come even if I don't feel like it? You see, the only grounds you'd have for breaking the custom of waiting a proper interval between visits would be if you took the position that social conventions might be necessary for stability in a social group, but that they aren't absolutes and you can dispense with them in special situations where your end justifies it. In other words, you're willing to have me to dinner tonight anyhow as long as that's what we all want—social stability isn't your end in this special situation. Well, then, suppose your end was to have another conversation and you had reason to believe that once I got there I'd talk to you whether I'd really wanted to come or not —most guests would—then it shouldn't matter to you whether I wanted to come or not, since your ends would be reached anyway."

"You're still making fun of me."

"Oh, now, that's too easy an out. It's beside the point whether I'm making fun of you or not. You're evading the question."

No answer.

"Now, I'm coming to dinner at six o'clock, whether I want to or not, and if you aren't ready to answer my argument by then, I'm going to tell Joe."

"Six-thirty is when the kids go to bed," Rennie said in a slightly injured voice, and hung up. I went back to my rocker and rocked for another forty-five minutes. From time to time I smiled inscrutably, but I cannot say that this honestly reflected any sincere feeling on my part. It was just a thing I found myself doing, as frequently when walking alone I would find myself repeating over and over in a judicious, unmetrical voice, *Pepsi-Cola hits the spot; twelve full ounces: that's a lot*—accompanying the movement of my lips with a wrinkled brow, distracted twitches of the corner of my mouth, and an occasional quick gesture of my right hand. Passers-by often took me for a man lost in serious problems, and sometimes when I looked behind me after passing one I'd see him, too, make a furtive movement with his right hand, trying it out.

At four-fifteen Dr. Schott telephoned and confirmed my appointment to the faculty of the Wicomico State Teachers College as a teacher of grammar and composition, at a starting salary of $3200 per year.

"You know," he said, "we don't pay what they pay at the big universities! Can't afford it! But that doesn't mean we're not choosy about our teachers! We're a pretty dedicated bunch, frankly, and we hired you because we believe you share our feelings about the importance of our job!"

I assured him that I did indeed share that feeling, and he assured me that he was sure I did. I was not pleased at being asked to teach composition as well as grammar—I was supposed to be strictly a prescriptive-grammar man—but, pending advice from the Doctor, I thought it best to accept the job anyway.

As a matter of fact I drove out to the Morgans' place at five-thirty, for no particular reason. My day was no longer weather-less, but I was quiescent. I found Joe and Rennie having a leisurely catch with a football on the lawn in front of their house, although the afternoon was fairly warm. They showed no great surprise at seeing me, greeted me cordially, and invited me to join their game.

"No, thanks," I said, and went over to where their two sons, ages three and four, were throwing their own little football at each other—adeptly for their age. I sat on the grass and watched everybody.

"I didn't mean to get upset on the phone today, Jake," Rennie said cheerfully between passes.

"Ah, don't pay attention to what I say on telephones," I said. "I can't talk on telephones."

I've never seen a girl who could catch and throw a football properly except Rennie Morgan. As a rule she was a clumsy animal, but in any sort of strenuous physical activity she was completely at ease and even graceful. She caught and threw the ball in the same manner and with the same speed and accuracy as a practiced man.

"What have you changed your mind about that you said, then?" Joe asked, keeping his eyes on the ball.

"I don't even remember what I said."

"You don't? Rennie remembers the whole conversation. Do you really not remember, or are you trying not to make her uncomfortable?"

"I really don't remember at all," I said, with some truth. "I've learned by now that you all don't believe in avoiding discomfort. The fact is I can never remember arguments, my own or anybody else's. I can remember conclusions, but not arguments."

This observation, which I thought arresting enough, seemed to disgust Joe. He lost interest in the conversation and stopped to correct the older boy's way of gripping the football. The kid attended his father's quiet advice as though it were coming from Knute Rockne; Joe watched him throw the ball correctly three times and then turned away.

"Here, Jake," he said, tossing me the other ball. "Why don't you pitch a few with Rennie while I put supper on, and then we'll have a drink. No use to wait till six-thirty, since you're here."

I was, as I said before, quiescent. I would not voluntarily have joined the game, but neither would I go out of my way to avoid playing. Joe went on into the house, the two boys following close behind, and for the next twenty minutes Rennie and I threw the football to each other. Luckily—for as a rule I dreaded being made to look ridiculous—I was no novice at football myself; though not so adept a passer as Joe, I was able to throw at least as accurately and unwobblingly as Rennie. She seemed to have nothing special to say to me, nor did I to her, and so the only sound heard on the lawn was the rush of passing-arms, the quiet spurts of running feet on the grass, the soft smack of catches, and our heavy breathing. It was all neither pleasant nor unpleasant.

Presently Joe called to us from the porch, and we went in to dinner. The Morgans rented half of the first floor of the house. Their apartment was very clean; what furniture they owned was the most severely plain modern, tough and functional, but there was very little of it. In fact, because the rooms were relatively large they seemed quite bare. There were no rugs on the hardwood floors, no curtains or drapes on the polished windows, and not a piece of furniture above the necessary minimum; a day bed, two sling chairs, two lamps, a bookcase, and a writing table in the living room; a small dining table and four metal folding chairs in the kitchen; and a double bunk, two bureaus, and a work table with benches in the single bedroom, where the boys slept. Because the walls and ceiling were white, the light pouring through the open venetian blinds made the living room blindingly bright. I squinted; there was too much light in that room for me.

While we drank a glass of beer, the children went into the bedroom, undressed themselves, and bathed themselves without help in the water that Joe had already drawn for them. I expressed surprise at such independence at ages three and four. Rennie shrugged.

"We make pretty heavy demands on them for physical efficiency," Joe admitted. "What the hell, in New Guinea the kids are swimming before they walk, and paddling bamboo logs out in the ocean at Joey's age. We figured the less they're in our hair the better we'll get along with each other."

"Don't think we drive them," Rennie said. "We don't really give a damn. But I guess we demand a lot tacitly."

Joe listened to this remark with casual interest.

"Why do you say you don't give a damn?" he asked her.

Rennie was a little startled at the question, which she had not expected.

"Well—I mean *ultimately*. Ultimately it wouldn't matter one way or the other, would it? But *immediately* it matters because if they weren't independent we'd have to go through the same rigmarole most people go through, and the kids would be depending on all kinds of crutches."

"Nothing matters one way or the other ultimately," Joe pointed out. "The other importance is all there is to anything."

"That's what I meant, Joe."

"What I'm trying to say is that you shouldn't consider a value less real just because it isn't absolute, since less-than-absolutes are all we've got. That's what's implied when you say you don't *really* give a damn."

Well, it was Rennie's ball—I watched them over my beer much as I'd watched them out on the lawn—but the game was interrupted by the timer bell on the kitchen stove. Rennie went out to serve up the dinner while Joe dried the two boys and assisted them into their pajamas: their physical efficiency apparently didn't extend to fastening their own snaps in the back.

"Why don't you have them snap each other up in the back?" I suggested politely. Rennie flashed me an uncertain look from the kitchen, where she was awkwardly dishing out rice with a spoon too small for the job, but Joe laughed easily and unsnapped both boys' pajama shirts so that they could try it. It worked.

Since there were only four chairs in the kitchen, Rennie and the two boys and I ate at the table while Joe ate standing up at the stove. There would have been no room at the table for one of the sling chairs, and anyhow it did not take long to eat the meal, which consisted of steamed shrimp, boiled rice, and beer for all hands. The boys— husky, well-mannered youngsters—were allowed to dominate the conversation during dinner; they were as lively and loud as any other bright kids their age, but a great deal more physically co-ordinated and self-controlled than most. As soon as we finished eating they went to bed, and though it was still quite light outside, I heard no more from them.

The Morgans had an arrangement with their first-floor neighbor whereby they could leave open a door connecting the two apartments and listen for each other's children if one couple wished to go out for the evening. Taking advantage of this, we went walking through a clover field and a small stand of pines behind the house after the supper dishes were washed. The Morgans tended to walk vigorously, and this did not fit well with my quiescent mood, but neither did refusing to accompany them. Rennie, an amateur naturalist, remarked on various weeds, bugs, and birds as we bounded along, and Joe confirmed her identifications. I can't say I enjoyed the walk, although the Morgans enjoyed it almost fiercely. When it was over, Rennie went inside the house to write a letter, and Joe and I sat on the lawn in the two sling chairs. Our conversation, by his direction, dealt with values, since they'd come up earlier.

"Most of what you told Rennie on the phone this afternoon was sensible," he granted. "I'm glad you talked to her, and I'm glad you told her it was beside the point whether you were making fun of her or not. That's exactly what she needs to learn. She's too sensitive about that."

"So are you," I said. "Remember the Boy Scouts."

"No, I'm not, really," Joe denied, in a way that left you no special desire to insist that he was. "The only reason I caught it up about the Scouts was that I'd decided I wanted to know you a little bit, and it seemed to me that too much of that might stand in the way of any sensible talking. It doesn't matter at all outside of that."

"Okay." I offered him a cigarette, but he didn't smoke.

"What really pleases me is that in spite of your making fun of Rennie you seem willing to take her seriously. Almost no man is willing to take any woman's thinking seriously, and that's what Rennie needs more than anything else."

"It's none of my business, Joe," I said quiescently, "but if I were Rennie I'd object like hell having anybody so concerned over my *needs*. You talk about her as if she were a patient of yours."

He laughed and jabbed his spectacles back on his nose. "I guess I do; I don't mean to. When Rennie and I were married we understood that neither of us wanted to make a permanent thing of it if we couldn't respect each other in every way. Certainly I'm not sold on marriage-under-any-circumstances, and I'm sure Rennie's not either. There's nothing intrinsically valuable about marriage."

"Seems to me you put a pretty high value on *your* marriage," I suggested.

Joe squinted at me in disappointment, and I felt that had I been his wife he would have corrected me more severely than he did.

"Now you're making the same error Rennie made a while ago, before supper: the fallacy that because a value isn't intrinsic, objective, and absolute, it somehow isn't *real*. What I said was that the marriage relationship isn't any more of an absolute than anything else. That doesn't mean that I don't value it; in fact I guess I value my relationship with Rennie more than anything else in the world. All it means is that once you admit it's no absolute, you have to decide for yourself the conditions under which marriage is important to you. Okay?"

"Suits me," I said indifferently.

"Well, do you agree or not?"

"Sure, I agree." And, so cornered, I suppose I *did* agree, but there was something in me that would have recoiled from so systematic an analysis of things even if I'd had it straight from God that such happened to be the case.

"Well," Joe said, "I'm not a man who needs to be married under any circumstances—in fact, under a lot of circumstances I couldn't tolerate being married— and one of my conditions for preserving any relationship at all, but particularly a marriage relationship, would be that the parties involved be able to take each other seriously. If I straighten Rennie out now and then, or tell her that some statement of hers is stupid as hell, or even slug her one, it's because I respect her, and to me that means not making a lot of kinds of allowances for her. Making allowances might be Christian, but to me it would always mean not taking seriously the person you make allowances for. That's the only objection I have to your making fun of Rennie: not that it might hurt her feelings, but that it means you're making allowances for her being a *woman*, or some such nonsense as that."

"Aren't you regarding this take-us-seriously business as an absolute?" I asked. "You seem to want you and Rennie to take each other seriously under any circumstances."

This observation pleased Joe, and to my chagrin I noticed that I was unaccountably happy that I'd said something he considered bright.

"That's a good point," he grinned, and began his harangue. "The usual criticism of people like me is that somewhere at the end of the line is the *ultimate* end that gives the whole chain its relative value, and this ultimate end is rationally unjustifiable if there aren't any absolute values. These ends can be pretty impersonal, like 'the good of the state,' or else personal, like taking your wife seriously. In either case if you're going to defend these ends at all I think you have to call them subjective. But they'd never be *logically* defensible; they'd be in the nature of psychological *givens*, different for most people. Four things that I'm not impressed by," he added, "are unity, harmony, eternality, and universality. In my ethics the most a man can ever do is be right from his point of view; there's no general reason why he should even bother to defend it, much less expect anybody else to accept it, but the only thing he can do is operate by it, because there's nothing else. He's got to expect conflict with people or institutions who are also right from *their* points of view, but whose points of view are different from his.

"Suppose it were the essence of my nature that I was completely jealous of Rennie, for instance," he went on. "Now it happens that that's not the case at all, but suppose it were true that because of my psychological make-up, marital fidelity was one of the *givens*, the subjective equivalent of an absolute, one of the conditions that would attach to any string of ethical propositions I might make for myself. Then suppose Rennie committed adultery behind my back. From my point of view the relationship would have lost its *raison d'être*, and I'd probably walk out flat, if I didn't actually shoot her or shoot myself. But from the state's point of view, for example, I'd still be obligated to support her, because you can't have a society where people just walk out flat on family relationships like that. From their point of view I should be forced to pay support money, and I would have no reason to complain that their viewpoint isn't the same as mine: it couldn't be. In the same way, the state would be as justified in hanging me or jailing me for shooting her as I would be in shooting her—do you see? Or the Catholic Church, if I were officially a Catholic, would be as justified from their point of view in refusing me sacred burial ground as I'd be in committing suicide if the marriage relationship had been one of the *givens* for my whole life. I'd be a fool if I expected the world to excuse my actions simply because I can explain them clearly.

"That's one reason why I don't apologize for things," Joe said finally. "It's because I've no right to expect you or anybody to accept anything I do or say—but I can always *explain* what I do or say. There's no sense in apologizing, because nothing is ultimately defensible. But a man can act coherently; he can act in ways that he can explain, if he wants to. This is important to me. Do you know, for the first month of our marriage Rennie used to apologize all over herself to friends who dropped in, because we didn't have much furniture in the house. She knew very well that we didn't want any more furniture even if we could have afforded it, but she always apologized to other people for not having their point of view. One day she did it more elaborately than usual, and as soon as the company left I popped her one on the jaw. Laid her out cold. When she came to, I explained to her very carefully why I'd hit her. She cried, and apologized to me for having apologized to other people. I popped her again."

There was no boastfulness in Joe's voice when he said this; neither was there any regret.

"What the hell, Jake, the more sophisticated your ethics get, the stronger you have to be to stay afloat. And when you say good-by to objective values, you really have to flex your muscles and keep your eyes open, because you're on your own. It takes *energy;* not just personal energy, but cultural energy, or you're lost. Energy's what makes the difference between American pragmatism and French existentialism—where the hell else but in America could you have a cheerful nihilism, for God's sake? I suppose it was rough, slugging Rennie, but I saw the moment as a kind of crisis. Anyhow, she stopped apologizing after that."

"Ah," I said.

Now it may well be that Joe made no such long coherent speech as this all at once; it is certainly true that during the course of the evening this was the main thing that got said, and I put it down here in the form of one uninterrupted whiz-bang for convenience's sake, both to illustrate the nature of his preoccupations and to add a stroke or two to my picture of the man himself. I heard it all quiescently; despite the fact that I was accustomed to expressing certain of these opinions myself at times (more hopefully than honestly), arguments against nearly everything he said occurred to me as he spoke. Yet I would by no means assert that he couldn't have refuted my objections —I daresay even I could have. As was usually the case when I was confronted by a really intelligent and lucidly exposed position, I was as reluctant to give it more than notional assent as I was unable to offer a more reasonable position of my own. In such situations I most often adopted what in psychology is known as the "non-direc-

tive technique": I merely said, "Oh?" or "Ah," and gave the horse his head.

But I was interested in the story of Rennie's first encounter with the Morgan philosophy, and the irresistible rhetoric Joe had employed to open her eyes to the truth about apologies. It demonstrated clearly that philosophizing was no game to Mr. Morgan; that he lived his conclusions down to the fine print; and Rennie became a somewhat more interesting figure to me. Indeed, I should say that that particular little anecdote was doubtless the main thing that made me amenable to a proposal which Joe made later on, after Rennie had joined us out on the lawn.

"Do you like horseback-riding, Jake?" Rennie had happened to ask.

"Never rode before, Rennie,"

"Gee, it's fun; you'll have to try it with me sometime."

I raised my eyebrows. "Yes, I suppose it would be better to do that before I tried it with a horse."

Rennie giggled, whipping her head from side to side, and Joe laughed loudly, but not, I think, enthusiastically. Then I saw his frowning forehead suddenly illuminate.

"Hey, that's an idea!" he exclaimed to Rennie. "Teach Jake how to ride!" He turned to me. "Rennie's folks have riding horses on their farm, down the road, but I seldom get a chance to ride and Rennie hates to ride by herself. I'm busy nearly all day reading for my thesis before school starts. Why don't you let Rennie teach you to ride? It'll give her a chance to get outdoors more, and you all will be able to do some talking."

I was embarrassed both by Joe's deliberate enthusiasm for his project and by his poor taste in implying that talking to me would do Rennie good. It pleased me, perversely, to see Rennie squirm a little, too: she was apparently not yet so well educated by her husband that his ingenuousness did not sometimes embarrass her, though she was careful to conceal her discomfort from Joe.

"What do you think?" he demanded of her.

"I think it's a swell idea, if Jake wants to learn," Rennie said quickly.

"*Do* you?" Joe asked me.

I shrugged. "Doesn't make a damn to me."

"Well, if it doesn't make a damn to you, and Rennie and I think it's a good idea, then it's settled, if you're not willing to refuse, just like this dinner business!"

We all chuckled, and the subject was dropped, Joe explaining to me happily that as a matter of fact my statement on the telephone (that I would come to dinner whether I wanted to or not) was unintelligible.

"Rennie would've told you if you hadn't flustered her by making fun of her," he smiled; "the only demonstrable index to a man's desires is his acts, when you're speaking of past time: what a man did is what he wanted to do."

"What?"

"Don't you see?" asked Rennie, and Joe sat back and relaxed. "The idea is that you could have conflicting desires—say, the desire not to have dinner with us and the desire not to offend us. If you end by coming to dinner it's because the second desire was stronger than the first: other things being equal, you wouldn't want to eat with us, but other things never are equal, and actually you'd rather eat with us than insult us. So you eat with us—that's what you *finally* wanted to do. You shouldn't say you'll eat with us whether you want to or not; you should say you'll eat with us if it satisfies desires in you stronger than your desire *not* to eat with us."

"It's like combining plus one hundred and minus ninety-nine," Joe said. "The answer is just barely plus, but it's completely plus. That's another reason why it's silly for anybody to apologize for something he's done by claiming he didn't really want to do it: what he *wanted* to do, in the end, was what he did. That's important to remember when you're reading history."

I observed that Rennie colored slightly at the reference to apologizing.

"Mmm," I replied to Joe, non-directively.

Questions

1. Horner has no "personality" without a "mood." Since his moods need to be set by something external, whatever he *stands for* depends upon the external, and there is no telling how he might be struck by one thing or another. Contrast this sort of character—if that is the right word—with that of Socrates. Give special attention to the part that intelligence and reflection have in their lives.

2. "The fact is I can never remember arguments, my own or anybody else's. I can remember conclusions, but not arguments." What does this mean in terms of Jacob's character? Does it indicate that to him intelligence is something to be used only in service of the moment?

3. Joe says of his and Rennie's children, "the less they're in our hair the better we'll get along with each other." What does this mean?

4. What is Joe saying and what is he opposing in the following sentence? "There's nothing intrinsically valuable about marriage."

5. Joe holds the view that values may be *real* without being "intrinsic, objective, and absolute." Though his meaning is unclear, he seems to mean this as an analysis of *moral* value. However, Socrates would seem to hold that moral value must be intrinsic and absolute. What *sort* of disagreement is this? What kind of arguments would be used in defending one side or the other?

6. Here we have two intellectuals discussing something which is obviously important. Why don't they get any further?

7. If you are working with a text of ethical theories, respond to Joe in terms of the theories you have studied. It might be particularly helpful to contrast Joe's attitude with the thoughts expressed by Plato, Kant, Mill, and Prichard.

17

Telling the Truth

Selection from
All Creatures Great and Small

Chapter 28

There were three of us in the cheerless yard, Isaac Cranford, Jeff Mallock and myself. The only one who looked at ease was Mallock and it was fitting that it should be so, since he was, in a manner of speaking, the host. He owned the knacker yard and he looked on benignly as we peered into the carcass of the cow he had just opened.

In Darrowby the name Mallock had a ring of doom. It was the graveyard of livestock, of farmers' ambitions, of veterinary surgeons' hopes. If ever an animal was very ill somebody was bound to say: "I reckon she'll be off to Mallock's afore long," or "Jeff Mallock'll have 'er in t' finish." And the premises fitted perfectly into the picture; a group of drab, red-brick buildings standing a few fields back from the road with a stumpy chimney from which rolled endlessly a dolorous black smoke.

It didn't pay to approach Mallock's too closely unless you had a strong stomach, so the place was avoided by the townspeople, but if you ventured up the lane and peeped through the sliding metal doors you could look in on a nightmare world. Dead animals lay everywhere. Most of them were dismembered and great chunks of meat hung on hooks, but here and there you could see a bloated sheep or a greenish, swollen pig which not even Jeff could bring himself to open.

Skulls and dry bones were piled to the roof in places and brown mounds of meat meal stood in the corners. The smell was bad at any time but when Jeff was boiling up the carcasses it was indescribable. The Mallock family bungalow stood in the middle of the buildings and strangers could be pardoned if they expected a collection of wizened gnomes to dwell there. But Jeff was a pink-faced, cherubic man in his forties, his wife plump, smiling and comely. Their family ranged from a positively beautiful girl of nineteen down to a robust five-year-old boy. There were eight young Mallocks

From *All Creatures Great and Small* by James Herriot. Copyright © 1972 by James Herriot. Reprinted by permission of St. Martin's Press, Inc.

and they had spent their lifetimes playing among tuberculous lungs and a vast spectrum of bacteria from Salmonella to Anthrax. They were the healthiest children in the district.

It was said in the pubs that Jeff was one of the richest men in the town but the locals, as they supped their beer, had to admit that he earned his money. At any hour of the day or night he would rattle out into the country in his ramshackle lorry, winch on a carcass, bring it back to the yard and cut it up. A dog food dealer came twice a week from Brawton with a van and bought the fresh meat. The rest of the stuff Jeff shovelled into his boiler to make the meat meal which was in great demand for mixing in pig and poultry rations. The bones went for making fertiliser, the hides to the tanner and the nameless odds and ends were collected by a wild-eyed individual known only as the "ket feller." Sometimes, for a bit of variety, Jeff would make long slabs of strange-smelling soap which found a brisk sale for scrubbing shop floors. Yes, people said, there was no doubt Jeff did all right. But, by gaw, he earned it.

My contacts with Mallock were fairly frequent. A knacker's yard had a useful function for a vet. It served as a crude post-mortem room, a place where he could check on his diagnosis in fatal cases; and on the occasions where he had been completely baffled, the mysteries would be revealed under Jeff's knife.

Often, of course, farmers would send in an animal which I had been treating and ask Jeff to tell them "what had been wrong wi't" and this was where a certain amount of friction arose. Because Jeff was placed in a position of power and seldom resisted the temptation to wield it. Although he could neither read nor write, he was a man of great professional pride; he didn't like to be called a knacker man but preferred "fellmonger." He considered in his heart that, after twenty-odd years of cutting up diseased animals, he knew more than any vet alive, and it made things rather awkward that the farming community unhesitatingly agreed with him.

It never failed to spoil my day if a farmer called in at the surgery and told me that, once more, Jeff Mallock had confounded my diagnosis. "Hey, remember that cow you were treating for magnesium deficiency? She never did no good and ah sent 'er into Mallock's. Well, you know what was really the matter wi' 'er? Worm i' the tail. Jeff said if you'd nobbut cut tail off, that cow would have gotten up and walked away." It was no good arguing or saying there was no such thing as worm in the tail. Jeff knew—that was all about it.

If only Jeff had taken his priceless opportunities to acquire a commonsense knowledge it wouldn't have been so bad. But instead, he had built up a weird pathology of his own and backed it up by black magic remedies gleaned from his contacts with the more primitive members of the farming community. His four stock diseases were Stagnation of t'lungs, Black Rot, Gastric Ulsters and Golf Stones. It was a quartet which made the vets tremble for miles around.

Another cross which the vets had to bear was his unique gift of being able to take one look at a dead animal on a farm and pronounce immediately the cause of death. The farmers, awestruck by his powers, were always asking me why I couldn't do it. But I was unable to dislike the man. He would have had to be more than human to resist the chance to be important and there was no malice in his actions. Still, it made things uncomfortable at times and I liked to be on the spot myself whenever possible. Especially when Isaac Cranford was involved.

Cranford was a hard man, a man who had cast his life in a mould of iron austerity. A sharp bargainer, a win-at-all-cost character and, in a region where thrift was general, he was noted for meanness. He farmed some of the best land in the lower Dale, his shorthorns won prizes regularly at the shows but he was nobody's friend. Mr. Bateson, his neighbour to the north summed it up: "That feller 'ud skin a flea for its hide." Mr. Dickon, his neighbour to the south, put it differently: "If he gets haud on a pound note, by gaw it's a prisoner."

This morning's meeting had had its origin the previous day. A phone call mid afternoon from Mr. Cranford. "I've had a cow struck by lightning. She's laid dead in the field."

I was surprised. "Lightning? Are you sure? We haven't had a storm today."

"Maybe you haven't, but we have 'ere."

"Mmm, all right, I'll come and have a look at her."

Driving to the farm, I couldn't work up much enthusiasm for the impending interview. This lightning business could be a bit of a headache. All farmers were insured against lightning stroke—it was usually part of their fire policy—and after a severe thunderstorm it was common enough for the vets' phones to start ringing with requests to examine dead beasts.

The insurance companies were reasonable about it. If they received a certificate from the vet that he believed lightning to be the cause of death they would usually pay up without fuss. In cases of doubt they would ask for a post-morten or a second opinion from another practitioner. The difficulty was that there are no diagnostic post-morten features to go on; occasionally a bruising of the tissues under the skin, but very little else. The happiest situation was when the beast was found with the tell-tale scorch marks running from an ear down the leg to earth into the ground. Often the animal would be found under a tree which itself had obviously been blasted and torn by lightning. Diagnosis was easy then.

Ninety-nine per cent of the farmers were looking only for a square deal and if their vet found some other clear cause of death they would accept his verdict philosophically. But the odd one could be very difficult.

I had heard Siegfried tell of one old chap who had called him out to verify a lightning death. The long scorch marks on the carcass were absolutely classical and Siegfried, viewing them, had been almost lyrical. "Beautiful, Charlie, beautiful, I've never seen more typical marks. But there's just one thing." He put an arm round the old

man's shoulder. "What a great pity you let the candle grease fall on the skin."

The old man looked closer and thumped a fist into his palm. "Dang it, you're right, maister! Ah've mucked t'job up. And ah took pains ower it an' all—been on for dang near an hour." He walked away muttering. He showed no embarrassment, only disgust at his own technological shortcomings.

But this, I thought, as the stone walls flipped past the car windows, would be very different. Cranford was in the habit of getting his own way, right or wrong, and if he didn't get it today there would be trouble.

I drove through the farm gate and along a neat tarmac road across the single field. Mr. Cranford was standing motionless in the middle of the yard and I was struck, not for the first time, by the man's resemblance to a big, hungry bird. The hunched, narrow shoulders, the forward-thrust, sharp-beaked face, the dark overcoat hanging loosely on the bony frame. I wouldn't have been surprised if he had spread his wings and flapped his way on to the byre roof. Instead, he nodded impatiently at me and began to hasten with short, tripping steps to a field at the back of the house.

It was a large field and the dead cow lay almost in the centre. There were no trees, no hedges, not even a small bush. My hopeful picture of the body under a stricken tree melted immediately, leaving an anxious void.

We stopped beside the cow and Mr. Cranford was the first to speak. "Bound to be lightning. Can't be owt else. Nasty storm, then this good beast dropping down dead."

I looked at the grass around the big shorthorn. It had been churned and torn out, leaving patches of bare earth. "But it hasn't exactly dropped down, has it? It died in convulsions—you can see where its feet have kicked out the grass."

"All right then, it 'ad a convulsion, but it was lightning that caused it." Mr. Cranford had fierce little eyes and they darted flitting glances at my shirt collar, macintosh belt,

Wellingtons. He never could quite bring himself to look anybody in the eye.

"I doubt it, Mr. Cranford. One of the signs of lightning stroke is that the beast has fallen without a struggle. Some of them even have grass in their mouths."

"Oh, I know all about that," Cranford snapped, his thin face flushing. "I've been among livestock for half a century and this isn't the first beast I've seen that's been struck. They're not all t'same, you know."

"Oh, I realise that, but, you see, this death could have been caused by so many things."

"What sort o' things?"

"Well, Anthrax for a start, magnesium deficiency, heart trouble—there's quite a list. I really think we ought to do a post-mortem to make sure."

"Now see here, are you saying I'm trying to do summat I shouldn't?"

"Not at all. I'm only saying we should make sure before I write a certificate. We can go and see her opened at Mallock's and, believe me, if there's no other obvious cause of death you'll get the benefit of the doubt. The insurance people are pretty good about it."

Mr. Cranford's predatory features sank lower into his coat collar. He dug his hands viciously into his pockets. "I've had vitneries at these jobs afore. Proper, experienced vitneries, too." The little eyes flashed in the direction of my left ear. "They've never messed about like this. What's the use of going to all that trouble? Why do you have to be so damn particular?"

Why indeed, I thought. Why make an enemy of this man? He wielded a lot of power in the district. Prominent in the local Farmers' Union, a member of every agricultural committee for miles around. He was a wealthy, successful man and, if people didn't like him, they respected his knowledge and listened to him. He could do a young vet a lot of harm. Why not write the certificate and go home? This is to certify that I have examined the above-mentioned animal and, in my opinion, lightning stroke was the cause of death. It would be easy and

Cranford would be mollified. It would be the end of the whole thing. Why antagonise this dangerous character for nothing? Maybe it really was lightning, anyway.

I turned to face Mr. Cranford, trying in vain to look into the eyes that always veered away at the last moment. "I'm sorry, but I feel we ought to have a look inside this cow. I'll ring Mallock and ask him to pick her up and we can see her in the morning. I'll meet you there at ten o'clock. Will that be all right?"

"Reckon it'll have to be," Cranford spat out. "It's a piece o' nonsense, but I suppose I've got to humour you. But just let me remind you—this was a good cow, worth all of eighty pounds. I can't afford to lose that amount of money. I want my rights."

"I'm sure you'll get them, Mr. Cranford. And before I have her moved I'd better take a blood film to eliminate Anthrax."

The farmer had been under a mounting load of pressure. As a pillar of the Methodist chapel his range of language was restricted, so he vented his pent-up feelings by kicking out savagely at the carcass. His toe made contact with the unyielding backbone and he hopped around on one leg for a few seconds. Then he limped off towards the house.

I was alone as I nicked the dead ear with my knife and drew a film of blood across a couple of glass slides. It hadn't been a happy session and the one tomorrow didn't hold out much more promise. I enclosed the blood films carefully in a cardboard box and set off for Skeldale House to examine them under the microscope.

So it wasn't a particularly cheerful group which assembled at the knacker yard the following morning. Even Jeff, though he preserved his usual Buddha-like expression, was, in fact, deeply offended. The account he had given me when I first arrived at the yard was fragmentary, but I could piece the scene together. Jeff, leaping from his lorry at Cranford's, sweeping the carcass with a piercing glance and making his brilliant spot diagnosis. "Stagnation o' t'lungs. I can allus tell by the look in their eyes and the way their hair lies along t'back." Waiting confidently for the wondering gasps, the congratulatory speeches which always followed his *tour de force*.

Then Mr. Cranford, almost dancing with rage. "Shut your big, stupid mouth, Mallock, tha knows nowt about it. This cow was struck by lightning and you'd better remember that."

And now, bending my head over the carcass, I couldn't find a clue anyway. No sign of bruising when the skin was removed. The internal organs clean and normal.

I straightened up and pushed my fingers through my hair. The boiler bubbled softly, puffing out odoriferous wisps into the already highly-charged atmosphere. Two dogs licked busily at a pile of meat meal.

Then a chill of horror struck through me. The dogs had competition. A little boy with golden curls was pushing a forefinger into the heap, inserting it in his mouth and sucking with rapt enjoyment.

"Look at that!" I quavered.

The knacker man's face lit up with paternal pride. "Aye," he said happily. "It isn't only the four-legged 'uns wot likes my meal. Wonderful stuff—full of nourishment!"

His good humour completely restored, he struck a match and began to puff appreciatively at a short pipe which was thickly encrusted with evidence of his grisly trade.

I dragged my attention back to the job at hand. "Cut into the heart, will you, Jeff," I said.

Jeff deftly slicked the big organ from top to bottom and I knew immediately that my search was over. The auricles and ventricles were almost completely occluded by a cauliflower-like mass growing from the valves. Verrucose endocarditis, common in pigs but seldom seen in cattle.

"There's what killed your cow, Mr. Cranford," I said.

Cranford aimed his nose at the heart. "Fiddlesticks! You're not telling me them little things could kill a great beast like that."

"They're not so little. Big enough to stop the flow of blood. I'm sorry, but there's no doubt about it—your cow died of heart failure."

"And how about lightning?"

"No sign of it, I'm afraid. You can see for yourself."

"And what about my eighty pounds?"

"I'm truly sorry about that, but it doesn't alter the facts."

"Facts! What facts? I've come along this morning and you've shown me nowt to make me change my opinion."

"Well, there's nothing more I can say. It's a clear-cut case."

Mr. Cranford stiffened in his perching stance. He held his hands against the front of his coat and the fingers and thumbs rubbed together unceasingly as though fondling the beloved bank notes which were slipping away from him. His face, sunk deeper in his collar, appeared still sharper in outline.

Then he turned to me and made a ghastly attempt to smile. And his eyes, trained on my lapels, tried valiantly to inch their way upwards. There was a fleeting instance when they met my gaze before flickering away in alarm.

He drew me to one side and addressed himself to my larynx. There was a wheedling note in the hoarse whisper.

"Now look here, Mr.Herriot, we're both men of the world. You know as well as I do that the insurance company can afford this loss a lot better nor me. So why can't you just say it is lightning?"

"Even though I think it isn't?"

"Well, what the hangment does it matter? You can say it is, can't you? Nobody's going to know."

I scratched my head. "But what would bother me, Mr. Cranford, is that I would know."

"You would know?" The farmer was mystified.

"That's right. And it's no good—I can't give you a certificate for this cow and that's the end of it."

Dismay, disbelief, frustration chased

across Mr. Cranford's features. "Well, I'll tell you this. I'm not leaving the matter here. I'm going to see your boss about you." He swung round and pointed at the cow. "There's no sign of disease there. Trying to tell me it's all due to little things in the heart. You don't know your job—you don't even know what them things are!"

Jeff Mallock removed his unspeakable pipe from his mouth. "But ah know. It's what ah said. Stagnation o' t'lungs is caused by milk from milk vein getting back into the body. Finally it gets to t'heart and then it's over wi't. Them's milk clots you're looking at."

Cranford rounded on him. "Shut up, you great gumph! You're as bad as this feller here. It was lightning killed my good cow. Lightning!" He was almost screaming. Then he controlled himself and spoke quietly to me. "You'll hear more of this, Mr. Knowledge, and I'll just tell you one thing. You'll never walk on to my farm again." He turned and hurried away with his quick-stepping gait.

I said good morning to Jeff and climbed wearily into my car. Well, everything had worked out just great. If only vetting just consisted of treating sick animals. But it didn't. There were so many other things. I started the engine and drove away.

Chapter 29

It didn't take Mr. Cranford long to make good his threat. He called at the surgery shortly after lunch the following day and Siegfried and I, enjoying a postprandial cigarette in the sitting-room, heard the jangle of the door bell. We didn't get up, because most of the farmers walked in after ringing.

The dogs, however, went into their usual routine. They had had a long run on the high moor that morning and had just finished licking out their dinner bowls. Tired and distended, they had collapsed in

a snoring heap around Siegfried's feet. There was nothing they wanted more than ten minutes' peace but, dedicated as they were to their self-appointed role of fierce guardians of the house, they did not hesitate. They leaped, baying, from the rug and hurled themselves into the passage.

People often wondered why Siegfried kept five dogs. Not only kept them but took them everywhere with him. Driving on his rounds it was difficult to see him at all among the shaggy heads and waving tails; and anybody approaching the car would recoil in terror from the savage barking and the bared fangs and glaring eyes framed in the windows.

"I cannot for the life of me understand," Siegfried would declare, thumping his fist on his knee, "why people keep dogs as pets. A dog should have a useful function. Let it be used for farm work, for shooting, for guiding; but why anybody should keep the things just hanging around the place beats me."

It was a pronouncement he was continually making, often through a screen of flapping ears and lolling tongues as he sat in his car. His listener would look wonderingly from the huge greyhound to the tiny terrier, from the spaniel to the whippet to the Scottie; but nobody ever asked Siegfried why he kept his own dogs.

I judged that the pack fell upon Mr. Cranford about the bend of the passage and many a lesser man would have fled; but I could hear him fighting his way doggedly forward. When he came through the sitting-room door he had removed his hat and was beating the dogs off with it. It wasn't a wise move and the barking rose to a higher pitch. The man's eyes stared and his lips moved continuously, but nothing came through.

Siegfried, courteous as ever, rose and indicated a chair. His lips, too, were moving, no doubt in a few gracious words of welcome. Mr. Cranford flapped his black coat, swooped across the carpet and perched. The dogs sat in a ring round him and yelled up into his face. Usually they collapsed after their exhausting performance but there was something in the look or smell of Mr. Cranford that they didn't like.

Siegfried leaned back in his armchair, put his fingers together and assumed a judicial expression. Now and again he nodded understandingly or narrowed his eyes as if taking an interesting point. Practically nothing could be heard from Mr. Cranford but occasionally a word or phrase penetrated.

"...have a serious complaint to make..."
"...doesn't know his job..."
"...can't afford...not a rich man..."
"...these danged dogs..."
"...won't have 'im again..."
"...down dog, get by..."
"...nowt but robbery..."

Siegfried, completely relaxed and apparently oblivious of the din, listened attentively but as the minutes passed I could see the strain beginning to tell on Mr. Cranford. His eyes began to start from their sockets and the veins corded on his scrawny neck as he tried to get his message across. Finally it was too much for him; he jumped up and a leaping brown tide bore him to the door. He gave a last defiant cry, lashed out again with his hat and was gone.

Pushing open the dispensary door a few weeks later, I found my boss mixing an ointment. He was working with great care, turning and re-turning the glutinous mass on a marble slab.

"What's this you're doing?" I asked.

Siegfried threw down his spatula and straightened his back. "Ointment for a boar." He looked past me at Tristan who had just come in. "And I don't know why the hell I'm doing it when some people are sitting around on their backsides." He indicated the spatula. "Right, Tristan, you can have a go. When you've finished your cigarette, that is."

His expression softened as Tristan hastily nipped out his Woodbine and began to work away on the slab. "Pretty stiff concoction, that. Takes a bit of mixing," Siegfried said with satisfaction, looking at his bro-

ther's bent head. "The back of my neck was beginning to ache with it."

He turned to me. "By the way, you'll be interested to hear it's for your old friend Cranford. For that prize boar of his. It's got a nasty sore across its back and he's worried to death about it. Wins him a lot of money at the shows and blemish there would be disastrous."

"Cranford's still with us, then."

"Yes, it's a funny thing, but we can't get rid of him. I don't like losing clients but I'd gladly make an exception of this chap. He won't have you near the place after that lightning job and he makes it very clear he doesn't think much of me either. Tells me I never do his beasts any good—says it would have been a lot better if he'd never called me. And moans like hell when he gets his bill. He's more bother than he's worth and on top of everything he gives me the creeps. But he won't leave—he damn well won't leave."

"He knows which side his bread's buttered," I said. "He gets first-rate service and the moaning is part of the system to keep the bills down."

"Maybe you're right, but I wish there was a simple way to get rid of him." He tapped Tristan on the shoulder. "All right, don't strain yourself. That'll do. Put it into this ointment box and label it: 'Apply liberally to the boar's back three times daily, working it well in with the fingers.' And post it to Mr. Cranford. And while you're on, will you post this faeces sample to the laboratory at Leeds to test for Johne's disease?" He held out a treacle tin brimming with foul-smelling liquid diarrhoea.

It was a common thing to collect such samples and send them away for Johne's tests, worm counts, etc., and there was always one thing all the samples had in common—they were very large. All that was needed for the tests was a couple of teaspoonfuls but the farmers were lavish in their quantities. They seemed pleasantly surprised that all the vet wanted was a bit of muck from the dung channel; they threw aside their natural caution and shovelled the stuff up cheerfully into the biggest container they could find. They brushed aside all protests; "take plenty, we've lots of it" was their attitude.

Tristan took hold of the tin gingerly and began to look along the shelves. "We don't seem to have any of those little glass sample jars."

"That's right, we're out of them," said Siegfried. "I meant to order some more. But never mind—shove the lid on that tin and press it down tight, then parcel it up well in brown paper. It'll travel to the lab all right."

It took only three days for Mr. Cranford's name to come up again. Siegfried was opening the morning mail, throwing the circulars to one side and making a pile of the bills and receipts when he became suddenly very still. He had frozen over a letter on blue notepaper and he sat like a statue till he read it through. At length he raised his head; his face was expressionless. "James, this is just about the most vitriolic letter I have ever read. It's from Cranford. He's finished with us for good and all and is considering taking legal action against us."

"What have we done this time?" I asked.

"He accuses us of grossly insulting him and endangering the health of his boar. He says we sent him a treacle tin full of cow shit with instructions to rub it on the boar's back three times daily."

Tristan, who had been sitting with his eyes half closed, became fully awake. He rose unhurriedly and began to make his way towards the door. His hand was on the knob when his brother's voice thundered out.

"Tristan! Come back here! Sit down—I think we have something to talk about."

Tristan looked up resolutely, waiting for the storm to break, but Siegfried was unexpectedly calm. His voice was gentle.

"So you've done it again. When will I ever learn that I can't trust you to carry out the simplest task? It wasn't much to ask, was it? Two little parcels to post—hardly a tough assignment. But you managed to botch it. You got the labels wrong, didn't you?"

Tristan wriggled in his chair. "I'm sorry, I can't think how . . ."

Siegfried held up his hand. "Oh, don't worry. Your usual luck has come to your aid. With anybody else this bloomer would be catastrophic but with Cranford—it's like divine providence." He paused for a moment and a dreamy expression crept into his eyes. "The label said to work it well in with the fingers, I seem to recall. And Mr. Cranford says he opened the package at the breakfast table . . . Yes, Tristan, I think you have found the way. This, I do believe, has done it."

I said, "But how about the legal action?"

"Oh, I think we can forget about that. Mr. Cranford has a great sense of his own dignity. Just think how it would sound in court." He crumpled the letter and dropped it into the wastepaper basket. "Well, let's get on with some work."

He led the way out and stopped abruptly in the passage. He turned to face us. "There's another thing of course. I wonder how the lab is making out, testing that ointment for Johne's disease?"

Questions

1. Why didn't Herriot simply sign Isaac Cranford's insurance certificate and save himself some trouble? Why is he concerned with the truth in such a small matter?

2. Keeping in mind that whether or not we *like* what happened does not determine its justice, *is* justice done at the close of this episode? *Can* justice be done by accident? Suppose that Tristan had made the switch on purpose, would that make it a case of justice?

3. What would Socrates say about the outcome of this case?